IRPP

INSTITUTE FOR RESEARCH ON PUBLIC POLICY

INSTITUT DE RECHERCHE EN POLITIQUES PUBLIQUES

Founded in 1972, the Institute for Research on Public Policy is an independent, national, non-profit organization. Its mission is to improve public policy in Canada by promoting and contributing to a policy process that is more broadly based, informed and effective.

In pursuit of this mission, the IRPP

- identifies significant public policy questions that will confront Canada in the longer term future and undertakes independent research into these questions;

- promotes wide dissemination of key results from its own and other research activities;

- encourages non-partisan discussion and criticism of public policy issues in a manner which elicits broad participation from all sectors and regions of Canadian society and links research with processes of social learning and policy formation.

The IRPP's independence is assured by an endowment fund, to which federal and provincial governments and the private sector have contributed.

Créé en 1972, l'Institut de recherche en politiques publiques est un organisme national et indépendant à but non lucratif.

L'IRPP a pour mission de favoriser le développement de la pensée politique au Canada par son appui et son apport à un processus élargi, plus éclairé et plus efficace d'élaboration et d'expression des politiques publiques.

Dans le cadre de cette mission, l'IRPP a pour mandat:

- d'identifier les questions politiques auxquelles le Canada sera confronté dans l'avenir et d'entreprendre des recherches indépendantes à leur sujet;

- de favoriser une large diffusion des résultats les plus importants de ses propres recherches et de celles des autres sur ces questions;

- de promouvoir une analyse et une discussion objectives des questions politiques de manière à faire participer activement au débat public tous les secteurs de la société canadienne et toutes les régions du pays, et à rattacher la recherche à l'évolution sociale et à l'élaboration de politiques.

L'indépendance de l'IRPP est assurée par les revenus d'un fonds de dotation auquel ont souscrit les gouvernements fédéral et provinciaux, ainsi que le secteur privé.

INSTITUTE FOR RESEARCH ON PUBLIC POLICY

IRPP

INSTITUT DE RECHERCHE EN POLITIQUES PUBLIQUES

PULLING AGAINST GRAVITY:

ECONOMIC DEVELOPMENT
IN NEW BRUNSWICK
DURING THE MCKENNA YEARS

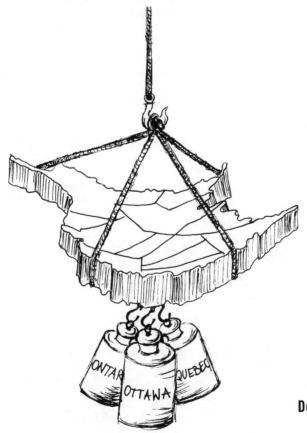

Donald J. Savoie

IRPP

Printed in Canada
Dépôt légal 2001

Bibliothèque nationale du Québec

National Library of Canada
Cataloguing in Publication Data

Savoie, Donald J., 1947-
Pulling against gravity: economic development in New
Brunswick during the McKenna years

Includes bibliographical notes.
ISBN 0-88645-192-2

1. New Brunswick–Economic policy. 2. New Brunswick–
Economic conditions–1991- 3. New Brunswick–Economic
conditions–1945-1991. 4. McKenna, Frank J. I. Institute for
Research on Public Policy. II. Title

HC117.N3S392 2001   338.9715'1   C2001-901480-

Suzanne Ostiguy McIntyre
Vice President, Operations

Copy Editor
Brian McIntyre

Design
Studio Duotone inc.

Production
Chantal Létourneau and
Studio Duotone inc.

Cover Illustration
Renata Czeczuk

Published by
The Institute for Research on Public Policy (IRPP)
l'Institut de recherche en politiques publiques (IRPP)
1470 Peel Street, Suite 200
Montreal, Quebec H3A 1T1
irpp@irpp.org / www.irpp.org

Contents

THE DENOUEMENT

List of Charts, Tables, Figures and Appendices

Chapter 2

Chapter 3

Chapter 4

Chapter 5

Chapter 6

Chapter 7

Foreword

Economic dependence is never desirable. So it is appropriate for public officials to aspire to replace dependency with self-sufficiency whenever possible. But indigenous factors, global economic trends and past policy decisions can make the task immensely difficult. Frank McKenna faced these challenges head-on.

Throughout his tenure as Premier of New Brunswick, McKenna's mantra was self-reliance, his energy boundless and the economic challenges facing his province enormous, turning them around often akin to pulling against gravity, the apt title of this book. Did he succeed? The jury is still out, but the policies McKenna put in place and the lessons learned in New Brunswick under his leadership will be of interest to all Canadians.

Donald J. Savoie has, as few scholars could, provided us with an account of the task and the obstacles McKenna faced, as well as the policy changes he brought forward and their outcomes. Drawing on his knowledge of New Brunswick's history, politics and economics, Savoie paints for us a comprehensive picture of the province, and he does so within a framework that is neither political nor ideological; it is analytical and exploratory – and fascinating.

It is Savoie's outstanding grasp of New Brunswick's history and governance structure that makes this work stand out. He conducted extensive interviews with the leading players, including several with Premier McKenna, and delved into the correspondence and reports of the period. He makes the reader keenly aware of the enormity of the challenges and of the weight past decisions carry in current events. Savoie makes us see that, in the words of Chapter 7, *history matters*.

Trying to turn the tide of history while experiencing both a North American recession and cutbacks in federal transfers proved daunting indeed. But McKenna did not use these factors as an excuse for what at times must have looked like discouraging economic outcomes. He worked through the problems and moved on, and in the process made what may have been his greatest contribution to his province: instilling in fellow New Brunswickers a sense that history need not pass them by, that entrepreneurial drive would overcome obstacles and that they could harness new technologies to create jobs.

While heartening in the sense that determination can create change for the better, *Pulling Against Gravity* nevertheless makes for sobering reading for students of the politics of economic development: Savoie makes the case that no matter how determined the provincial leader, the structure of Canadian politics must be fundamentally changed before the smaller provinces can overcome the political might of central Canada. He reserves his strongest words for the ability of politicians to turn regional economic development programs into national subsidies that do little to redress the imbalances that prompted the implementation of the programs in the first place.

The policy challenges and issues explored by Savoie's work extend well beyond the borders of New Brunswick. In today's climate of growing regional discontent, they are important to all Canadians.

ii   IRPP is proud to be associated with Professor Savoie's work. It is a reminder that decisions taken by a determined political leader at a particular time in history can have far-reaching effects.

As with all such efforts, the views expressed herein are those of the author; they do not necessarily reflect those of the IRPP staff or of its board of directors.

Hugh Segal, President

Preface

This book examines Frank McKenna's efforts to transform New Brunswick into a more self-reliant society. The purpose is to take stock of the McKenna years and to identify lessons learned that may be helpful to other small, have-less provinces as they plan their own economic development.

I would like to inform the reader at the outset that Frank McKenna and I are friends. I have known him for sixteen years. He sought my advice from time to time during his term as premier of New Brunswick and we co-authored a paper on Canadian federalism in 1995. I readily admit that I have a great deal of respect for Frank McKenna for his having served as premier of my province at a difficult moment in our history, given never-ending cuts in federal government spending, and for the level of energy and commitment he brought to the job. I must add, however, that I do not consider myself politically partisan. If I have a bias, it is on behalf of the economic interest of my province and of the Maritime region, as the reader will discover when reading this book.

It is also important for the reader to appreciate that since New Brunswick is a small province it is hardly possible for me, a long-term student of public policy and public administration, not to know the province's political and economic elite. Indeed, former Premier Richard Hatfield, a Progressive Conservative, also sought my advice from time to time while he was premier of New Brunswick. In other words, if friendship were a reason to deter one from undertaking research in New Brunswick, few New Brunswickers would be able to write much about their own province.

donald j. savoie

I have sought to paint an objective portrait of the McKenna years from an economic development perspective. I carried out a number of interviews, including two with Frank McKenna, and several with his key advisors and with senior public servants. My objective was to gain an appreciation of the challenges confronting the McKenna government and the policies it pursued rather than to determine the success of those policies. The reader will note that I looked to widely accepted economic indicators, to data produced by Statistics Canada and other published sources to take stock of the McKenna years. I also spent time in the provincial archives, going through government documents and correspondence. Finally, the reader will see that I let data from Statistics Canada do the talking when I reported on the success or lack of success in economic development during the McKenna years.

I cannot possibly thank everyone who assisted in my research, but I do wish to single out a few. Ginette Benoit again accepted with good cheer to type, and retype, the manuscript. Danick LaFrance helped me on this and other projects during the academic year 1999-2000, as my research assistant. I also owe a special thanks to Dale Cogswell of the provincial archives. Working with very limited resources, he made himself available and attended to all my requests with competence and civility. I want to express my thanks to Ronald Murray, former deputy minister in the government of New Brunswick, who agreed to read an earlier draft of the manuscript and to offer suggestions to improve it. Philippe Doucet, one of my former professors of Political Science here at l'Université de Moncton, and Peter Aucoin, a friend and professor of Political Science at Dalhousie University, also read an earlier draft of the manuscript and provided valuable advice to improve it. Tom Courchene, a friend and a colleague, also provided insightful comments and advice on how to improve the manuscript. Cynthia Williams, a friend and an excellent student of public policy in her own right also read the manuscript and made many suggestions to improve it. Daniel Schwanen generated important data and material for this study and I owe him a special thank you. Finally, two anonymous reviewers also made important suggestions to improve the manuscript. All defects in the book, however, are mine.

Donald J. Savoie

1

Introduction and Overview

In the summer of 1994, I was asked by the federal minister responsible for the Atlantic Canada Opportunities Agency (ACOA) to consult with a number of Atlantic Canadians, including the four Atlantic premiers, to plan a conference on future economic development efforts in the area. One of the first points the then Nova Scotia Premier John Savage made in our meeting was, "Do you know what one of my biggest obstacles in promoting economic development here in Nova Scotia is? – Frank McKenna." He went on to explain, "When I go to Toronto to meet with Chief Executive Officers to promote Nova Scotia as a place to invest, I very often discover that Frank McKenna has already been there. We need to coordinate our activities better." To be sure, his point was valid. But it also told me that McKenna was clearly "out-hustling" Savage in pursuing new investments for their respective provinces.

Probably the most damning criticism one can direct at a former prime minister or premier is to say he or she left office without a trace. That is, the government machinery was hardly disturbed during the leader's mandate and new government policies, if any were introduced, had precious little impact. Whatever else may be said about him, no one would claim McKenna left office without a trace. He overhauled the machinery of government, cut spending, repaired New Brunswick's balance sheet, reoriented the education system and promoted economic development in the province with a kind of missionary zeal. His goal, he repeatedly argued, was to make New Brunswick economically self-sufficient. The popular press, including the national media, reported time and again on

McKenna's "remarkable energy level" throughout his stay in office.[1] The media also often referred to the "McKenna miracle" in describing the economic transformation that, they argued, was taking root in New Brunswick.[2] Even several years after McKenna's being elected premier, The Globe and Mail referred to him in a front-page story as "one of the rare bright stars of the Canadian political firmament."[3]

The purpose of this book is to take stock of the McKenna years. Avec le recul du temps we seek to answer a number of questions. First, what kind of impact did McKenna have on the province and, second, have any lasting economic and social changes resulted from his policies? Some observers have argued that "policy makers and other opinion leaders in other regions have come to think of New Brunswick as a testing ground, a research laboratory for public policy."[4] If this is indeed the case, we need to answer this question: What are the lessons learned from the McKenna years and how may they be applied by other small, have-less provinces? In short, this book seeks to identify the challenges McKenna faced, to describe the reforms he implemented, to assess the impact of those reforms, and to draw lessons for other have-less provinces.

We know this much – something happened in New Brunswick during McKenna's tenure. Some journalists, as already noted, spoke of the "McKenna miracle," others about an economic turnaround, still others about an innovative approach to governing, and the list goes on.[5] Fully three years after McKenna had left office, he was still being invited to such countries as Jamaica, Wales, Scotland and Australia to speak about his experience.[6] What is less clear is what precisely happened in New Brunswick during that time and what, if any, economic transformation actually took place in the province. The first question, then, is to what extent are we dealing with substantial and lasting change or, as some of McKenna's critics have argued, has it all been just "smoke and mirrors?" The critics claim that the McKenna reforms had more to do with having top flight "spin doctors" on staff than with any genuine change.[7] Current New Brunswick Premier Bernard Lord, for example, has said, "The previous government was hype professionals. They were big on making announcements."[8]

In brief, then, the central purpose of this book is to take stock of the McKenna years from an economic development perspective. It is not, however, a political biography of Frank McKenna. That I leave to others.[9] Here, we want to determine if the McKenna experience was more show than substance or if it brought real progress as well as substantial and lasting change.

I hope this book will also contribute to our knowledge of Canadian public policy and public administration. There is no shortage of studies on the federal government and how decisions are made in Ottawa. There is also a wide variety of studies on public policy issues from a national perspective. The work of the former Economic Council of Canada comes to mind. The federal government today supports a number of policy networks, think tanks and research groups of one kind or another located in Ottawa and drawn to things national, rather than provincial or regional. Regrettably, the same can be said about the academic community.[10] The federal government has much more money than the provinces to fund research by academics and consultants. This and other reasons, including the fact that studies produced from a national perspective will invariably reach a broader audience than those that are provincial or regional in scope, probably explain why we have an abundance of national studies and precious few from a provincial perspective.

In the matter of policy, the provinces today are in many ways where the "rubber meets the road." Provincial governments hold jurisdiction over the more important policy fields such as health care and education. They are also responsible for natural resources and control most determinants of human resources and land use. Additionally, it is generally believed globalization will strengthen the hand of the provinces in the years ahead. That said, I am continually struck by the large number of federal officials, policy groups of one kind or another, and Ottawa-based consultants all doing research in fields which properly belong to provincial governments. One federal official employed in a policy branch put his finger on the problem when he observed, "I am being kept busy turning a crank that is not attached to anything."[11] All of the above is to say we need a better understanding of how provincial governments work and how public policy issues are viewed from their perspective. My hope is that this study will make a contribution on this front and encourage others to pursue the topic as well.

Although this book is not a biography of Frank McKenna, a few biographical facts are in order to provide a backdrop for understanding his passion for economic reform.[12] McKenna was born in 1948 on a farm in Apohaqui, a small hamlet with a population of 340 near Sussex, New Brunswick, to parents who scratched a living from a pig and dairy farm. Josh Beutel writes that his "rural upbringing, farm chores and long, muddy trudges to and from school nine kilometres away, helped produce in him a fixated Calvinist ethic for work and for life."[13] McKenna himself acknowledged that his upbringing gave him "a bit of a puritan ethic." He explained his wish to create jobs for New Brunswickers in this way: "It's almost spiritual for me. I believe in the value of work. I believe it's a value in itself and I believe that people need work for self-fulfillment and for pride and dignity."[14]

Frank McKenna was the eldest son in a family of eight. He embraced work from an early age. For example, as a child he trapped muskrats to sell their hides

3

for extra money. He was a good student and an athlete and was offered several university scholarships, including an athletic scholarship to attend Boston College. He opted instead for a scholastic scholarship to St. Francis Xavier University, where "he led the student union, won academic awards and became the first student appointed to the board of governors."[15]

People who knew him in high school and university, during his law practice and as a politician invariably point to McKenna's competitive nature to explain what motivates him. Before entering politics, he was a successful criminal lawyer in Chatham, New Brunswick, where he won national recognition. He successfully defended, for example, Maritime boxing champion Yvon Durelle, who had been charged with murder. Durelle described McKenna's performance at the trial in this fashion: "By the way his hands and face went, full of life, you could tell he really wanted to win."[16]

McKenna is not one to ponder problems for very long and contemplate several possible courses of action. He is not a patient man, nor is he a "policy wonk." In office, he had little time for position papers, strategic outlines, federal-provincial sectoral reviews and the like, and very few were produced at his urging. For the most part, he tolerated them as a necessary evil. As former Ontario Premier David Peterson once observed, "Frank isn't the kind of guy to go to a meeting with a bag full of problems. He'll go in there with some solutions."[17] McKenna, always impatient to get on with the tasks at hand, himself observed that "the best leadership comes from sprinters, not long-distance runners."[18]

4   New Brunswickers gave the sprinter probably more than he bargained for in the October 1987 general election. McKenna won every seat in the legislature, a clear mandate for Frank McKenna and his Liberal party. Still, it was also clear that New Brunswickers wanted the scandal-plagued Hatfield government out of power. Hatfield had been in power since 1970 and had stretched his last mandate to its full five years before calling a general election. The Globe and Mail summed up Hatfield's political career in this fashion: "Once widely admired, he ended his days in office under a cloud of scandal: tales of marijuana and cocaine and parties with college boys on government airplanes."[19]

Winning every seat in the legislature, however, was not all good news. McKenna himself commented that he felt "like a dog with a whole bunch of new puppies," later saying that when he first walked into caucus "they all started barking."[20] There followed constant demands for new schools, hospitals, roads and jobs, always from the government side. If nothing else, these demands had the potential of pushing the government off its agenda and its central purpose.

McKenna's central purpose was very clear, at least in his own mind – he wanted to make New Brunswick economically self-sufficient. He wanted to lessen the province's reliance on federal transfer payments and remake its image as "one of the worst places to do business," to one of the best in North America.[21] He wanted New Brunswick to pull itself up by its own bootstraps, to be self-reliant in most things, and to have a strong vibrant private sector. No small order – but, in McKenna's view, if a poor farm boy from Apohaqui could make it, so could his province. For McKenna, it was really that simple. Energy, willpower, enthusiasm and greater self-confidence could, he became convinced, turn things around for New Brunswick. He once made this observation: "Ultimately, a province such as ours can be what it wants to be. With a flourishing work ethic and entrepreneurship, you can stay as wealthy as you want to be."[22] For McKenna, then, it was up to his government and the people of New Brunswick to pull it off.

McKenna would often say, in speeches in Toronto or when meeting business executives in central Canada, he wanted to address them "not as a supplicant, but as an equal." He insisted, time and again, that "New Brunswick is not going to be the bellyache of Canada."[23] New Brunswick, he believed, could turn things around economically just by getting on with the job, saying, "If you give a man a fish, you feed him for a day. If you teach him how to fish, you feed him for life."[24] In the late 1980s it became fashionable for large private sector firms and government departments to tack vision or mission statements on their walls. McKenna's vision was straightforward: "I believe in a vision of New Brunswick self-sufficient, proud, and equal to every other Canadian province."[25]

McKenna would soon get a helping hand from the federal government, albeit perhaps not the kind he was looking for. By the time he came to power in the fall of 1987, Ottawa was increasingly sending out clear signals that it wanted to get its fiscal house in order. In his 1988 budget speech, Finance Minister Michael Wilson announced spending cuts of $300 million and declared, "Spending on non-statutory programs, excluding foreign aid and defence, will be lower in 1989-90 than it was when we took office. This is a real reduction after inflation of almost 20 percent over a five-year period."[26] Spending cuts followed in every federal budget tabled during McKenna's ten years in office. Only after he left office did Ottawa start to open its spending tap again. Cuts were made not just in transfer payments to the provinces and individuals, but also in economic development, notably in federal-provincial programming and in federal government operations in New Brunswick, including military bases. Thus, New Brunswick was increasingly told that it had to rely less and less on federal transfer payments and a federal presence in New Brunswick at the very same time that McKenna was seeking to make his province more self-reliant. To sum up then, when McKenna assumed power in 1987, the situation could almost be described as *come the moment, come the man.*

5

But McKenna could scarcely start with a clean slate, nor did he probably fully appreciate the magnitude of the challenge he had set out for himself and his government. The face of New Brunswick, one of the four original partners in the Canadian federation, had been fashioned by many events, policies and developments since Confederation. McKenna would soon discover, as other premiers had before him, that he had to work with the economic levers handed to him under the constitution and by powerful economic forces over which the provincial government had very limited control.

New Brunswick is a small province in terms of both its size and its population. No part of the province, for example, is more than 280 kilometres from the ocean. It ranks eighth in population and its economy can hardly be described as a picture of health. It has consistently ranked among the weakest provinces in terms of earned per capita income, unemployment rate and levels of public and private investment. As well, the south of the province is economically much stronger and more urban than the north, which is largely rural and continuously facing serious difficulties.

The forestry sector has always played an important role in the province's economy and continues to do so today. Timber, shipbuilding and, later, pulp and paper mills have contributed greatly over the years to economic development and job creation in the province. There are still several pulp and paper mills operating and they are strategically located in virtually all regions of the province. The province's mining industry, though relatively small, has made and continues to make a significant contribution to the economy. The same can be said for agriculture, though the closing down of family farms occurred faster in New Brunswick than anywhere in Canada in the critical years between 1951 and 1971 (26,431 farms were recorded in the 1951 census compared with 5,485 in the 1971 census). The fishery remains important in a number of communities, notably in the northeast, southeast and southwest regions.

The above would lead one to conclude that the province has little presence in the so-called "new economy," and one would be right. Indeed, this was one of the key areas McKenna sought to rectify.

It is often said that New Brunswick's population of 720,000 is unique in that it is highly representative of Canada as a whole, a kind of microcosm of the country. However, this is true on only one level. Some 33 percent of New Brunswickers have French as their mother tongue and 66.7 percent have English. There are about ten thousand New Brunswickers of Native ancestry (Micmac or Maliseet). New Brunswick is not, however, a microcosm of Canada in the sense that it remains, even today, largely untouched by the several important waves of immigration to Canada which took place during the twentieth century. For example, there are only 3,000 New Brunswickers of Asian origin and 440 of African origin. Much of the population is of European stock and for the most part from Western Europe. In brief, emigration rather than immigration has been the rule in New Brunswick.

In addition, the fiscal capacity of the province is weak. New Brunswick has been on the receiving end of Ottawa's equalization payments ever since they were first introduced in 1957. Though New Brunswick's tax burden is very high by national standards, the province could not provide anywhere near current levels of public services without access to these payments. Yet, New Brunswick has one of the finest provincial public services in the country.[27] It is interesting to note, for example, that New Brunswick was the first province to establish a Department of Health.

This brief glimpse of the circumstances that Frank McKenna would have to take into account as he set out to transform New Brunswick into a self-reliant society is itself sufficient to make one believe that he would be "pulling against gravity." Indeed, one can hardly imagine a more daunting public policy challenge.

Outline

How is it that New Brunswick came to be dependent in the first place? What is the problem that needs fixing? In economic development, as in other things, history matters, and economic history has not been kind to New Brunswick. The reader will note that we spend a great deal of time looking to history 7 and to New Brunswick's place in Confederation. It is essential that we do so in order to understand the province's current economic circumstances and McKenna's efforts to promote economic development. When I started work on this book, my intentions were to focus on economic development during the McKenna years. I soon discovered, however, that this would tell only part of the story and that there is a great deal more to the economic development of a region than reporting on the efforts of a provincial government over a ten-year period. Accordingly, this book ended up being not just about the McKenna years. While it is about McKenna, his economic development efforts and his attempt to reform government operations, it is also about New Brunswick, its economic history, its place in the Canadian federation and the impact of national policies on its development.

McKenna did not start from ground zero nor could he work in a vacuum. The underlying theme of the first section of this book is that one has to appreciate the roots of New Brunswick's current economic realities to assess properly the scope and impact of the McKenna years. Much of the economic literature in Canada is ahistorical and most economists are much too quick to define immediate solutions to immediate problems. If things were only that simple. We take a different tack and, accordingly, this study is not limited to the McKenna efforts and policies. At the risk of sounding repetitive, we became convinced that – to fully appreciate the McKenna years and their impact on New Brunswick – we had to look to history and to past and current federal government economic policies.

In the second chapter, we examine the impact of various national policies and measures on the Maritime economy and reports on regional grievances, how the province and the region became "supplicants" and how they organized to apply pressure on the federal government. We make the case that national policies have been, over the years, damaging to the New Brunswick economy.

The federal government has, particularly since the 1960s, responded to regional concerns and put in place a number of measures to promote economic development in New Brunswick and other smaller provinces. The third chapter reviews these measures.

Chapter 4 provides a snapshot of New Brunswick's economic circumstances at the time McKenna came to power. We look to a number of standard economic indicators to assess New Brunswick's economic circumstances. Given the far-reaching changes in Canada's economy in recent years, it is important to compare New Brunswick's performance not only with national averages but also with other provincial economies of comparable size, notably Nova Scotia and Manitoba. Additionally, we look at the state of the provincial public service, the province's public finances and key economic sectors.

In Chapter 5, we review and analyze the various measures the McKenna government introduced to promote economic development and reform government operations. We review how McKenna sought to reform government operations and the public service and his efforts to repair the public finances of the province. We look to his job creation measures in the new economy, changes to the province's income assistance programs, efforts to expand traditional economic sectors and his dealings with Ottawa. The focus is on economic development: For this reason we do not review, for example, policies in health care or municipal government reform measures.

In the following chapter, we provide a report card on the McKenna efforts. We seek to answer several questions: Have things actually changed? How? What is the likely lasting impact? We compare New Brunswick's economic circumstances in 1997 when McKenna left office with those he found in 1987 when he came to power. This chapter looks to key economic indicators to establish any gains New Brunswick made during the McKenna years.

We conclude in Chapter 7 by reporting on lessons learned and on the traces, if any, McKenna left on New Brunswick's economic landscape. We also consider what the McKenna efforts hold for future economic development in the smaller, have-less provinces. Finally, we look at the new forces shaping the economic landscape and offer suggestions for New Brunswick and other Maritime provinces in their dealings with national political institutions and on new economic development measures.

9

Notes

1. John Lownsbrough, "The Energizer Premier," *Report on Business* (March 1993), p. 29.

2. Lownsbrough, "The Energizer Premier," p. 29.

3. "McKenna bets his job on jobs," *The Globe and Mail*, 9 September 1995, p. A1.

4. William J. Milne, *The McKenna Miracle: Myth or Reality* (Toronto: University of Toronto Press, monograph series on public policy and public administration, 1996), p. 9.

5. "Run, Frank, Run," *The Ottawa Citizen*, 27 July 1999, p. 8.

6. See "New Brunswick's Own Wise Man," *Times and Transcript*, Moncton, 24 December 1999, p. G9.

7. Elizabeth Weir, "Let's Be Frank," in Josh Beutel (ed.), *True Blue Grit: A Frank McKenna Review* (Saint John: Lanceman Productions, 1996), p. 9. See also Milne, *The McKenna Miracle*.

8. "200 days," *The Globe and Mail*, Toronto, 7 January 2000, p. A12.

9. A leading New Brunswick journalist, Philippe Lee, has decided to produce a political biography of Frank McKenna. See "Une biographie de Frank McKenna intéresse une maison d'édition," in *L'Acadie Nouvelle*, Caraquet, 11 January 2000, p. 8.

10. I freely admit that I am as guilty as any of my colleagues on this front. See, for example, Donald J. Savoie, *The Politics of Public Spending in Canada* (Toronto: University of Toronto Press, 1990) and *Governing from the Centre: The Concentration of Power in Canadian Politics* (Toronto: University of Toronto Press, 1999).

11. Quoted in Savoie, *The Politics of Public Spending in Canada*, p. 161.

12. Josh Beutel, "What Makes Frankie Run?" in Josh Beutel (ed.), *True Blue Grit*, p. 9.

13. Beutel, "What Makes Frankie Run?", p. 9.

14. Quoted in "McKenna hunts jobs worldwide," *The Globe and Mail*, 9 September 1995, p. A6.

15. Lownsbrough, "The Energizer Premier," p. 29.

16. Yvon Durelle, "Frank's a Helluva Fighter," in Josh Beutel (ed.), *True Blue Grit*, p. 177.

17. Lownsbrough, "The Energizer Premier," p. 22.

18. Lownsbrough, "The Energizer Premier," p. 21.

19. "McKenna hunts jobs worldwide," p. A6.

20. Lownsbrough, "The Energizer Premier," p. 25.

21. See, among others, Charles W. Magill, "Frank McKenna, Hands-on Premier," *Reader's Digest* (January 1994), p. 52.

22. Lownsbrough, "The Energizer Premier," p. 31.

23. Lownsbrough, "The Energizer Premier," p. 25.

24. Lownsbrough, "The Energizer Premier," p. 25

25. Quoted in "McKenna hunts jobs worldwide," p. A6.

26. Canada, *The Budget Speech*, Department of Finance, 10 February 1988, p. 7.

27. See, for example, Donald J. Savoie, "New Brunswick: A Have Public Service in a Have-less Province," in Evert Lindquist (ed.), *Government Restructuring and Career Public Services* (Toronto: Institute of Public Administration of Canada, 2000), pp. 260-86.

THE SETTING

2

Pulling Against Gravity

In economic development, no less than in other things, success breeds success, failure breeds failure and history matters. New Brunswick can boast a number of individual success stories, ranging from the McCain frozen food empire to the Irvings' successful presence in several economic sectors. Indeed, when one compares the New Brunswick record with that of other regions and individuals around the world, one could easily conclude that New Brunswick has performed well and continues to do so. But economic analysts, the national media, Statistics Canada and New Brunswickers themselves invariably look to national indicators and to other regions of the country to gauge acceptable economic performance rather than to international indicators of well-being. Bluntly stated, national comparisons matter to New Brunswickers (and, for that matter, to other Canadians), while those with Eastern Europe or Asia do not. And on the national front, the New Brunswick economy has not fared very well.

New Brunswick has long been classified as a have-less province. Any economic progress made in the past century was very tentative and even then only in a few areas. Moreover, in many fields the region has actually lost ground. Significantly, many of the gains in per capita income and in high-quality public services that have been achieved over the last forty years or so in New Brunswick can be directly attributed to federal transfer payments. Though these can provide the basis for higher per capita income and high quality public services, they can also create an economic dependency, precisely what McKenna decided to fight when he spoke about the need to promote economic self-sufficiency for his province.

For much of the twentieth century, leaving aside federal transfer payments, economic development in Canada was concentrated in the Quebec-Windsor corridor, in the oil and gas producing provinces of Western Canada, and in resource-rich British Columbia. Anyone calling for economic development elsewhere in the country was shouting into the wind. Nowhere was this more the case than in New Brunswick and Atlantic Canada.

Frank McKenna had no choice but to come to terms not only with Canadian economic history, but also with powerful new forces already at play in the New Brunswick economy as he was being sworn into office. There are, of course, many factors that explain a region's economic development: resource endowment, proximity to markets, the quality of the workforce, the urban-rural structure, research and development capacity, availability of risk capital, and so on. There is also no denying that chance or luck, call it what you may, enters the picture. For example, had Henry Ford decided to set up his business in Calais, Maine, rather than in Michigan, the economies of both New Brunswick and southern Ontario would be vastly different today. Likewise, Confederation has had a profound impact on the New Brunswick economy which, overall, has been negative and continues to be felt today. This chapter reviews the effects of Confederation on New Brunswick and the Maritimes. It also discusses how the region tried, over the years, to influence national policies to promote its own development.

Betrayed by Confederation?

The New Brunswick economy was once prosperous. It developed rapidly in the first half of the nineteenth century largely to meet British demands for timber and ships. As Hugh Thorburn writes, "Up to 1850 New Brunswick prospered as part of the closed trading system of the British Empire. It sold over 90 percent of its exports in British markets and was controlled politically from London."[1] However, as Britain turned to freer trade and loosened its political and economic ties to its North American colonies, New Brunswick had to adjust. The adjustment was not very painful or, for that matter, very demanding, in part because of the reciprocity in trade with the United States and the high demands for goods generated by the Crimean War and the American Civil War. The reciprocal free trade agreement with the United States included timber, coal, fish and farm products, which suited New Brunswick very well.

All three Maritime provinces prospered in this era. Historian D.A. Muise writes about the "emergence of a powerful locally-based merchant marine that carried regional products and also made regionally-based shippers a force to be reckoned with...later generations would look back upon this era as the region's golden age."[2] By the 1860s, New Brunswick had a growing population of about 250,000. Given the province's economic structure and its main exports, New Brunswickers resided mostly in small rural villages and hamlets. For example, Saint John, the province's major city, had at the time a population of about 25,000. The communities were also economically self-reliant. What would later become known as the social safety net had not yet come into being.

While all was well in New Brunswick and the other two Maritime provinces, at least when compared with some of the other British colonies in North America in the early 1860s, there were new forces at play that threatened to change the game. The end of the Crimean War and the chances that the reciprocity agreement with the United States would be terminated became stronger day by day as it became clear that the protectionist North was going to win the civil war. In brief, the end of the Crimean War and the American Civil War would also have a profound impact on New Brunswick exports. Although the burgeoning economy of the 1850s and 1860s often demanded all the human resources available, there was a flip side to the situation since the "staples trades that were the backbone of regional productivity were notoriously fickle – a year of plenty was all too likely to be followed by a year of want."[3] Thus, though New Brunswick and the Maritimes in general were enjoying growth, they also needed to lay the groundwork for future economic stability. It is probably difficult for many Canadians to imagine today, but the Maritimes were at the time an economic powerhouse and, naturally, they wanted to stay that way. Even as late as 1890, the Maritimes accounted for 24 percent of Canada's manufacturing enterprises, though it represented only 18 percent of the nation's population. Prior to Confederation, the Maritimes also had a number of dynamic firms in the financial sector which later formed the basis for the Royal Bank and the Bank of Nova Scotia. In 1885, the region had three of the country's five sugar refineries, both Canadian steel mills and six of the twelve rolling mills.[4]

Many in New Brunswick and Nova Scotia felt that railway construction held the key to future economic stability. But the Maritimes could not agree on a comprehensive approach, so railway construction proceeded on a piecemeal basis. For example, Halifax was linked to Truro and Windsor, and Saint John with Moncton. This suggests that some of the economic problems confronting the region were homegrown.

High profile political leaders in New Brunswick (for example, Leonard Tilley) and Nova Scotia (Charles Tupper) began to promote a political union of the three Maritime provinces as a means to ensure greater economic stability for the region. The two men arranged a meeting in 1864 in Charlottetown to explore Maritime political union. They felt that political union held a number of advantages, including a solid foundation to construct the Intercolonial Railway. At the time, there was also public support for political union. Donald Creighton wrote that support for union "had become a public issue, openly discussed and strongly supported. It even showed some...signs of becoming a popular movement."[5] There were several reasons for this support, including a "negative one of antagonism toward Canada...swept along...on a wave of hatred of Canadian duplicity and domination."[6] In any event, by the mid-1860s, one by one the legislative assemblies of the three Maritime provinces agreed to participate in a conference to devise an appropriate blueprint for Maritime union. Unexpectedly, however, the governor of British North America asked if the Canadian government could send delegates to the conference to make a case for a larger political union. The rest of the story is, of course, well known.

But not long after New Brunswick and Nova Scotia signed on as partners in Confederation, a number of Maritimers began to have second thoughts about joining Canada. Indeed, from the 1870s to the late 1920s, there was deep resentment in some quarters of the region toward Confederation and its growing economic impact on the Maritime economy. More than a few Maritime politicians argued publicly that they felt betrayed by the terms of the union and some even recommended that the region should leave the Canadian federation before it was too late. Feelings ran high. One politician argued that a "loyal and contented people had been converted by an act of parliament into a state of serfdom to Canadian greed and spoliation."[7] Another suggested that "the iron-gloved hand of Canadian greed will still be clutching at the tax strings of the Maritime provinces and meanwhile the stream of emigration will be like the brooks as described by Tennyson as running on forever and the cities will be drying up."[8]

The reasons for the resentment were varied. New Brunswick historian Phillip Buckner claims that "the majority of Maritimers had never opposed the idea of Confederation, only the unpalatable terms imposed upon the region at the Quebec Conference."[9] The Maritimes objected to these terms and Prince Edward Island decided to opt out of Confederation in 1867. The concerns were many, including the apparent inability "to protect the interest of a smaller province in a federal rather than a legislative union where the Canadians would inevitably dominate any House of Commons selected on the basis of representation by population."[10] Quite apart from the terms drawn up in Quebec, New Brunswick and Nova Scotia resented the fact that they were greatly underrepresented in the federal public service. The new service consisted of "little more than" the old bureaucracy of the old United Provinces of Canada.[11] But there were also other concerns, perhaps related. For instance, Maritimers became convinced that Ottawa could never appreciate that harbours were as critical to many Maritime communities as roads and canals were to communities in central Canada. Nor would it give proper attention to trade issues affecting the region.

For many in New Brunswick, more critical still was the issue of where to concentrate industry in the country, since the Maritimes simply could not compete with the vote-rich provinces of Ontario and Quebec. Ernest Forbes explains that it soon became clear that whenever there was regional competition, Ottawa would invariably opt for Ontario and perhaps also Quebec. He points out, for example, that Ottawa simply said, "We can't have a tariff on coal because Ontario needs to import it from the United States. They took the tariff off and were able to create an iron and steel industry in Ontario."[12] That decision alone shifted economic power to central Canada and served to eliminate the advantages previously enjoyed by Cape Breton coal producers.

Historians have also produced a veritable catalogue of misguided federal policies, at least from the perspective of the Maritimes, and have documented their negative impact on the region's economy. Hugh Thorburn sums it up well when he observes that "In the long run the federal government's tariff, transportation, and monetary policies have worked to the general disadvantage of New Brunswick."[13] Policies were struck in Ottawa to meet national objectives and, to a New Brunswicker, national objectives became a code phrase meaning the economic interests of Ontario and Quebec only. What was good for central Canada was invariably perceived in Ottawa to be good for Canada, but the same reasoning would never apply to the Maritimes. Ottawa's monetary policy during the 1930s – and for that matter ever since – reflected economic circumstances in Ontario and Quebec, often at the expense of the Maritimes. Canada, it will be recalled, refused to devalue its currency during the depression of the 1930s while many other countries did. New Brunswick, like the other two Maritime provinces, "was exposed to a two-way squeeze: from high and rigid prices for the manufactured goods she had to buy, and from difficult selling conditions in the export markets upon which she depended."[14] The impact on central Canada, meanwhile, was much less severe, given its greater reliance on east-west trade within Canada. This is not to suggest for a moment that Confederation explains all of the economic

19

woes confronting the Maritimes from the 1860s to the late 1880s. As already noted, a number of the economic difficulties were homegrown and the lapse of the reciprocity treaty with the United States did not help matters. Railway debts were also high and the region's shipbuilding industry required a major adjustment. Still, historians have made the case that Confederation hardly helped matters.[15]

The impact of Sir John A. Macdonald's National Policy on the Maritimes has been well documented and there is no need to review it in any detail. Suffice to note that, over time, economic protectionism and the National Policy forced producers in the Maritimes to ship their goods on expensive rail routes to central Canada rather than on ships to their traditional export markets in the New England states and elsewhere. Canada's east-west trade patterns, which were artificially created through the National Policy, promoted a shift to overland trade, for which New Brunswick was geographically ill-suited and, in time, served to make the province an "isolated extremity of Canada."[16] The emerging trade patterns were artificial in the sense that they were created by political decisions, not by market forces.

The National Policy and protectionism served to undercut the region's trading advantages in water-borne shipping. David Alexander summed up the impact of the National Policy on the region in this way: "In the Maritimes, underdevelopment seems a sorry descent from those heady days when the region possessed one of the world's foremost shipbuilding industries, the third or fourth largest merchant marine, financial institutions which were the core of many of the present Canadian giants, and an industrial structure growing as fast as that of central Canada."[17] The National Policy also encouraged American firms to establish branch plants in Canada. However, because of the imposed east-west trade patterns, understandably, precious few of these firms picked a Maritime location to serve the "national" domestic market. Thus, Maritimers could legitimately claim there was no place for them in the National Policy.

C.D. Howe's decision to locate the bulk of wartime production in central Canada also had serious implications for New Brunswick. C.D. Howe was an extremely powerful minister in the government of Mackenzie King and Louis St. Laurent. He served as minister in various departments between 1936 and 1957, including transport, munitions, reconstruction and industry. At the start of the Second World War, there were fifteen crown corporations. Thirty-two were added during the war years as being better suited to lure business people to manage war programs than a typical government department would be. In addition, C.D. Howe also felt that a successful war effort required a highly decentralized form of administration, such as provided by the crown corporation model. Sir Robert Borden, who established the Canadian National Railways as a crown corporation in 1919, explained the advantages of crown corporations in that they were designed to promote business-like management, financial autonomy and a degree of freedom from direct political interference.[18] Howe saw these attributes as being tailor-made for a successful war industry. At the same time, crown corporations represented a significant new source of investments, with the potential to generate a great deal of new economic activities. Indeed, they would also provide the basis for future development in the manufacturing sector in the post-war years.[19] For example, the wartime crown corporations gave rise to aircraft manufacturers, synthetic rubber producers, an advanced technology company called Research Enterprises and the list goes on. Virtually all of the new corporations, however, were established in the Montreal-Windsor corridor; not one was located in the Maritime region.[20]

Although many of the crown corporations established during the war were later disbanded, some continued, including Polysar and Canadian Arsenals Limited. Crown corporations served the war effort very well, but they also served in the long run to strengthen considerably central Canada's manufacturing sector. And that was not all. The Department of Munitions and Supply made extensive new investments in Canadian industries. But by 1944 only about 3.7 percent of these investments had been made in the Maritimes, mainly for aircraft and naval repair. In fact, even the bulk of the shipbuilding for the war was carried out elsewhere. Historians are now agreed that "C.D. Howe and his bureaucrats favoured the concentration of manufacturing in central Canada."[21]

Thus, the Maritimes essentially were left on the outside looking in, as the country's manufacturing sector started to take shape. To make matters worse, the migration or the "assignment" of skilled labour to war industries in central Canada made it very difficult for the region to promote its own manufacturing sector in the post-war years. Here again, political decisions rather than market forces strengthened central Canada's position in the manufacturing sector.

It is now well established that the manufacturing sector in the Maritimes stagnated during much of the twentieth century. In addition, though the region again was fairly strong economically, relative to both national and international standards at the moment of Confederation, its position deteriorated during the first half of the twentieth century. We now know, for example, that relative to Canada, the Maritimes accounted for 14 percent of goods produced in 1880, only 9 percent in 1911, and 5 percent in 1939.[22]

It is important to note that population growth in the Maritimes, by and large, followed the Canadian average from 1851 to the early 1880s. However, from 1891 to today, the region's population growth rate has stagnated, as Figure 1 clearly indicates.

A good number of economists maintain that the economic vitality of a region is tied directly to the development of an urban structure.[23] Urban areas,

Figure 1
Population Growth Rates in the Maritimes and Canada
1851–1931

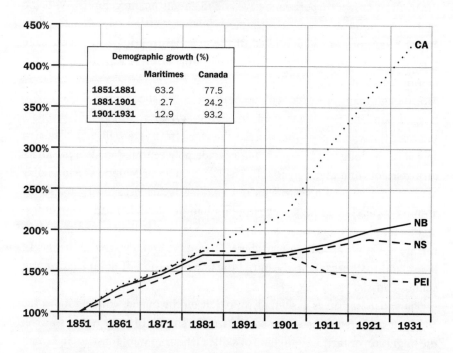

Demographic growth (%)		
	Maritimes	Canada
1851-1881	63.2	77.5
1881-1901	2.7	24.2
1901-1931	12.9	93.2

Source: Statistics Canada, *Historical Statistics of Canada*, cat. 11-516-XIE.

notably in the twentieth century, became in no small measure the shapers of economic development. Larry McCann explores what he labels the Great Transformation in Canadian society that lasted from Confederation to 1929.[24] At the turn of the twentieth century, the Maritime economy shared an overall urban-rural structure similar to Canada's.

Twenty-nine years later, however, central Canada was making great strides toward industrial and urban maturity, but not the Maritimes. There are many indicators confirming this development. For example, at the end of the First World War, Ontario and Quebec were passing the halfway point in climbing the urbanization ladder, while the Maritimes were barely a quarter of the way up the same ladder. New Brunswick today is only where Ontario and Quebec were at the end of the First World War.

Table 1 compares developments in the Maritimes and Canada during the Great Transformation. The findings are revealing. The gross value of production in the manufacturing sector tripled in Canada between 1850 and 1931 while it doubled in the Maritimes. Between 1920 and 1926 alone, the number of manufacturing jobs in Amherst, Dartmouth, Halifax, New Glasgow, Sydney, Truro, Moncton and Saint John fell to 14,000 from 25,000 (or by 44 percent) and about 150,000 Maritimers left the region. Between 1890 and 1937 the Maritimes' position relative to Canada in manufacturing gross value per capita shrank to 42 from 68 percent. One reason for this drop is that the Maritimes did not benefit from federal government decisions to establish defence-related industries during the First World War.

If one isolates Ontario from the national average, we see that the province's urbanization level increased the most of any province, from 1891 and 1931, to 63.1 percent from 35.0 percent.[25] The Maritimes, meanwhile, increased to only 36.0 percent from 16.5 percent. The impact of the National Policy may not in itself entirely explain this development, but it does explain some of it.

In the introduction we noted that in economic development, success breeds success. Given the findings in Figure 1, it should come as no surprise that the last influx of immigrants from southern and eastern Europe would pick Ontario and the western provinces over the Maritimes to find a job or create new economic activities and seek a new life.[26] It is no exaggeration to suggest that the big Canadian immigration waves left the Maritimes virtually untouched. Indeed, many Maritimers joined new Canadians in choosing to leave their homes and move to central and, later, western Canada.

Canada witnessed strong economic growth starting in 1940, which extended well beyond the immediate post-war period. As already noted, the war industries created new economic activities and generated employment. But there were two other important forces at play – Keynesian economics, which came in fashion in the post-war period, and a high level of foreign investment.

The Keynesian revolution captured the Department of Finance and the federal treasury of Canada, as it did elsewhere. The Canadian government presented a major policy paper to parliament toward the end of the Second World War, which was clearly Keynesian in outlook. It said, "The Government will be prepared, in periods where unemployment threatens, to incur deficits and increases

Table 1
The Industrialization and Urbanization of the Maritimes and Canada During the Great Transformation, 1890-1929[a]

	Maritimes		Canada	
	1890, 1891	**1929, 1931**	**1890, 1891**	**1929, 1931**
Total population[1]	880,737	1,009,103	4,883,239	10,376,786
Percentage of population, urban	16.5	36.3	29.8	52.5
Number of urban places (1,000+ population)	41	53	274	503
GROSS VALUE OF PRODUCTION[2]				
Primary industries ($000s)	77,993	150,163	585,625	2,061,585
Manufacturing ($000s)	56,514	108,354	623,205	1,802,960
LABOUR FORCE DISTRIBUTION (%)[3]				
Primary	54.8	47.9	50.0	34.0
Secondary	21.4	17.0	25.3	25.3
Tertiary	23.8	35.1	24.7	40.7

[a] Population and labour force data are for 1891 and 1931 (Ottawa).
Sources: 1) Canada, *Census of Canada* for 1891 and 1931 (Ottawa); 2) D. Alexander, "Economic Growth in the Atlantic Region," *Acadiensis*, Vol. 8 (1978), p. 60; 3) Alan G. Green, *Regional Aspects of Canadian Economic Growth* (Toronto: University of Toronto, 1971), Appendix C.

in the national debt resulting from its employment and income policy...in periods of buoyant employment and income, budget plans will call for surpluses."[27] Not only the government, but also Canadians in general willingly accepted the new direction. They had emerged from the war determined never to permit another depression of the kind witnessed in the 1930s. By war's end, the public's belief in the ability of government to intervene and to manage the economy was high. Large latent demand and rapid population increase, combined with the realization that the government management of the war effort had been successful, gave governments carte blanche to expand. Canadians had learned during the war "that governments were able, in moments of crisis, and when moved by an all-consuming goal, to lead the country to high levels of economic activity and employment."[28] Not only did the allies win the war but the government had also run the war economy well. Unemployment had fallen to zero, yet prices had been held down. Growth of productivity and real GNP was accelerated, inequalities among social groups diminished, civilian consumption actually increased, there were no balance of payment crises and foreign exchange rates remained stable. When the war ended, everyone was prepared for measures to counter a return of the depression years. But the expected severe economic downturn did not materialize and the Keynesian-inspired measures proved unnecessary. Still, governments (in particular, the federal government) were now convinced that they possessed "a new arsenal of economic policy" to achieve high employment and generally manage the economy.

But Keynesian economics had precious little to offer the Maritimes. It spoke to the notion of balance in the national economy and to the development and management of the national economy, not regional economies. The prevailing belief was that a strong and well-managed economy based on east-west trade would benefit all regions. That belief, as history now reveals, was ill-founded.

Harold Innis, arguably Canada's leading economist of the twentieth century, was one of the first senior scholars to see a basic flaw in Keynesian economics from a regional perspective. He argued that Keynesian demand and management techniques would serve to aggravate rather than attenuate existing regional differences in economic well-being. He claimed that Keynesian economics would not allow for the simple reality that each region had a different relationship with the rest of Canada. He bluntly stated that full employment policies would "become a racket on the part of the central provinces for getting and keeping what they can."[29]

Keynesian economics did enable Ottawa to fine tune the national economy, but the economic slide that started a few years after the implementation of the National Policy in the Maritimes simply continued. Canada's overall population grew from 12 to 18 millions between 1946 and 1961, thanks to a strong birth rate and 2 million new immigrants. Meanwhile, the Maritimes witnessed a net out-migration of 90,000, or 8 percent of the population in the 1940s, 85,000 or 7 percent in the 1950s, and 95,000 or 6.6 percent in the 1960s. Maritimers were continuing to go down the road to central Canada to secure a job, often in the growing manufacturing sector. And this trend was not without political implications, given that the Senate has not been able to perform its role on behalf of the regions. The population of the Maritimes dropped to 8 percent of the nation in 1961 from 20 percent in 1871.[30]

The Economic Council of Canada carried out an ambitious study of regional economic development in 1977. The study provides revealing data on the state of Canada's regions between the immediate post-war period to 1976, precisely when Keynesian economics held sway in Ottawa. The council scarcely paints a picture of economic health for New Brunswick or the Atlantic region during this period.

The Maritimes emerged from the Second World War with a per capita income 24 percent below the Canadian average. By 1955 it had dropped to 33 percent. Still, between 1955 and 1976 we see a slow convergence toward the national

25

average in per capita income.[31] The bad news, however, is that the convergence was in no small measure the result of increased federal transfer payments to individuals rather than from earned income.

In other areas, however, there was precious little progress. From 1953 to 1975, the Atlantic provinces consistently had the highest unemployment rate in the country and, further, when unemployment across Canada increased, the rate increased still more in the four Atlantic provinces. Accordingly, when Canada saw an increase of, say, 2 percentage points in its unemployment rate, it was typically accompanied by an increase of 3.7 points in the Atlantic provinces.[32]

American investments in the Canadian manufacturing sector between 1945 and 1965 built both on the National Policy and on C.D. Howe's war effort to further consolidate central Canada's position. Indeed, C.D. Howe's post-war industrial strategy was developed around converting wartime industries to peacetime production. Special government incentives were made available which ensured that wartime industries would be the first to convert to the newest technologies. The result, as Janine Brodie explains, is that "the end of the war brought both expansion and modernization to industries at the centre, making it almost impossible for industry elsewhere to compete for the booming post-war market."[33] We now know that between 1949 and 1967 over 70 percent of Ontario counties (about 40 out of 53) experienced an increase in total manufacturing employment, while only one of the 29 counties in the Maritimes did so.[34] Again, the National Policy, Howe's decision to concentrate wartime manufacturing capacity in Ontario, and later government incentives to make the transition to peacetime production, explain in no small measure Ontario's success in the manufacturing sector.

But Ottawa's success in promoting growth in Ontario's manufacturing sector came, it seems, at a price. By the 1960s the federal government became deeply concerned with the level of American investment in Ontario's manufacturing sector. Because of the federal government's preoccupation with the growth of American investment in central Canada, new measures were introduced in the 1970s to control the flow of investment, mostly coming from south of the border. Federal agencies such as FIRA (Foreign Investment Review Agency) were established to review and screen new foreign investments. Maritime politicians, including New Brunswick ones, were left scratching their heads trying to understand why Ottawa felt the need to monitor and control the flow of foreign investment when they themselves were out actively seeking it. In fact, they had become convinced that the region was suffering precisely from a lack of outside investment. For New Brunswick politicians, it would have made much more sense for Ottawa to deliberately "exclude" the region from the new

26

legislation. But, Ottawa would argue, it had a responsibility to apply "national" policies and it was simply doing its job. For Maritimers, however, it was simply another example of what was good for Ontario was good for Canada.

By the 1960s and early 1970s, it had already become clear that research and development, new technology and, in particular, computers would in the future become the key factors in strengthening a region's productivity and its capacity to compete. There were only four computers in Canada in 1956 and they were in Ontario and Quebec. It took the other eight provinces anywhere from one to four years to get them. But progress in the other provinces remained slow, so that by 1963 fully 76 percent of the country's computers were still located in Ontario and Quebec.

Table 2 shows that Atlantic Canada trailed the national average very badly in the number of computers per million workers in the critical early years. The facts that Ottawa is the home to the head offices of federal government departments and Toronto and Montreal are now home to the head offices of virtually all of Canada's large financial institutions explain in no small measure why central Canada led the nation by a wide margin in introducing computers in the workplace.

Table 2
Number of Computers per Million Workers
Canada, by Region, 1963, 1973

27

	Computers per million workers			
	1963		1973	
	Number per million	Percentage of Canadian average	Number per million	Percentage of Canadian average
Atlantic region	19	28	475	75
Quebec	66	96	540	86
Ontario[1]	94	136	771	122
Prairie region	54	78	584	93
British Columbia	65	94	533	84
Canada (avg.)	69	100	630	100

[1] Excluding computers used by the federal government in Ottawa.
Source: Richard Beaudry, *Les aspects régionaux de la diffusion de la technologie au Canada, le cas des ordinateurs*, Economic Council of Canada Discussion Paper 50, 1976, p. 44; and CANSIM data on regional development.

donald j. savoie

The Region as a Supplicant

From time to time, the federal government has come to terms with the fact that Confederation dealt the Maritimes a bad hand. One keen observer of New Brunswick politics wrote in 1961 about the "enormous economic disabilities under which [the] region has been labouring since the inauguration of the National Policy" with the result that New Brunswick and, more generally, Maritime politicians have been "cast in the role of supplicants pressing on whatever pretext that can be devised for better terms from Ottawa."[35]

The Confederation controversy, as already noted, did not die down in the Maritimes when they joined the new union. Maritimers became convinced that Confederation came about because of the political skills of pro-Confederation politicians, the role of British officials and the failure to renegotiate reciprocity. The region itself, many were convinced, never truly, or at least enthusiastically, embraced Confederation, at least in its early years.[36]

Some Maritime politicians even sought to turn back the clock and take the region out of Confederation. As late as May 1886, the Fielding government in Nova Scotia proposed that "the financial and commercial interests of the people of Nova Scotia, New Brunswick and Prince Edward Island would be advanced by these provinces withdrawing from the Canadian federation and uniting under one government."[37] But in reality few in the Legislature actually believed this would happen. For one thing, there was no indication, let alone assurance, that the British government would agree to let Nova Scotia, or any other Maritime province, leave Confederation. For another, the purpose may well have been to demonstrate to Ottawa that the region was paying too high a price by being in the Confederation. It was more of a *cri du coeur* than the basis for a true secessionist movement. Indeed, the region's anti-Confederation movement, never large to begin with, would eventually disappear without leaving much of a trace. But the region's deep sense of betrayal and grievance would not.

As time passed, Maritimers saw their economy whittled away and their political influence wane. The number of Maritime seats in the House of Commons declined from 43 seats in the 1870s to 31 in 1921. New Brunswick's fell from 16 to 11. Yet, the size of the House of Commons increased from 206 seats in 1874 to 235 in 1921. Worse still, it was clear even then that the Senate, the upper house, did not have the political clout or legitimacy to safeguard regional interests in national policy-making as the United States Senate had. The result is that political leaders from the two largest provinces of the country could put in place a national policy that favoured their own provinces over the others, establish wartime crown corporations in their own regions, and ignore other regions, and establish tariffs that benefited largely their own regions, all the time knowing that they would never be held in check by an upper house speaking on behalf of regional interests.

For their part, Maritime members of Parliament became well versed in the rhetoric of regional protest and in calling for "better terms" from Confederation. But things began to change as far back as the early 1890s as party loyalty started to take precedence over regional loyalty in Ottawa. Apart from a brief period in the 1920s, Maritime interests took a back seat to partisan politics at election time and in the House of Commons.[38]

By the 1920s, however, regional grievances in the Maritimes reached the boiling point. One of the reasons that led the Maritimes to sign on to a larger political union – railway construction – had been turned on its head, at least from the region's perspective. The Canadian National Railway was mandated to play a key role in managing Canada's railway system, with the result that the integration of the Intercolonial into the national railway system spelled bad news for the Maritimes. Freight rates for Maritime producers to ship to central Canada skyrocketed and it became all too clear that they could no longer compete in that market. The railway became a *bête noire* for the Maritimes and "probably the single most important source of anti-Ottawa animus."[39] Western farmers were able to obtain a renewal of the Crowsnest Pass freight rates in 1922 but Maritimers were unable to secure assistance to deal with a "40 percent increase in freight rates."[40]

As is well known, a Maritime Rights Movement came into being in the 1920s. There is now a whole body of literature on the movement, its supporters, its demands, its successes and its failures.[41] One point is worth stressing – it was non-partisan. As Ernest Forbes explains, the movement had no specific founder or leader and all the political parties tried to use the protest movement. But, he adds, the movement was essentially a spontaneous expression of the economic and social frustrations of Maritimers. In the process, however, it also brought home the point that the region had now been turned into a supplicant. There was less talk of secession from Canada (in fact, key members of the movement declared their full support for the nation) and more about the region becoming an equal participant in the country's economic development. The agenda was one of redress, of bringing pressure to bear on Ottawa to see the light and to deal with real regional grievances. The movement, in time, would gain credibility to the point that in the 1921 general election "regional anger had created a force stronger than party loyalty."[42]

The supplicants also met with some success. First, the Conservatives under Meighen responded to some of the movement's demands, as then did the Liberals, under King. The region used its political clout to punish Meighen in 1921 (the Liberals won twenty-five of the region's thirty-one seats) and then

King in 1925 (the Conservatives won twenty-three of twenty-nine seats). The results of the 1925 election, as is well known, led to a period of political and even constitutional instability in Ottawa. Through the efforts of the movement and its political impact, the supplicant was able to secure *some* concessions. For example, in 1922 it saw a 7.5 percent decrease in freight rates and the "re-establishment" of Atlantic regional headquarters in Moncton.

But these measures were not enough to satisfy the region and so King finally decided to appoint a royal commission – the Duncan Commission – to "focus the discussion into a practicable program."[43] The Chair of the commission, Sir Andrew Duncan, deliberately set out to concentrate on finding "practical solutions" to economic problems and, as he wrote in the conclusion of his report, he avoided trying to find "palliatives for the dissatisfaction and political unrest which have been prevailing in that part of the Dominion."[44] Still, Duncan, a British coal mining authority, did challenge the view that Confederation was the sole reason for the Maritime's economic difficulties. The Nova Scotia government in its presentation to the commission argued that national policies had forced the region into a condition of "dilapidation and decay."[45] The Duncan Commission did acknowledge the region's economic difficulties and decline since joining Confederation. But it insisted that factors other than Confederation had been at play, buying into the argument that the decline of the Maritime economy was a result of the obsolescence of "wind, wood and sail."[46]

30 The contribution of the Duncan Commission was limited by several restrictions placed on its mandate. It was told, for example, not to deal with tariff and trade issues because they were "a matter properly to be considered by the Tariff Advisory Board."[47] It did, however, urge the board to move on several issues of direct interest to the Maritimes.

On the question of freight rates and transportation, the commission reported that it had,

> ...definitely [come] to the conclusion that the rate structure as it has been altered since 1912 has placed upon the trade and commerce of the Maritime Provinces a) a burden which, as we have read the pronouncements and obligations undertaken at Confederation, it was never intended it should bear and b) a burden which is, in fact, responsible in very considerable measure for depressing abnormally in the Maritimes today business and enterprise which had originated and developed before 1912 on the basis and faith of the rate structure as it then stood.[48]

The commission also looked at the steel industry in the region. Again, it noted that it was beyond its mandate to deal with tariff and trade issues. But it observed,

> [I]ndependent evidence of an expert character was given to us, that if due regard were paid to the economic unit of production in steel, there was no reason why it should not be produced as efficiently and cheaply in Nova Scotia as anywhere else in Canada.

It added,

> [A] calculation was given to us [which] shows that as a result of the operations of the Customs Tariff, if labour employed in the production of iron and steel and its raw products is taken as the unit for measuring protective value, the protection afforded to Nova Scotia is only 28 percent and whereas in Canada the protection to labour is between 85 percent and 100 percent.[49]

There is no denying that the fact that the commission was not allowed to deal properly with tariff and trade issues – which in many ways went to the heart of the problem, given that it was increasingly clear that many of its producers could not compete in the national market – inhibited its ability to come up with a complete set of practical solutions. In addition, as it became all too clear later, King's objective in establishing the commission was to defuse Maritime agitation and to engage in a policy of delay. He succeeded.

The region would never again be able to embrace the kind of non-partisan approach to applying pressure on the federal government as it did under the Maritime Rights Movement. Never again would the region vote strategically as it did in the 1921 and 1925 general elections. Maritimers, even more than the other regions, came to embrace established national political parties and remain loyal to them. Regional grievances would eventually give rise to new political parties in the west (Reform) and Quebec (Bloc Québécois), but not in the east.

Strong regional ministers from Roméo LeBlanc in New Brunswick and Allan J. MacEachern in Nova Scotia, under the Liberals, to Hugh John Flemming in New Brunswick and John Crosbie in Newfoundland and Labrador, under the Progressive Conservatives, would represent Atlantic Canada in Ottawa. But they did so behind the scenes, and few outside Ottawa would ever know what battles they were fighting or if they were meeting with any success. In more recent years, regional ministers have lost a great deal of their power and for the most part tend to concentrate on securing specific projects. As Alan Cairns writes,

> Early Cabinets were collections of regional notables with independent bases of their own who powerfully asserted the needs of their provinces at the highest political level in the land... Now, however, regional spokesmen of such power and authenticity are only memories, although the regional basis of Cabinet appointment continues.[50]

One thing is certain, regional ministers from small provinces invariably work from a position of weakness. They too must pull against gravity. Political power always begins on the government side of the House of Commons and ministers from Ontario and Quebec could always command more attention if only because general elections are won or lost in these two provinces. Actual power, then, flows from cabinet and, more recently, from the prime minister and a handful of key advisors. They will accommodate regional interests as they see fit from a political perspective and remain virtually unchecked by other national political institutions in doing so.

Provincial premiers have become high profile spokespersons for provincial and regional economic interests. They do not have to work in secret when dealing with Ottawa and they never hesitate to press provincial demands, knowing they will always be applauded back home for doing so. New Brunswick has been fortunate in that since the 1940s it has been served by highly respected premiers from John McNair, Hugh John Flemming, Louis Robichaud and Richard Hatfield (until his last term in office) to Frank McKenna. The work of regional ministers and premiers, combined with events (the national unity debate, for one) and economic forces such as east-west trade patterns, eventually moved Ottawa to respond with new measures to promote economic development in New Brunswick and in other supplicant provinces.

Notes

1. Hugh G. Thorburn, *Politics in New Brunswick* (Toronto: University of Toronto Press, 1961), p. 13.

2. D.A. Muise, "Prologue: The Atlantic Colonies before Confederation," in E.R. Forbes and D.A. Muise (eds.), *The Atlantic Provinces in Confederation* (Toronto: University of Toronto Press, 1993), p. 9.

3. D.A. Muise, "The 1860s: Forging the Bonds of Union," in E.R. Forbes and D.A. Muise (eds.) *The Atlantic Provinces in Confederation*, p. 29.

4. T.W. Acheson, "The National Policy and the Industrialization of the Maritimes, 1880-1910," *Acadiensis*, Vol. 1, no. 2 (Spring 1972).

5. Donald Creighton, *The Road to Confederation: The Emergence of Canada 1863-67* (Toronto: Macmillan of Canada, 1964), p. 26.

6. W.M. Whitelow, *The Maritimes and Canada Before Confederation* (Toronto: Oxford University Press, 1934), p. 201.

7. Nova Scotia, *Debates and Proceedings of the Nova Scotia House of Assembly*, 1885, p. 105.

8. Nova Scotia, *Debates and Proceedings of the Nova Scotia House of Assembly*, 1885, p. 110.

9. Phillip A. Buckner, "The Maritimes and Confederation: A Reassessment," *Canadian Historical Review*, Vol. 71, no. 1 (March 1990), pp. 114-29.

10. Forbes and Muise (eds.), *The Atlantic Provinces in Confederation*, p. 37.

11. Phillip A. Buckner, "The 1870s: Political Integration," in Forbes and Muise (eds.), *The Atlantic Provinces in Confederation*, p. 49.

12. Ernest Forbes quoted in "Shafted," *Atlantic Progress* (June 1999), p. 36.

13. Thorburn, *Politics in New Brunswick*, p. 16.

14. Thorburn, *Politics in New Brunswick*, p. 16.

15. See, among many others, E. R. Forbes and D. A. Muise (eds.), *The Atlantic Provinces in Confederation* (Toronto: University of Toronto Press, 1993).

16. Forbes and Muise (eds.), *The Atlantic Provinces in Confederation*, p. 14.

17. David A. Alexander, *Atlantic Canada and Confederation: Essays in Canadian Political Economy* (Toronto: University of Toronto Press, 1983), p. 4.

18. J.R. Mallory, *The Structure of Canadian Government* (Toronto: Macmillan, 1971), p. 124.

19. Donald J. Savoie, *The Politics of Public Spending in Canada* (Toronto: University of Toronto Press, 1990), chap. 10.

20. E.R. Forbes, "Consolidating Disparity: The Maritimes and the Industrialization of Canada during the Second World War," *Acadiensis*, Vol. 15, no. 2 (Spring 1986), p. 13.

21. Carmen Miller, "The 1940s: War and Rehabilitation," in Forbes and Muise (eds.), *The Atlantic Provinces in Confederation*, p. 325.

22. Alexander, *Atlantic Canada and Confederation*, p. 68.

23. See, among others, Paul Bairoch, *Cities and Economic Development: From the Dawn of History to the Present* (Chicago: Christopher Braider, 1988).

24. L.D. McCann, "Shock Waves in the Old Economy: The Maritime Urban System During the Great Transformation 1867-1939," in George J. DeBenedetti and Rodolphe H. Lamarche (eds.), *Shock Waves: The Maritime Urban System in the New Economy* (Moncton: Institut canadien de recherche sur le développement régional, 1994), pp. 9-42.

25. McCann, "Shock Waves in the Old Economy," DeBenedetti and Lamarche (eds.), *Shock Waves*, p. 12

26. McCann, "Shock Waves in the Old Economy," DeBenedetti and Lamarche (eds.), *Shock Waves*, p. 14.

27. Canada, Department of Reconstruction and Supply, *Employment and Income with Special Reference to the Initial Period of Reconstruction* (Ottawa: King's Printer, 1945), p. 21.

28. A.W. Johnson, *Social Policy in Canada: The Past as It Conditions the Present* (Halifax: Institute for Research on Public Policy, 1987), p. 1.

29. Harold Innis, "Decentralization and Democracy," in H. Innis (ed.), *Essays in Canadian Economic History* (Toronto: University of Toronto Press, 1956), p. 371.

30. Canada, *The Atlantic Region of Canada: Economic Development Strategy for the Eighties* (Saint John's, Newfoundland: Atlantic Development Council, 1978), p. 39.

31. Canada, *Living Together: A Study of Regional Disparities* (Ottawa: Economic Council of Canada, 1977), p. 35.

32. Canada, *Living Together: A Study of Regional Disparities*, p. 49.

33

33. Janine Brodie, *The Political Economy of Canadian Regionalism* (Toronto: Harcourt Brace Javanovich, 1990), p. 156.

34. Brodie, *The Political Economy of Canadian Regionalism*, pp. 156-57.

35. Thorburn, *Politics in New Brunswick*, p. 16.

36. See, among others, G.A. Rawlyk and Doug Brown, "The Historical Framework of the Maritimes and Confederation," in G.A. Rawlyk, *The Atlantic Provinces and the Problems of Confederation* (Atlantic Canada: Breakwater, 1979), p. 15.

37. Nova Scotia, Journal of the Nova Scotia Assembly, 1886, pp. 147-48.

38. Forbes and Muise, *The Atlantic Provinces in Confederation*, chap. 7.

39. Rawlyk and Brown, "The Historical Framework of the Maritimes and Confederation," p. 26.

40. Forbes and Muise, *The Atlantic Provinces in Confederation*, p. 253.

41. For an excellent history of the movement, see Ernest R. Forbes, *Maritime Rights: The Maritime Rights Movement, 1919-1927* (Montreal: McGill-Queen's University Press, 1979).

42. Forbes, *Maritime Rights*, p. 29.

43. Forbes, *Maritime Rights*, p. 158.

44. Canada, *Report of the Royal Commission on Maritime Claims* (Ottawa: King's Printer, 1927), p. 44.

45. Quoted in Forbes and Muise, *The Atlantic Provinces in Confederation*, p. 258.

46. Quoted in Alexander, *Atlantic Canada and Confederation*, p. 53.

47. Quoted in Forbes and Muise, *The Atlantic Provinces in Confederation*, p. 36.

48. Forbes and Muise, *The Atlantic Provinces in Confederation*, p. 21.

49. Forbes and Muise, *The Atlantic Provinces in Confederation*, p. 37.

50. Alan C. Cairns, *From Interstate to Intrastate Federalism in Canada* (Kingston, Ontario: Institute of Intergovernmental Relations, 1979), p. 6.

34

3

Dealing with the Supplicant

During the period from Confederation to the mid-1950s, Ottawa preferred to deal with the Maritimes issue by issue. There was never an overarching strategy, an explicit regional development policy or even a consistent approach. Only when the situation became too heated, as with the rise of the Maritime Rights Movement, would Ottawa react and establish a royal commission to look for practical solutions to defuse the crisis.

It was only with the introduction of equalization payments in 1957 that Ottawa engaged in concerted efforts to deal with regional disparities. But equalization payments were designed to help poorer provinces provide public services, not to assist them promote economic development. Other federal measures that followed did seek to do this. However, they can hardly be termed a picture of consistency, as federal commitment to the economic development of the Maritimes has waxed and waned over the years. Moreover, the success of these efforts is doubtful.

This chapter seeks to understand what motivated the federal government to intervene in provinces like New Brunswick with special measures to promote economic development and to determine how far it was prepared to go. Accordingly, instead of providing a descriptive account of these efforts, readily available elsewhere,[1] we seek to understand the forces that have influenced the federal government in shaping its economic development policies and programs. It also seeks to shed new light on how the Maritimes, in particular New Brunswick, responded and how they would define their place in Confederation as the federal government sought to expand its role and responsibilities through its spending power.

donald j. savoie

In the Beginning There Was Duncan

Canada has always had federal-provincial problems. In some provinces, fiscal difficulties started to manifest themselves shortly after Confederation. Ottawa responded by making a number of special and even supposedly final federal subsidies and grants to the provinces. But the subsidies were never final and regional discontent would never disappear.

In the previous chapter we discussed the rise of the Maritime Rights Movement. The movement gained credibility if only because by the early 1920s the region had come to acknowledge its economic difficulties and decline relative to central Canada. There was a widely held consensus that the single most important factor behind the region's malaise was discriminatory federal government policies. The solution then was to fix things in Ottawa and to force the federal government to be more sensitive to economic circumstances in the Maritimes.

In the 1920s New Brunswick and its sister Maritime provinces still held some political advantages and clout, as the elections of 1921 and 1925 so clearly demonstrated. As well, the fact that regional inequalities existed in Canada was something that surprised and, at the time, concerned Canadians as a whole.[2] Ontario better than any understood the importance of public policy to economic development well before the era of big government. By the early 1920s, the benefits of the National Policy to the Ontario economy were already obvious. The economic difficulties of the Maritimes, it was assumed, could be resolved only if the right mix of public policy measures was implemented.

The federal government began to sponsor a series of special studies, inquiries and royal commissions to deal with specific issues confronting the region. The Duncan Commission was the most important of these. The commission was allowed to find practical solutions to the Maritimes' difficulties, but not at the expense of Ontario's economic interests. The fact that Duncan was instructed not to deal in any concrete terms with tariffs and trade issues is ample evidence of this. Duncan also completely ignored the impact of the region's declining representation in the House of Commons and its implications for the three Maritime provinces.

Clearly, the commission was also established to deal with a problem not on the official agenda. When things appeared to get out of hand in political terms, as they did in 1921 and 1925, commissions and special inquiries could serve a useful purpose: They could be used as diversionary tactics. Mackenzie King (of the famed comment, "conscription if necessary but not necessarily conscription") was, as history now makes clear, a master in the art of delay to avoid dealing with pressing public policy issues. King successfully employed his considerable skills in the case of the Maritime Rights Movement.

That said, the Duncan Commission's findings did have some impact. It recommended a reduction in Canadian National Railway rates with the carrier compensated by federal subsidy. Though the King government was able to sidestep much of what the Duncan Commission had to say and recommend, it did not ignore this recommendation. A special assistance program was introduced in 1927, establishing Maritime rates at 20 percent lower than rates elsewhere. It was revised in 1957 to 30 percent and in 1969 was extended to highway carriers. A further revision in 1974 provided an additional 20 percent reduction for selected commodities moving to markets outside the Atlantic region. A federal-provincial committee determined which products were eligible for the rate subsidy. New products manufactured in the region could be added to the list. For example, wheel weights for automobiles were declared eligible when a firm in Nova Scotia began manufacturing them. Total payments under the freight-assistance programs amounted to $60 million in 1980 and $63 million in 1981. By 1990-91, payments under the Maritime Freight Rates Act (railway) and under the Atlantic Region Freight Assistance Act (railway, marine and trucking) amounted to nearly $100 million.[3] This program remained in place until the mid-1990s when the Chrétien government launched a major program review in 1994 to repair Ottawa's balance sheet. All departments were asked to make significant spending cuts. Doug Young, the then Transport minister and New Brunswick's representative in the federal cabinet, volunteered to sacrifice the subsidies as part of his department's contributions to the program review exercise and the freight rates assistance for the region is now history.

The report's findings did lead to some new measures but they were hardly as ambitious or (in the end) as effective as the Maritime Rights Movement had initially hoped. Historian David Frank sums up the legacy of the Duncan report in this fashion:

[T]he failure of the report and the weakness of subsequent action may simply have increased Maritime cynicism about the prospects for achieving significant changes through the political process...for many Maritimers it simply confirmed their skeptical appreciation of the weakness of the hinterland within the Canadian state.[4]

But again for King it had served an important purpose: it had defused a delicate political situation. Maritime grievances would never again enjoy the kind of national prominence that the Maritime Rights Movement had been able to generate. Regional ministers from New Brunswick and the other Maritime provinces would still do their best to secure the odd project for their province, but there was little appetite left in Ottawa to take a broad, comprehensive approach to economic development in the Maritimes. The Great Depression was soon on Canada's doorstep and the prime minister was in no mood to make concessions to the Maritimes. Some follow-up measures from the Duncan Commission were introduced, including further modest adjustments to federal subsidies to the three Maritime provinces, but slowly and surely the findings of the commission disappeared from the public policy agenda.

This, combined with the fact that the Maritimes' political influence in the House of Commons continued to decline as western Canada kept adding new seats, pushed Maritime concerns to the background. If Maritimers look back to the period just before Confederation as the region's golden age in economic terms, they can look to the 1920s, when they were able to put aside partisan considerations at election time, as its golden age in political terms.

This is not to suggest that Maritime provincial governments gave up on pressing their claims on Ottawa. The Nova Scotia government, for example, appointed in 1944 a royal commission containing high profile and credible members from outside the province to review the "province's disabilities in Confederation." The commission decided to focus on tariff issues. Commission staff sought to provide a cost-benefit estimate of tariffs by calculating the amount by which the tariffs raised prices in each province and by subtracting any increases deemed beneficial. To the surprise of no one, the three Maritime provinces came out the heavy losers.[5]

But there has never been any market in Ottawa for this line of thinking and the Nova Scotia Royal Commission had precious little impact. Federal government payments to the three provinces could be adjusted but tariffs went to the heart of the Ontario and Quebec economy. The nation's political power, concentrated in these two provinces, would decide on its own terms if tariffs could be changed and by how much.

Defining the Nation Through Government Initiatives

From the mid-1930s onward, Maritime concerns became subsumed into the nation's broader socioeconomic problems. By then, many in Ottawa probably started to accept as inevitable the decline of the Maritime economy, given its location on the periphery of a tariff-protected Canadian market. In any event, the nation had bigger issues to address. The Great Depression was one, but

40

so was the federal government's apparent inability to respond to the challenges it presented. If the National Policy constituted the first phase in Canadian nation building, the federal government spending power would constitute the second.

The Great Depression had, in a very harsh manner, revealed Ottawa's inability to use public policy to deal with a disastrous economic downturn. In addition, many leading intellectuals and Canadian nationalists in Ontario became disturbed over the resurgence of provincial rights. The establishment of the Bank of Canada in the late 1930s brought a new policy capacity to Ottawa, and the Department of Finance, during this same period, started to hire bright young economists, one of whom (Bob Bryce) had actually studied at the feet of Lord Keynes at Cambridge. Keynesian economics, which advocated a government's spending its way out of economic depressions, had, as already noted, come into fashion in Ottawa. But Ottawa could not do this, if only because provincial governments were, on the whole, more concerned with trying to balance their budgets by cutting spending and raising taxes than with introducing new spending measures to stimulate economic activities. This is precisely what Lord Keynes argued would serve only to make things worse.

Mackenzie King decided in 1937 to establish a royal commission to carry out "a re-examination of the economic and financial basis of Confederation and of the distribution of legislative powers in light of the economic and social developments of the last seventy years."[6] The problem, as seen from Ottawa, was straightforward. Canada's constitution, the BNA Act, had granted the federal government all the necessary power to implement the National Policy, but times had changed and the Act was now ill suited to respond to current realities. In light of the Depression years and the development of the modern state, Canada required access to public policy levers given by the Act to the provinc es. The key ones were in the areas of social welfare and the implementation of macroeconomic policies, such as inspired by Keynesian economics, and no longer in managing tariffs and trade issues.[7]

It came as no surprise then that the 1940 Rowell-Sirois Report stressed the need for integrating federal-provincial fiscal policies more effectively and, at the same time, sought to give Ottawa a much stronger hand in managing them. By the time the report was tabled, Ottawa had already moved to carve a role for itself in the social policy field. It had, for example, secured a constitutional amendment to allow the federal government to assume full responsibility for unemployment relief, which enabled it to establish an Unemployment Insurance Fund. In addition, as part of managing the wartime economy, the federal government was able to convince the provinces to leave the income tax field for the duration of the war in return for grants calculated on estimates of what the provinces would have collected. When the war ended, Ottawa tried to retain its monopoly of income tax. But the provinces were in no mood to agree. It had been only thirty years since the provincial governments had granted "consent" for the federal government to enter the income tax field. They were not about to vacate the field completely only to let Ottawa have a free hand in imposing new taxes. The result was the development of an elaborate system of sharing of both revenues and responsibilities, the remnants of which can still be found today in health, education and social services spending. It was not Ottawa's preferred option, but it would have to do. It did, however, hand the federal government a great deal of power over the country's fiscal policies. Historian W.L. Morton has labeled the 1936-1949 period "The Revival of National Power."[8]

Why, one may ask, would New Brunswick premiers agree to an expanding role for the federal government? Certainly, premiers Allison Dysart and later J.B. McNair would know from memory the havoc the National Policy had wreaked on their province and the reasons for the rise of the Maritime Rights Movement. They would also have had a first-hand appreciation of the bias C.D. Howe and his bureaucrats had for central Canada. In addition, Oxford-educated McNair understood the finer points of the Canadian constitution probably better than many of the other provincial premiers and one can only assume he was well aware New Brunswick no longer had the political clout to influence Ottawa in the event the federal government was able to carve out a greater role for itself. Furthermore, McNair had repeatedly stressed the importance of provincial autonomy.

There were, it appears, two reasons for New Brunswick's support for an expanded role for the federal government. First, when McNair replaced Dysart as premier in 1940, New Brunswick was literally on the edge of bankruptcy and the "province's Montreal bankers were threatening to foreclose."[9] With the bankers at its throat, the province was hardly in a position to bargain with Ottawa from a position of strength. Indeed, it needed Ottawa's financial help simply to continue to operate. Added to all of this was the fact that McNair was both a partisan Liberal and a strongly committed supporter of Ottawa's war effort. Partisan politics had come to matter a great deal more in New Brunswick in the 1940s than it had in the 1920s and McNair took a back seat to no one when it came to partisan politics.

Second, McNair and the other Maritime premiers would have had reason for some optimism in supporting the findings of the Rowell-Sirois Report. While it is true the report did not look directly at tariff issues, trade patterns or, for that matter, economic development, it did the next best thing, at least from a New

Brunswick perspective. It recommended "that the wealth produced nationally should be taxed nationally and redistributed on a national basis, instead of being taxed in the main by the central provinces for the benefit of the central provinces."[10] In other words, while the commission did not want to change where wealth was being produced in the country, it argued that the benefits from it should be shared nationally. The commission heard briefs from both the Maritimes and the Prairie provinces that their economic woes were largely the result of the National Policy. It agreed with this assessment and concluded that those provinces which were impoverished by the National Policy, which was implemented in the "general interest," should now be compensated with "public expenditures." Though the commission had precious little to say about how to go about this, it had plenty to say about the fiscal capacity of the provinces. It recommended the introduction of national adjustment grants that would have favoured the poorer provinces. Janine Brodie sums up the findings of the Rowell-Sirois Commission well when she writes that "the grants would simply help to underwrite some of the social costs of uneven development within certain political jurisdictions [for example, New Brunswick] while the economic relationships that promoted uneven development remained unchallenged."[11] For this reason, the idea of some form of fiscal equity in Canada was born.

But when Prime Minister Mackenzie King sought to overhaul Canada's taxation and social policy infrastructure and implement the findings of the Rowell-Sirois Report at a federal-provincial conference, he met with firm and highly vocal opposition from both Ontario and Quebec. Indeed, he was told in no uncertain terms by the premiers of Ontario and Quebec that the initiative was a non-starter, so much so that Ontario Premier, George Drew, "hysterically characterized [the reform package] as Hitlerism."[12] But Quebec and Ontario's opposition served another purpose: "The central Canadian premiers' opposition confirmed the Maritime premiers' good opinion of King's plans."[13] Given Ontario and Quebec's opposition and the preoccupation with the war effort, Ottawa was not able to proceed with a massive overhaul of the country's social policy infrastructure, secure control of an important source of provincial revenues – income tax – or introduce a national adjustment grant initiative. Still, Ottawa would continue to expand its role in many policy areas through its spending power, and the idea of introducing unconditional grants to the provinces with a bias to poorer provinces would re-emerge later.

Some fifteen years after the Rowell-Sirois Commission tabled its findings, the St. Laurent government asked Walter Gordon to chair yet another royal commission, this one on Canada's economic prospects. Again, the Atlantic region decided to play an active role in the work of the Gordon Commission

43

and the region submitted 23. Virtually all of them "were couched in the now familiar language of regional grievance."[14]

The Gordon Commission is probably best known for expressing deep concerns over the impact of foreign ownership in the Canadian economy. But it also had important things to say about the deepening patterns of uneven development. It went beyond the issue of fiscal need to suggest ways to improve the performance of regional economies. Still, the commission decided not to address "the causes of uneven development" between the regions.[15] This was taken as a given which needed not to be revisited. Instead, the challenge, as the commission saw it, was to find ways to promote economic development in slow growth regions without hurting the stronger provinces, in particular Ontario.

Hugh John Flemming, the then New Brunswick premier, played a lead role on behalf of Atlantic Canada in the work of the Gordon Commission and in making representations to Ottawa in support of the region. He decided to organize a major conference in New Brunswick on the region's economic prospects and invited the other three Atlantic premiers to participate. They agreed and the first ever conference of Atlantic premiers was held in Fredericton on 9 July 1956. Flemming led the charge, arguing the region should press Ottawa for subsidies based on fiscal need, assistance for resource development, a new regional transportation policy, different monetary and fiscal policies to stimulate economic development, and a new tariff policy geared to the region's economic interests. Nova Scotia Premier Henry Hicks recommended they ask Ottawa to place more defence industries and contracts in the region.[16] The "supplicant" had become more demanding. The focus was no longer restricted to fiscal needs for provincial governments but on a helping hand to promote economic development.

At the same time, however, there were concerns increasingly being heard in Ottawa that the federal government ought not to play regional favourites. That is, Ottawa should not agree to any special concessions for Atlantic Canada unless it was prepared to make them also available to the other regions. Equalization in the mid-1950s meant something very different than it does today and the prevailing view was that all federal payments to the provinces should be made on an "equal" basis. New Brunswick historian W.S. MacNutt rebutted this view by writing, "Where is the equalization in the operation of tariff policy...in the St. Lawrence Seaway, in the pipeline contract? We can say that, since we started on fairly even terms in 1867, equalization as seen from Ottawa has had some curious results."[17] The last budget of the St. Laurent government announced plans to introduce annual equalization payments to the have-less provinces. By that time, the Gordon Commission had also submitted an interim report and recommended that "a bold, comprehensive and coordinated approach" be implemented to resolve the underlying problems of the Atlantic region which, in the commission's opinion, required special measures to improve its economic framework. These included a federally sponsored capital-projects commission to provide needed infrastructure facilities to encourage economic growth and measures to increase the rate of capital investment in the region.

In many ways the commission was breaking new ground in advocating the involvement of the private sector in promoting development in slow-growth regions. Perhaps for this reason the commission expressed concerns about any negative impact on other regions. It argued, "Special assistance put into effect to assist these areas might well adversely affect the welfare of industries already functioning in more established areas of Canada."[18] The point was clear enough: The government could assist Atlantic Canada, but not at the expense of other regions, notably Ontario.

A New Approach for the Supplicant

Looking back, it is now clear that the election of John Diefenbaker as prime minister constituted a kind of watershed for Atlantic Canada. Unlike the long-serving prime ministers, Sir John A. Macdonald, Sir Wilfred Laurier, Mackenzie King and Louis St. Laurent, Diefenbaker was not from either Ontario or Quebec. He also had a healthy distrust of central Canada's political and economic elite.[19] Furthermore, he had strong political ties to the region. Hugh John Flemming, it will be recalled, moved Diefenbaker's nomination at the party's national leadership convention and Robert Stanfield, newly elected premier of Nova Scotia, delivered the convention's keynote address. In addition, Diefenbaker garnered 121 members of Parliament in the June 1957 general election, 16 more than his party had in the previous general election. He went on to form a minority government, having won only seven seats more than the Liberals. In forming his government, he appointed a 22-member cabinet including four ministers from Atlantic Canada and, for the first time in Canadian history, there were more ministers from Atlantic Canada and the West than from central Canada.

Diefenbaker had included an "Atlantic Manifesto" as an important part of his 1957 election platform. The manifesto borrowed heavily from the Flemming Fredericton conference of Atlantic premiers and the Gordon Commission. It urged federal government aid to electrical power development in the region, further freight-rate adjustment, capital projects, adjustment grants to the provinces, a Canadian coast guard and a national resource-development program.[20] Though the federal Department of Finance was quick to recommend a "go-slow" approach to Atlantic Canada, Diefenbaker had, within a year of coming to power, implemented several significant measures for the region, including a loan to help develop the Beechwood dam in New Brunswick and a $25 million special adjustment grant to Atlantic Canada.[21] In addition, measures to promote economic development in the Prairies would indirectly help Atlantic Canada.

The 1960 budget speech unveiled the first of many measures Ottawa has developed to combat regional disparities. The budget permitted firms to obtain double the normal rate of capital-cost allowances on most of the assets they acquired to produce new products, if they located in designated regions (with high unemployment and slow economic growth). Shortly after this measure was introduced, Parliament passed the Agriculture Rehabilitation and Development Act (ARDA). ARDA began as a federal-provincial effort to stimulate agricultural development in order to increase income in rural areas. It was an attempt to rebuild the depressed rural economy and represented Ottawa's first "regional" development program.[22] Later still, the Diefenbaker government established the Atlantic Development Board (ADB), an idea that first surfaced in the work of the Gordon Commission. A planning staff was put together and the board was given a special fund to improve the region's basic economic infrastructure.

The Diefenbaker government was also the first to turn to the private sector to promote economic development in Atlantic Canada, a bold step in its day. It introduced the Area Development Incentives Act (ADIA) and the Area Development Agency (ADA) within the Department of Industry. Legislation establishing ADIA was passed in 1963.[23] The central purpose behind these initiatives was to turn to the private sector to stimulate growth in economically depressed regions. This was to be done by enriching existing tax incentives and by introducing capital grants in designated areas. Regions of high unemployment and slow growth were the target of both. Only regions with unemployment rates above a specified threshold would become eligible.

By contrast, the succeeding Pearson government was not particularly creative in this respect. It essentially played at the margins, expanding some existing programs and revising others. It repackaged ARDA, expanded its scope and relabeled it the Fund for Rural Economic Development (FRED). It also designated new regions that could benefit from the program and added new money.

The Rise and Fall of DREE

Pierre Trudeau declared during the 1968 national election campaign that the problem of regional development was as threatening to national unity as the language issue.[24] He was no sooner elected to power than he moved to establish the Department of Regional Economic Expansion (DREE) and appointed his close friend and the senior Quebec minister Jean Marchand as its first minister. There was no secessionist movement in Atlantic Canada threatening national unity, so one can only assume that Trudeau had Quebec in mind when he suggested that regional underdevelopment posed a threat to national unity. The fact that he named Marchand to head DREE rather than, say, the senior Atlantic minister Allan J. MacEachern, also spoke to Trudeau's preoccupation with Quebec.

To be sure, Trudeau had ambitious plans for regional development and for DREE. There is also no denying that DREE introduced or supported a great number of measures for New Brunswick during its fourteen years of existence. The reader may wish to consult[25] one of the several publications that discuss these in considerable detail. We will not, however, review them here.

Given the purpose of this study, we need to focus on Ottawa's commitment to New Brunswick in its regional development policies. Jean Marchand made it very clear at the outset that federal regional development efforts would be concentrated on eastern Quebec and Atlantic Canada. He bluntly stated that if the bulk of federal government spending for regional development (something like 80 percent of the budget) was not spent east of Trois-Rivières, then Ottawa's regional development efforts would fail.[26] This is also precisely what Marchand and Tom Kent (DREE's first deputy minister) did in defining DREE policies and programs. The regions initially designated under the industrial incentives program accounted for only 30 percent of the Canadian labour force and included all the Atlantic provinces, eastern and northern Quebec, parts of northern Ontario and the northernmost regions of the four western provinces. The department's other important program, built around the growth pole concept to promote economic development, was even more restricted in its regional application.

Before too long, however, strong political pressure was exerted on Marchand to extend the programs. Initially at least, he stood firm, declaring that "the more you extend it [i.e., DREE], the more you weaken it. We have to stick to our guns."[27]

The other key issue in establishing DREE was whether it would have enough clout in Ottawa to push other departments to accept its mandate as a priority for their own programs. In reviewing the proposed DREE legislation, the then opposition leader Robert Stanfield expressed concern that the department would be left alone to carry the entire load while other federal departments simply went on with their sectoral responsibilities. Said Stanfield, "There may well be a tendency on the part of other Ministers to say, 'Let Jean do it'... This bill does not assure anything like the degree of coordination which there must be among the departments of the government if regional disparity is to be attacked effectively."[28] Both

47

the prime minister and Marchand dismissed Stanfield's concerns. Trudeau argued the establishment of DREE was necessary "to achieve real coordination...of our endeavours and undertakings in such a worthy and vital sphere in respect of our country's future." Marchand added his new department "[was] the only way to secure the coordination of federal efforts in regional development."[29]

DREE , however, would soon become vulnerable on both fronts. Cabinet ministers and MPs from the Montreal area frequently made the point that Montreal was Quebec's growth pole and if DREE were serious about regional development, then it ought to designate Montreal under its growth-pole-inspired program. By the early 1970s, it had become clear that Montreal's economic performance could no longer keep pace with that of Toronto. The city's unemployment rate stood at 7.0 percent in 1972 compared with 4.6 percent for Toronto. The rise of the Parti Québécois and the actions of the Front de Libération du Québec (FLQ) had pushed Quebec concerns high on the national agenda. Ottawa would make every effort to demonstrate to Quebec that Canadian federalism could be made to work to its advantage. It was thought that promoting the country's two official languages and introducing federal regional development in the province were as good a place as any to start to make federalism work for Quebec.

In the end, Marchand agreed to designate Montreal as a special region eligible for federal regional development programming. To no one's surprise, other communities also began to apply strong pressure for similar treatment. If DREE could justify a presence in Montreal, why not also in Vancouver and Toronto? Better yet, why not smaller communities in Ontario, like Cornwall or Windsor? Before long, DREE 's spending patterns were changing. Atlantic Canada was the big loser, in that it could make the case that it needed DREE expenditures far more than the other regions, and Quebec the clear winner, as Table 3 below shows.

History would prove Stanfield right and Trudeau and Marchand wrong. It very quickly became clear that other federal departments had little interest in promoting regional development through their own programs. Indeed, virtually all federal regional development efforts came from DREE alone. Tom Kent explains why: "From the point of view of almost all conventional wisdom in Ottawa, the idea of regional development was a rather improper one that some otherwise quite reasonable politician brought in like a baby on a doorstep from an election campaign."[30]

In any event, there were dark clouds on the horizon that would spell the end of DREE. With the energy crisis and other developments in the mid-1970s, there were signs that economic power was shifting away from Ontario to western Canada. The sharp increase in oil prices led to a transfer of wealth from

Table 3

Regional Distribution of DREE Expenditures

REGION	1969-70	1973-74
	(%)	
Atlantic	51	38
Quebec	12	39
Ontario	9	3
West	24	14

Source: DREE, Annual Reports 1970-71 and 1974-75.

the oil-consuming to the oil-producing provinces. The shift was such that by the end of the decade Ontario became eligible for equalization payments and the federal government had to introduce legislation to prevent the provincial government from collecting it.

By the early 1980s, the Trudeau government became convinced that it had to act. Ottawa might have thought Ontario was losing some of its economic power, but it knew full well the province still held considerable political power. The minister of Finance tabled a document as part of his 1981 budget papers titled "Economic Development for Canada in the 1980s." The document maintained that the regional balance was changing as a result of buoyancy in the West, optimism in the East, and unprecedented softness in key economic sectors in central Canada. Underpinning this view were the economic prospects associated with resource-based megaprojects. Atlantic Canada, in contrast to historical economic trends, was expected to enjoy a decade of solid growth, largely as a result of offshore resources. The West, meanwhile, would capture over half of the investment in major projects. Ontario and Quebec would face problems of industrial adjustment, brought about by increased international competition.

In brief, Canada's regional problem was changing and Ottawa felt it had to adjust its policies. Looking into their crystal ball, Department of Finance officials actually believed that Atlantic Canada would soon be experiencing an economic boom and Ontario-Quebec an economic downturn. In other words, anticipated major energy projects would fuel the economics of the West and the Atlantic provinces and these regions would be able to take care of themselves. The new regional problem was the weakening of the manufacturing sector in

49

central Canada. It was in these two regions that new employment opportunities ought to be created.

But there was another problem with DREE. There has always been a great deal of tension in Ottawa between the Department of Industry, operating as it does from a sectoral perspective, and any regional development department or agency. The tension spilled over to the national media in the early 1980s over the location of an automotive plant. The then DREE minister Pierre De Bané and Industry minister Herb Gray exchanged strong words in public over Volkswagen's decision to locate a new parts plant in Barrie, Ontario, in order to take advantage of Ottawa's duty-remission program, under which the duty on automobile imports was waived if a company established a plant in Canada.[31] At De Bané's urging, a delegation of federal officials was sent to Germany to meet with Volkswagen. DREE selected two sites, Montreal and Halifax, and offered a cash grant to Volkswagen to locate in either one. De Bané also suggested the federal government should refuse the duty remission for Volkswagen if the company pressed ahead with its Barrie location rather than a DREE-designated region. Gray and Trudeau rejected De Bané's argument and Volkswagen went to Barrie.

On 12 January 1982, Prime Minister Trudeau unveiled a major government reorganization for economic development. He issued a lengthy statement explaining the reasons for the new reorganization but said nothing about regional disparities. Although regional development would be central to policy-making, it involved something significantly different from fourteen years earlier. Regional development now referred less to alleviating regional disparities than to development at the regional level. It also meant Atlantic Canada would lose its preferred status in federal regional development programs which had, in any event, already become shaky.

Now that regional development policy would apply to all regions of Canada, Ottawa sought to give it much more weight in its decision-making process. Apparently oblivious to what he had told Stanfield fourteen years earlier, Trudeau pointed out that the key reason for the new organization was that it was "no longer enough that one department alone is primarily responsible for regional economic development."[32] In brief, the new organization involved the establishment of a central agency, the Ministry of State for Economic and Regional Development (MSERD), by adding regional policy and coordination to the functions of the existing Ministry of State for Economic Development. It also established a new line department, the Department of Regional Industrial Expansion (DRIE), through the amalgamation of the regional programs of DREE and the programs of the Department of Industry.

The first DRIE minister was Ed Lumley, who rose in the House of Commons on 27 June 1983 to explain the new program. Lumley cautioned that "combating regional disparities is difficult even in good economic times.... It is much more difficult in a period when, because of a worldwide downturn, [Canada's] traditional industries are suffering from soft markets, stiff international competition, rapid technological change and rising protectionism from the countries that make up our market." A new program to meet these circumstances would have to be one that he could "clearly recommend to the business community, to the Canadian public and to all Members of Parliament." DRIE, Lumley reported, had come up with such a program. It was a "regionally-sensitized, multifaceted program of industrial assistance in all parts of Canada.... This is not a program to be available only in certain designated regions. Whatever riding any Member of this House represents, his or her constituents will be eligible for assistance."[33] Toronto, Vancouver and Calgary would now join the ranks of communities eligible for regional development programs. It would also ensure, as a Privy Council Office official declared shortly after the reorganization, that there would be no more "public squabbling" between two ministers over the location of an automotive parts plant. The clear signal to former DREE employees was that the sectoral perspective had won over the regional one and that the Industry Department was the clear winner.[34] There was no longer any pretense that Ottawa's regional development efforts would favour Atlantic Canada.

During his brief tenure as prime minister, John Turner abolished MSERD, but left DRIE intact, as did Brian Mulroney, for a while at least. Mulroney had ambitious plans for regional development. During the 1984 election campaign, he declared that DRIE would receive a "specific legislative mandate to promote the least developed regions," and "every department will be required to submit to the Standing Committee of Parliament on Economic and Regional Development annual assessments of the effect of departmental policies on specific regions."[35] Barely a year after he came to office, Mulroney would see the four Atlantic premiers taking dead aim at Ottawa's regional development efforts, in particular DRIE, even though they were all partisan allies of the Mulroney Progressive Conservative party. The bulk of DRIE spending, over 70 percent, was being directed to Ontario and Quebec. It did not take long for the Atlantic and even Western premiers to point to DRIE as part of the problem rather than part of the solution. The point was even made that DRIE programming was, in fact, increasing regional disparities rather than contributing to their alleviation. Some provincial government officials in Atlantic Canada also began to report that on occasion firms hovering between establishing a plant in either Atlantic Canada or southern Ontario, received more generous offers from DRIE to locate in southern Ontario.[36]

51

By the mid-1980s, it was clear that Department of Finance predictions about new regional patterns of economic development in Canada had been wrong, with far-reaching implications for Atlantic Canada. Indeed, some observers were already pointing to the likelihood that the economies of southern Ontario and Quebec would soon overheat. Meanwhile, the Atlantic economy, where unemployment rates had fallen only slightly, was still in the doldrums. The anticipated mega-energy projects did not materialize for the region. In a meeting with Mulroney, the four Atlantic premiers made the case that, if he did nothing else, he should abolish DRIE. Mulroney decided to do something else.

He established the Atlantic Canada Opportunities Agency (ACOA) on 6 June 1987 and, never one for understatement, declared, "We begin with new money, a new mission and a new opportunity...the Agency will succeed where others have failed."[37] He gave it $1.05 billion in new money over five years, new in the sense that it would be over and above the $1 billion already committed to the region under existing programs.[38]

Mulroney was not done with regional development announcements. He had some political fence mending to do in western Canada since his government had in 1987 awarded the CF-18 fighter planes maintenance contract to a Quebec firm, although a Winnipeg firm had submitted the lowest bid. The public outcry in western Canada against this decision was very vocal and a general election was expected in 1988. A few months after he unveiled plans for ACOA, Mulroney went to Alberta to bring the news of a new Western Diversification Department, together with a $1.2 billion fund in *new* money. A month earlier, the Mulroney government had announced yet another regional development agency, this time in Northern Ontario. The Federal Economic Development Northern Ontario Agency (FEDNOR) was given about $160 million of new money over five years.

And southern Ontario and Quebec certainly could not be overlooked. A new Department of Industry, Science and Technology was created essentially for these two regions. Table 4, which reports on the department's defence industry productivity program in 1988-89, one year after McKenna came to office in New Brunswick, speaks to this point. At about the same time the department also signed a five-year $1 billion agreement to develop the Quebec regions. In fact, the agreement covered all of Quebec since it simply divided the province into two regions: the central region and the resource region.[39]

The Supplicant Is Not Alone

When McKenna came to office in 1987 he had to come to terms with the fact that federal economic development policies had a bias that hardly favoured his

Table 4
Defence Industry Productivity Program:
Accepted Offers and Authorized Assistance, 1988-89

PROVINCE OR TERRITORY	Offers accepted	Authorized assistance ($ million)
Newfoundland	0	0
Nova Scotia	0	0
Prince Edward Island	0	0
New Brunswick	2	0.4
Quebec	49	100.6
Ontario	65	102.2
Manitoba	2	2.8
Saskatchewan	0	0
Alberta	7	5.8
British Columbia	7	1.5
Yukon and Northwest Territories	0	0
Total	132	213.3

Source: Department of Regional Industrial Expansion and Ministry of State for Science and Technology, Minister of Supply and Services, *Annual Report* 1988-89, 1990.

province. This was clearly true historically and was still true in the fall of 1987. Worse, the federal government had lost its way in its regional development programs. The public perception was that Atlantic Canada was the biggest recipient of federal largesse. However, though the Atlantic region was getting the bad press, it was not getting the greatest benefits. Other regions were.

Diefenbaker had set a policy and a course of action in regional development that clearly favoured Atlantic Canada. Trudeau, in establishing DREE, initially at least, had, it appears, a similar objective, although he would, at the same time, add a new focus on eastern Quebec. Within a few years however, federal regional development efforts became an integral part of Ottawa's plans to strengthen national unity. Montreal was designated eligible, which served to open the floodgates. In DREE's last days, Atlantic Canada was no longer DREE's main client.

Looking back, we see that every region and every community, strong or weak, has had its hand in the federal government's regional development pot. By 1991, one of ACOA's main concerns was that its programs had become "uncompetitive with other federal economic development assistance offered to the private sector in other regions."[40] Highly profitable firms in every region of the country have, at one point or another, turned to federal assistance to build office buildings in major cities, ski resorts and golf courses.

53

Other economic programs of the federal government have been of far greater benefit to the richer regions over the years. Grants and repayable loans to industry are highly visible and at times give rise to heated public debate over their value. Less visible, but often more lucrative for firms, are tax credits, which do not involve a direct transfer of money. Nevertheless, they represent government revenue forgone. The federal Department of Finance produced a study on tax expenditure in 1985. The "economic development and support" and the "corporate income" categories were the second most important categories of tax expenditures (at the time, behind health and welfare). The study provided sufficient information to break down tax expenditures on a province-by-province basis. Ontario, Quebec, Alberta and British Columbia were the recipient of the lion's share of tax expenditures – over 80 percent of all corporate tax expenditures. On a per capita basis, Alberta led all provinces in corporate tax expenditures, while the four Atlantic provinces trailed badly. In fact, corporations declaring taxable income in the Yukon and Northwest Territories received more tax expenditures than did any of the four Atlantic provinces. The point here is that, though tax expenditures constituted at the time over 35 percent of the total federal expenditure budget, they played only a negligible role in Ottawa's fostering of regional development. One federal finance official speculated that tax expenditures with a specific regional development purpose never amount to more than two percent of the total federal tax expenditure budget.[41]

New Brunswick, along with the other Atlantic provinces, continues to benefit annually from federal equalization payments. It is important to bear in mind, however, that interregional transfer payments have never, as an Ontario-based economist argues, stemmed from "an interregional altruism intrinsic to Canadian culture."[42] Canadians appear to have lost sight of the fact that the idea dates back to the Rowell-Sirois Report, the thinking behind which was that the payments would compensate for discriminatory federal policies, starting with the National Policy, which had led to uneven development and which clearly favoured central Canada, in particular Ontario. In addition, central Canada was able, in a protected market, to export manufactured goods to Atlantic Canada and the transfers enabled the region to purchase the goods, since local natural resources did not yield sufficient rent.

Still, the transfer payments continue to help New Brunswick provide a high level of public service without having to impose an unduly high level of taxes. By the same token, transfer payments to individuals, particularly those made under the unemployment insurance program (later relabeled employment insurance) have represented, over the years, an important transfer of money from the wealthier provinces to certain regions in slow-growth provinces.

54

At no point however, at least until McKenna came to office, had the federal government been prepared to attack the causes of uneven economic development. The historical impact of the National Policy, the management of tariffs and trade, and the decision to concentrate war industries in central Canada are all important factors explaining the location of economic activities in Canada. Moreover, as we saw in this chapter, Ottawa is all too quick to react to a mere hint of vulnerability in the economies of central Canada. Indeed, the federal government's regional development policy was completely overhauled when the Department of Finance saw reasons for economic "optimism" on the east coast due to energy-related megaprojects and for concern over a pending unprecedented softness in Canada's industrial heartland. The federal response was to stimulate "job creation" in Ontario and Quebec.

McKenna came to power in New Brunswick with fresh ideas. He repeatedly insisted, as noted in the introductory chapter, that he did not want to go to Ottawa or Toronto as a "supplicant," or see New Brunswick as "the bellyache" of Canada. The message was, of course, well received in central Canada. By the mid-1980s, the Maritime Rights Movement, the impact of the National Policy and C.D. Howe's war efforts properly belonged to the history books, at least from the view of central Canada. The country's political and economic elite, not always well versed in their country's economic history, applauded the view that there is no point in dredging up old grievances to solve today's problems. Moreover, as this chapter makes clear, even federal regional economic policies in place before McKenna came to power were hardly any more helpful to New Brunswick than to other regions. For the most part, the national media have chosen to ignore the fact that these programs were as present in downtown Montreal and southern Ontario as they were in Atlantic Canada, if not more so.

McKenna would tap into a new fashion in public policy: Everyone who had the capacity and certainly every region should be responsible for their own economic well being. In part because of Ottawa's serious fiscal problems – and because Keynesian economics had fallen on hard times and neo-conservative economics was clearly in ascendancy – the conventional view was that New Brunswick and other slow-growth provinces should be submitted to a good dose of market discipline. In fact, by the mid-1980s, New Brunswickers were being told by some observers that transfer payments were actually never in their economic interests in the first place because they gave rise to an economic dependency.[43]

New Brunswick had been left on the outside as Canada's economic development took shape, first under the guiding hand of the National Policy of

55

the 1880s and, second, under Ottawa's spending power and its various industrial strategies starting with the war effort and then the transition to a postwar economy. Both of these national policies were now under attack by the Mulroney government's decision in 1985 to initiate free trade talks with the United States, which culminated in an agreement in 1987 and the widely held view that government had promised more than it could deliver and delivered more than it could afford. It was under this public policy environment that the McKenna government was sworn into office.

56

Notes

1. See, among others, Donald J. Savoie, *Regional Economic Development: Canada's Search for Solutions*, 2nd ed. (Toronto: University of Toronto Press, 1992).

2. David A. Alexander, *Atlantic Canada and Confederation: Essays in Canadian Political Economy* (Toronto: University of Toronto Press, 1983), p. 53.

3. Savoie, *Regional Economic Development*, p. 167.

4. Quoted in E.R. Forbes and D.A. Muise (eds.), *The Atlantic Provinces in Confederation* (Toronto: University of Toronto Press, 1993), p. 261.

5. Forbes and Muise (eds.), *The Atlantic Provinces in Confederation*, p. 229.

6. D. Smiley (ed.), *The Rowell-Sirois Report, Book 1* (Toronto: McClelland and Stewart, 1963), p. 2.

7. Janine Brodie adds, "measures to reconstruct a peacetime economy." See Janine Brodie, *The Political Economy of Canadian Regionalism* (Toronto: Harcourt Brace Javanovich, 1990), p. 149.

8. W.L. Morton, *The Kingdom of Canada* (Toronto: McClelland and Stewart, 1963), p. 465.

9. Forbes and Muise, *The Atlantic Provinces in Confederation*, p. 326.

10. Forbes and Muise, *The Atlantic Provinces in Confederation*, p. 479.

11. See, among others, Brodie, *The Political Economy of Canadian Regionalism*, p. 145.

12. Forbes and Muise, *The Atlantic Provinces in Confederation*, p. 328.

13. Forbes and Muise, *The Atlantic Provinces in Confederation*, p. 328.

14. Forbes and Muise, *The Atlantic Provinces in Confederation*, p. 407.

15. See, among others, H. Lithwick, "Federal Government Regional Economic Development Policies: An Evaluative Survey," in K. Norrie (ed.), *Disparities and Interregional Adjustment* (Toronto: University of Toronto Press, 1986), p. 116.

16. See, among others, "The Fredericton Conference of Atlantic Premiers," *Atlantic Advocate*, Fredericton (September 1956), p. 28. See also Forbes and Muise, *The Atlantic Provinces in Confederation*, chap. 11.

17. W.S. MacNutt, "The Fredericton Conference: A Look Backward and a Look Forward," *Atlantic Advocate*, Fredericton (September 1956), p. 13.

18. Canada, *Report of the Royal Commission on Canada's Economic Prospects* (Ottawa: The Queen's Printer, 1957), p. 404.

19. See Peter C. Newman, *Renegade in Power* (Toronto: McClelland and Stewart, 1963).

20. See the *Atlantic Advocate*, Fredericton (July 1957), p. 11.

21. See Forbes and Muise, *The Atlantic Provinces in Confederation*, p. 413.

22. Savoie, *Regional Economic Development*, p. 27.

23. Anthony Careless, *Initiative and Response: The Adaptation of Canadian Federalism to Regional Economic Development* (Montreal: McGill-Queen's University Press, 1977), pp. 91-108.

24. Savoie, *Regional Economic Development*, p. 1.

25. See, among others, Donald J. Savoie, *Federal-Provincial Collaboration and Regional Economic Development*, as well as the various DREE annual reports.

26. Quoted in Savoie, *Regional Economic Development*, p. 244.

27. Canada, House of Commons, Standing Committee on Regional Development, *Minutes Proceedings*, 1970, 2:62.

28. See Geoffrey Stevens, *Stanfield* (Toronto: McClelland and Stewart, 1973), pp. 3-11, and Canada, *Commons Debates*, 27 February 1969, Stanfield: 6020; Douglas: 6024.

29. Canada, *Commons Debates*, 27 February 1969, Trudeau: 6016; Marchand: 6894.

30. Canada, *Proceedings of the Standing Senate Committee on National Finance*, Issue no. 12, 22 March 1973, 14:24.

31. "Bickering Over Car Plant Led to Cabinet Shake-up," *Sunday Star*, Toronto, 17 January 1982, p. 1.

32. Ottawa, Office of the Prime Minister, "Reorganization for Economic Development," news release, 12 January 1969.

33. DRIE, Speaking Notes, The Right Honourable Ed Lumley to the House of Commons on the Industrial and Regional Development Program, 27 June 1983, pp. 1-2.

34. See Savoie, *Regional Economic Development*, chap. 7.

35. Statement by the Right Honourable Brian Mulroney at Halifax, Nova Scotia, 2 August 1984 (Progressive Conservative Party of Canada), Annex A, p. 1.

36. See, for example, Donald J. Savoie, *Establishing the Atlantic Canada Opportunities Agency* (Ottawa: Office of the Prime Minister, May 1987), p. 14.

37. "PM Launches New Agency for Atlantic Canada," *Sunday Herald*, Halifax, 7 June 1987, p. 1.

38. "Atlantic Canada Gets Big Boost," *Daily Gleaner*, Fredericton, 8 June 1987, p. 1.

39. See Savoie, *Regional Economic Development*, p. 159.

40. Donald J. Savoie, *Transition to Maturity* (Moncton: The Canadian Institute for Research on Regional Development, 1990), p. 47.

41. Ottawa, *Account of the Cost of Selective Tax Measures* (executive summary) (Ottawa: Department of Finance, August 1985).

42. Serge Coulombe, *Vision Paper: Regional Questions* (Ottawa: Department of Industry, August 1996), p. 43.

43. See, among many others, Thomas J. Courchene, "A Market Perspective on Regional Disparities," *Canadian Public Policy*, Vol. VII, no. 4 (1981), pp. 506-08.

58

THE PLAY

4

New Brunswick in 1987

A few months before Frank McKenna came to power, a federal report on Atlantic Canada was tabled. Its opening sentences warned, in the future, "solid and self-sustaining economic development in Atlantic Canada must in large part be endogenous and Atlantic Canadians themselves will have to provide the energy, the skills and the imagination to conceive and organize economic activity if the region is to prosper."[1] The message was blunt enough. But, to make the point clearer still, the report compared the situation to a story from the Second World War:

> Natives of some Pacific islands saw the arrival of American troops. The Americans cleared and leveled an oblong piece of the jungle, set lights along the edges, and, lo! after a while, a giant silver bird arrived, bearing all manner of gifts and things. This gave rise to a "cargo cult" among the natives, who, having seen what the Americans had done to attract the silver bird, similarly set about clearing portions of the jungle and then waited by their fires, patiently and reverently, for the arrival of the bird.[2]

The analogy was obvious – don't sit by waiting for the cargo to arrive. Make it happen.

To make things happen, all the public policy levers available to promote entrepreneurship in Atlantic Canada and growth in the region's more mature private sector were to be employed. In establishing the Atlantic Canada Opportunities Agency (ACOA), Prime Minister Brian Mulroney explained that the agency would have, as its main focus, the promotion of entrepreneurial development. He also declared, however, that the agency was to play an advocacy role on behalf of the region before national policies and programs. But clearly, the main message was that in the future the region would have to look within, to its own skills and workforce, to achieve economic success.

This message was not in fact directed only to Atlantic Canada. There were signs everywhere that the binge of post-World War II state worship had ended.[3] The confidence of many of those reared on the merits of Keynesian economics began to sag as they discovered that the scope and cost of government kept growing in good economic times as well as bad. By the late 1970s, a good number of countries were experiencing double-digit inflation and a growth in the cost of government that outstripped the growth in the economy. The standard Keynesian solution – that increased government spending would counter the problem of rising unemployment – appeared even more inappropriate in the face of inflationary pressure and growing government deficits. Observers began to write about a crisis of "governability" or "governmental overload." Political parties favouring a greater role for government in society and increased public spending were fast losing public support. For instance, in California, a grass-roots movement in 1978 successfully championed Proposition 13, a measure designed to limit taxation and, by extension, government spending.[4]

64 One concern was related to the apparent inability of governments to deal simultaneously with the issues of unemployment, inflation, balance of payments, and debt. Another extended to the apparatus of government itself, specifically the bureaucracy, which was regarded as a barrier to, rather than a vehicle for, progressive change. Those few who still argued against tampering with the existing machinery of government and its "armies" of entrenched officials were dismissed by both political left and right. They had become the new conservatives, seeking to protect a status quo. However, under the crushing burden of deficits and debts, the status quo was no longer sustainable. The message to politicians then was to redefine not only the role of government in society, but also how government itself operates.

Though he would have had, in fact, little choice but to accept this message, Frank McKenna was nevertheless quite comfortable with it. He saw considerable merit in submitting New Brunswick to a good dose of market discipline. He was also not one to wait patiently by a fire for the arrival of a big bird. He wanted a "hands-on" approach to economic development and his own hand became visible at all times.

This chapter takes stock of New Brunswick and its economy in the mid-1980s when the McKenna government came to power. At that time, a number of highly contentious issues were emerging on the national agenda, ranging from the proposed Meech Lake constitutional reform package to a possible free trade agreement with the United States. McKenna would have to stake out a position on both issues within weeks of assuming office. Economically, New Brunswick was enjoying relatively solid growth. The deep recession of the early 1980s was past, and several sectors were expanding rapidly. But there were also disturbing trends and deep-seated problems.

New Brunswick Before McKenna

The massive immigration that changed the face of Canada in the twentieth century had, as we have seen, little impact on New Brunswick society. In fact, there are still only three major cultural groups in New Brunswick: the English-speaking majority, a sizeable French-speaking minority, and Native communities. They are all from old stock communities, which explains in part why change comes slowly in New Brunswick's conservative and fragmented society.

The nucleus of the English majority in New Brunswick is descended from the United Empire Loyalists who left the American colonies in 1775 during the War of Independence. The Loyalists, essentially English and Scottish, were later joined by immigrants coming from Scotland and Northern Ireland. It has been reported that one half of New Brunswickers of British origin are from England, one quarter from Scotland, and one quarter from Ireland.[5] French New Brunswick, meanwhile, has two components. There are the Acadians, survivors of the 1755 expulsion, who returned to settle in remote river and coastal communities along the Northumberland Strait and Chaleur Bay. The other French New Brunswickers came over the Quebec border to settle in the northwestern part of the province. This last component is the smaller of the two, representing about only 20 percent of the total French-speaking population. The Native community also has two components: the Micmac, who live in eastern and northern New Brunswick, and the linguistically related Maliseet, living to the south and west.

The province's political and social stability is rooted in its static social situation and in its economic structure: New Brunswick has had no frontier economy and no dominating economic sector or urban centre. It is also a society that has remained far more rural than the other provinces. In the last century, a number of New Brunswickers joined immigrants from overseas in

Ontario, the West and New England in search of more prosperous lives. Those who stayed behind typically had a small business, a farm, a fishing boat or other such means of livelihood in the peaceful "serenity of a community that only changed slowly."[6]

Radical politics and third parties have not had much success in the province. The New Democratic Party, the Social Credit Party and the former Co-operative Commonwealth Federation Party have never been a factor in provincial elections. The one exception was the short-lived Confederation of Regions Party (CoR) which was able to win eight seats in the 1991 election and form the official opposition. CoR was a right wing, anti-bilingual party and its rise could be traced back to reactions against Premier Richard Hatfield's expansion of bilingualism. As R.K. Carty and David Stewart write, the Progressive Conservative Party, once out of office, fell into disarray and proved vulnerable to CoR's mobilization of Anti-French sentiments held by many former Tory supporters.[7] CoR's rise, however, was short lived and today it is no longer much of a factor in New Brunswick politics.

The province did, however, witness significant changes in the 1960s during the Robichaud era. Indeed, it was a remarkable period of political and social change. It was all the more remarkable not only because it occurred in New Brunswick, but also because the man behind it was the first elected Acadian premier of the province. Louis J. Robichaud was elected in July 1960, and he set in motion a series of events and measures that transformed New Brunswick society. Robichaud's program, Equal Opportunity, which would in time redesign the province's socioeconomic infrastructure, together with the passing of an *Official Languages Act* and the establishment of the Université de Moncton have had a profound impact on both New Brunswick Acadians and the province itself.

Historian Della Stanley wrote that "Robichaud...transformed New Brunswick society [and] dragged it into the modern age with massive reform legislation."[8] The degree of change and the administrative capacity required to implement Robichaud's program of Equal Opportunity were far more ambitious, for example, than were the various measures introduced under Quebec's Quiet Revolution. Indeed, the Equal Opportunity program required 130 legislative bills, eliminated one level of local government (county councils) and completely overhauled the province's social services, education, health care, municipal government, tax administration, and justice system. Robichaud's goal was as simple as it was courageous: "Provide an acceptance of minimum standards of service and opportunities for *all* citizens regardless of the financial resources of the locality in which they live."[9]

Other provinces kept a watchful eye but,

> While they watched, New Brunswick had the audacity and courage to
> rush in where others feared to tread. Ontario, Saskatchewan and
> Quebec, for example, were more cautious and restrained, holding their
> provincial, municipal and social reform reports on local government
> organization in reserve until they were more certain of the future....
> Subsequent social reforms in Ontario, Manitoba, Nova Scotia and Prince
> Edward Island in the areas of health, education, justice and munici-
> pal structure and taxation were reminiscent of Robichaud's program.
> The big difference remained that where New Brunswick attempted a
> massive, far-reaching reform of social conditions, other provinces
> moved with greater caution, introducing change step by step....[10]

Richard Hatfield defeated Robichaud in the 1970 election. Anyone wanting
to put things back as they were before the Robichaud storm hit the province
would have voted for Hatfield and would have had every reason to expect him
to undo much of the Robichaud reforms. Thus, the pressure on Hatfield to
turn back the clock was considerable. Hatfield, however, courageously decided
to support the changes Robichaud had set in train. In addition, he oversaw
much of the implementation of the province's *Official Languages Act* and gave
New Brunswickers a much needed period of calm.

McKenna, meanwhile, although enthusiastically endorsing Robichaud's
reforms and admiring Hatfield for standing firm on the program for Equal
Opportunity, also often argued that the province now needed to ensure that it
would have the means to continue to support this important but expensive
socioeconomic infrastructure. The best way to accomplish this, in his opinion,
was to create jobs, strengthen the economy and repair the provincial government's balance sheet.

Hatfield left a crucial piece of unfinished business for McKenna – he never
got around to getting legislative ratification of the Meech Lake constitutional
changes. Hatfield, it will be recalled, was one of the "ten white men in suits"
who, behind closed doors, had agreed to the Meech Lake accord in June 1987,
and he had done so barely five months before losing power in New Brunswick.
McKenna, while in opposition, had expressed strong reservations about the
Meech Lake package, insisting that modifications must be made before the
Legislative Assembly ratified it, modifications ensuring a strong central government and guarantees of the rights of women and of francophones outside
Quebec. Once in office, he made it clear that the New Brunswick legislature

67

would not ratify the accord without these changes. As the Meech Lake proposals began to fall out of favour with Canadians across the country, attention soon turned to McKenna to lead the charge against the accord. One journalist wrote, "Meech Lake foes pin hopes on McKenna."[11] The Meech Lake debate dominated the front pages of Canada's newspapers for a few years and consequently had a profound impact on McKenna's agenda throughout his first term in office.

In December 1987, McKenna also jumped into the Canada-US free trade debate and, although he had reservations about certain aspects of the deal, declared his support for the proposed agreement. He observed, "New Brunswick's economy is driven largely by its resource-based industries.... Our economy is dependent on export markets and, naturally, very dependent on our major trading partner – the United States." He added, "our view is that it is better to expend our energies preparing for the new liberalized environment than in resisting the thrust of the federal government's action in this area."[12]

McKenna's support of the Canada-US Free Trade Agreement meant he would break ranks with his fellow Liberals in Ottawa and elsewhere. John Turner, the then federal Opposition leader, made clear his opposition to the deal, as did David Peterson. Peterson explained,

> In 1980 and 1981, for example, we used the Auto Pact commitments to get Chrysler and American Motors to modernize and expand their Canadian operations.... The federal government gave away the option of extending auto parts status to offshore companies.... Ironically, the federal government which cooperated with us to attract Japanese assembly plants to Canada has now severely limited our ability to expand these facilities and attract new ones.[13]

What is not ironic, however, is that some 100 years after the introduction of Canada's National Policy, the Ontario government would stand four square against the proposed free-trade agreement between Canada and the United States. The Ontario government approved the federal government's shaping of public policy to favour central Canada and its promotion of the region's manufacturing sector and now feared that these gains would be compromised under free trade. By contrast, the premier of New Brunswick was prepared to cross party lines to support the proposed agreement, convinced that it was in his province's economic interests. It is interesting to note, however, that McKenna also broke with party ranks during the Meech Lake debate. Still, there were former senior federal Liberal politicians (e.g., Trudeau and Chrétien) and other provincial Liberals (e.g., Clyde Wells) who opposed the Meech Lake Accord.

68

The New Brunswick Economy, Circa 1987

What were economic circumstances like when McKenna was sworn into office? Where were the province's strengths? What was its growth rate? How did these compare with other provinces of similar size? We will return to these questions later by comparing key economic indicators between 1987 and 1997 when assessing McKenna's impact on New Brunswick. First, we need to give the reader a broad appreciation of New Brunswick's socioeconomic circumstances on the day McKenna came to office.

By 1987 New Brunswick had enjoyed five consecutive years of economic expansion and the province's growth rate throughout this period had matched the national average. Between 1982 and 1987, 34,000 jobs were created. Total employment in the province rose by 3.7 percent in 1987 and for the third consecutive year its employment growth rate exceeded the national average. The unemployment rate fell from 14.4 percent in 1986 to 13.2 percent in 1987, as the total number of unemployed New Brunswickers fell by 3,000.[14]

The labour force also increased by 2.2 percent in 1987 and the participation rate reached 58.8 percent, a record high for New Brunswick, up from 52.5 percent in 1986. This compared favourably with the participation rate of Newfoundland and Labrador (52.7 percent), but not with the national average (66.1 percent) or Nova Scotia (60.4 percent) or even Prince Edward Island (63.6 percent). Total employment in New Brunswick, however, rose by 10,000 from 1986 to 1987 to reach 277,000, which represented the highest rate of growth in employment of any province in 1987. Moreover, part-time employment dropped by 1,000 but full-time employment rose by 11,000.[15]

Several sectors in the province were showing signs of good health by the time McKenna came to office. The value of foreign exports increased by an impressive 13.9 percent in 1987 over 1986, reaching $2.95 billion. The United States continued to be the key export market, accounting for about two-thirds of total exports. Retail trade, manufacturing shipments, mineral production, investment, farm cash receipts and exports all showed renewed strength after the recession of the early 1980s. The provincial gross domestic product increased by 7.8 percent in 1987 over the previous year in constant dollars. There was also increased capital investment in trade, finance and commercial services, housing, institutions and government departments and utilities.

Several specific economic sectors also reported good news in 1987. Demand for the province's forest products, notably pulp and paper, was strong and led to a 16.6 percent increase in the value of shipment. The manufacturing sector also had a good year in 1987. There was an increase of 6.8 percent in the value

69

of shipments, over 1986, and a number of industries witnessed solid growth, including food processing, wood products, non-metallic mineral products, fabricated metal products and furniture. In fact, there were few weak spots in the sector. Even the province's shipyard in Saint John was prospering: It had a workforce of 2,000 in 1987 and had just been awarded a $2.7 billion contract to build six frigates.

The mining sector also continued to expand in 1987. The total value of mineral production was up by 39.7 percent over 1986. Even the fishery sector was sharing in the general growth. Exports of fish products increased substantially in 1987, with several species gaining a significant rise in price. The aquaculture industry was also flourishing and by the end of 1987 there were thirty salmon farms operating in the Bay of Fundy.[16]

In brief, though he would end up losing every seat, when Premier Hatfield called a general election for the fall of 1987, he did so in a climate of seeming optimism. On the face of it, 1987 was a good year for a new government to assume power in New Brunswick.

But a closer look revealed that not all was well. Any progress, at least in relation to the national economy, had been at best tentative in the previous twenty-five years or so. Moreover, there were ominous signs that the province was not keeping pace in areas that would shape future economic growth.

If economists agree on one thing, it is that an economy's Gross Domestic Product (GDP) is an important sign of its health or weakness. New Brunswick's GDP in relation to the national GDP did not expand substantially from 1961 to 1987, as Table 5 reveals. In 1987, its GDP as a percentage of the Canadian GDP stood at 68.5 percent, 7 percentage points stronger than it was in 1961.

The people factor, as we stressed in the introduction, is a key, if not the most important, determinant of a region's economic development. For example, it explains, at least in part, the strong performance of the economies of both Japan and Switzerland, two countries not particularly well endowed with natural resources. New Brunswick's population stood at 712,300 on 1 June 1987, an increase of only 0.3 percent from the previous year. In addition, the province had only a modest annual population growth of less than one percent from 1982 to 1987. Two factors explained that development: strong out-migration and a declining birth rate. This, in turn, would have an impact on the average age of the province's population. In fact, New Brunswick's residents were aging faster than the national average, with the median age increasing to 31.0 in 1987 from 28.6 in 1982.

The age distribution of the population reflected this trend. Those under the age of 25 represented 50 percent of the total population, down from 52 percent in 1971. In addition, this age group had also declined in the previous ten

Table 5

Gross Domestic Products for New Brunswick and Canada

YEAR	GDP New Brunswick ($million)	GDP Canada ($million)	GDP per capita New Brunswick ($thousand)	GDP per capita Canada ($thousand)	New Brunswick as % of Canada
1961	718	35,819	1,201	1,964	61.2
1962	746	38,928	1,233	2,095	58.9
1963	797	41,860	1,309	2,211	59.2
1964	897	45,619	1,468	2,365	62.1
1965	982	49,948	1,597	2,543	62.8
1966	1,094	55,990	1,774	2,797	63.4
1967	1,160	59,982	1,871	2,943	63.6
1968	1,249	65,488	1,998	3,164	63.1
1969	1,371	72,381	2,183	3,447	63.3
1970	1,482	77,259	2,364	3,628	65.2
1971	1,620	84,370	2,553	3,912	65.3
1972	1,832	94,774	2,862	4,347	65.8
1973	2,179	111,956	3,367	5,079	66.3
1974	2,664	134,725	4,076	6,024	67.7
1975	3,032	154,217	4,558	6,795	67.1
1976	3,457	176,924	5,105	7,695	66.3
1977	3,691	193,425	5,395	8,311	64.9
1978	4,085	216,680	5,937	9,214	64.4
1979	5,107	249,497	7,381	10,506	70.3
1980	5,254	282,408	7,555	11,746	64.3
1981	5,852	319,190	8,403	13,113	64.1
1982	6,223	334,990	8,933	13,627	65.6
1983	6,760	363,127	9,613	14,650	65.6
1984	7,561	400,755	10,681	16,044	66.6
1985	7,946	429,636	11,193	17,072	65.6
1986	8,777	453,885	12,355	17,903	69.0
1987	9,367	491,652	13,161	19,228	68.5

Source: Statistics Canada, *Provincial Economic Accounts*, cat. 13-213, various issues.

years. Meanwhile, the post-war "baby boom" had made the 25-44 group the fastest growing group during this period. Also continuing to increase its share was the 65+ group, which reached 11.4 percent of the total population in 1987, up from 10.1 percent in 1981 and 7.8 percent in 1961.

New Brunswick's net interprovincial migration for the 1986-87 census year (June 1 to May 31) was -2,536, which equaled the total loss in the previous two years combined. Over the previous four years, or from 1982 to 1986, both the number of persons moving to New Brunswick and the number departing had been on the rise. But the balance was not in the province's favour.

William J. Milne, in his review of the McKenna years, reported on a very disturbing development in New Brunswick's demographics. He reviewed data from the 1971, 1981 and 1991 census and concluded that "in contrast...to Canada, in New Brunswick there is no evidence of the echo generation, that is the bottom of the (population) pyramid has continued to shrink."[17] It is well known that the important characteristics of the structure of Canada's population are built around the baby boom generation, those born between 1947 and 1966, the baby bust generation, born between 1966 and 1980, and the echo generation, those born after 1980 who are the children of the baby boomers. It takes only a moment's reflection to appreciate the implications the lack of an echo generation would have on the province's economic growth. Indeed, the reverberations would be felt in virtually every sector, from health care to educational facilities and, of course, in the province's workforce.

Milne pointed to another worrisome development in the province's demographics. As had been the case for much of the twentieth century, out-migration remained a problem throughout the 1980s. Making the situation even worse was the fact that it was the younger and better educated who were leaving the province. Milne reported that in the case of New Brunswick, "out-migrants with at least some university education accounted for over 36 percent of total out-migrants" and added that the majority of these were moving to Ontario. The fact that 21.6 percent of New Brunswickers (aged 15 years and over) who left the province had a university degree (for Canada as a whole only 11.4 percent of those 15 years and over had a university degree) would, he correctly argued, have "important effects on the province's future and type of economic growth."[18]

The out-migration of highly educated New Brunswickers would also have an impact on the province's unemployment rate. As is well known, New Brunswick trails the national level and several provinces in employment levels. Indeed, since 1961 there has been only one year (1971) when the New Brunswick unemployment rate was roughly at the national average. From 1971 to 1987, its unemployment rate increased considerably in relation to the national average, as Table 6 reveals. In fact, by 1987, only Newfoundland and Labrador and Prince Edward Island were worse off than New Brunswick.

New Brunswick and the other smaller provinces made some progress in reducing disparities in per capita income between 1961 and 1987. Among the components of personal income, both earnings and transfers from government served progressively to reduce regional income inequalities between small

Table 6
Provincial Unemployment Rates
Selected Years, 1961–87: relationship to national average
(Canada = 100)

	1961	1966	1971	1976	1981	1986	1987
Newfoundland	275	171	135	189	186	202.1	203.4
Prince Edward Island	–	–	–	135	150	141.0	150
Nova Scotia	114	138	113	134	134	137.9	139.8
New Brunswick	148	156	98	155	154	150.5	148.9
Quebec	130	121	118	123	137	115.8	117.1
Ontario	77	76	87	87	87	73.7	69.3
Manitoba	70	82	92	66	79	81.1	84.1
Saskatchewan	58	44	56	55	61	81.1	84.1
Alberta	66	74	92	56	50	103.2	109.1
British Columbia	120	135	116	121	88	131.6	135.2
Disparity gap (ratio of highest to lowest)	4.74	3.88	2.41	3.43	3.72	2.74	2.94

Source: Statistics Canada, *The Labour Force*, cat. 71-001, various issues.

provinces and the rest of Canada. New Brunswick either kept pace with some provinces or actually moved ahead of others (see Table 7 below).

But not all news on this front was good between 1961 and 1987. It should be noted that per capita income includes government transfer payments to individuals. Accordingly, the per capita income can be misleading when assessing a region's economic health. For this reason, some observers suggest that earned income per capita provides a much better measure of a region's economic performance. Earned income per capita excludes relative gains from interregional transfer payments. According to this measurement, income disparities were more pronounced, and the disparity did not narrow between 1961 and 1987. As Table 8 reveals, New Brunswick made some progress, but it was only tentative.

The merit of government transfers to individuals is a subject that has been hotly debated in recent years. There is now a view increasingly being heard, even in Atlantic Canada, that transfers are not, and never have been, in the real long-term economic interests of either the individual or the region. A province, for example, in which residents derived 15 percent of their income from government transfer payments has less favourable economic circumstances and a weaker economic structure than one in which such payments comprised only 5 percent of income. Very few critics of transfer payments, however, have been able to suggest how to move a region from a 15 percent to a 5 percent dependency.

donald j. savoie

Table 7

Personal Income Per Capita, by Province and Territory
Selected Years, 1961-88: relationship to national average
(Canada = 100)

	1961	1966	1971	1976	1981	1986	1987	1988
Newfoundland	58.2	59.9	63.8	68.1	64.9	69.6	70.7	71.1
P.E.I.	58.8	60.1	63.7	68.2	67.4	74.3	72.5	73.9
Nova Scotia	77.8	74.8	77.5	78.47	79.0	83.7	83.4	82.5
New Brunswick	68.0	68.9	72.3	75.3	71.3	77.4	77.4	77.3
Quebec	90.1	89.2	88.7	93.2	93.3	94.3	94.8	95.0
Ontario	118.4	116.4	111.0	109.6	107.7	110.2	111.8	112.2
Manitoba	94.3	91.9	94.1	93.1	93.0	90.3	88.8	88.1
Saskatchewan	71.0	93.1	80.3	98.8	99.5	89.0	83.4	80.8
Alberta	100.0	100.1	99.0	102.4	110.2	105.9	101.8	102.4
British Columbia	114.9	111.6	109.0	108.8	101.7	100.4	99.6	98.4
Yukon and Northwest Territories	96.6	80.8	86.8	91.4	101.7	116.5	112.8	114.0
Disparity gap (ratio of highest to lowest)	2.03	1.94	1.83	1.60	1.69	1.67	1.59	1.60

Source: Statistics Canada, *Provincial Economic Accounts*, cat. 13-213, various issues.

74   Cutting transfer payments will obviously reduce a region's dependency, but it can also set in motion an economic downturn that can be difficult to arrest. In any event, by 1987 the federal government was already sending out clear signals that it intended to reduce substantially its future transfer payments.

By the time McKenna came to office it had already become clear to all economic observers that research and development, along with the knowledge industries, would be the fuel required for future economic activities worldwide. Table 9 is quite revealing on this point and shows the extent of the challenge confronting McKenna. New Brunswick was not keeping pace with other provinces in this area. In fact, it trailed every province except Prince Edward Island and Newfoundland and Labrador. It should be noted that Atlantic Canada's share of the Canadian population amounts to 8.3 percent.

Service industries in Atlantic Canada were also lagging those elsewhere in the country in applying new technologies. The percentage of firms in the region making use of computer-based applications trailed other regions by as much as 10 to 15 percent, the only exception being computerized financial systems, inventory control and property management systems. On the manufacturing front, food

Table 8
Earned Income per Capita, by Province and Territory
Selected Years, 1961-87: relationship to national average
(Canada = 100)

	1961	1966	1971	1976	1981	1986	1987
Newfoundland	53.2	52.5	54.8	56.1	53.4	57.4	58.6
Prince Edward Island	53.5	53.6	57.0	60.2	59.0	66.1	64.4
Nova Scotia	75.0	71.5	74.2	74.2	73.4	79.5	79.1
New Brunswick	64.1	65.1	68.1	69.0	64.9	70.2	70.5
Quebec	89.5	89.2	87.8	90.4	89.9	91.3	92.4
Ontario	121.1	118.3	119.2	112.5	110.6	114.5	116.1
Manitoba	93.5	91.0	93.7	93.9	92.9	89.8	88.0
Saskatchewan	67.2	92.3	78.7	99.5	98.9	86.5	80.0
Alberta	100.3	99.0	98.6	105.0	114.4	106.6	101.6
British Columbia	113.7	111.0	109.5	109.5	109.7	99.8	98.9
Yukon and Northwest Territories	103.1	85.1	91.9	94.7	105.3	122.6	118.3
Disparity gap (ratio of highest to lowest)	2.27	2.25	2.17	2.00	2.14	2.13	2.02
Canada (1961 = $1,514 = 100; current dollars)	100	142.6	203.9	395.6	696.1	943.4	1018.7

Source: Statistics Canada, *Provincial Economic Accounts*, cat. 13-213, various issues.

and beverage, wood, primary and fabricated metal, machinery, transportation equipment, petroleum and chemical industries were also lagging the national average in the use of advanced technologies. According to the Economic Council of Canada, Atlantic Canada, and New Brunswick was no exception, had the lowest levels of technological intensity over the 1980-85 period. Only 66.7 percent of establishments had introduced automation, compared to a national average of 75.5 percent. In Atlantic Canada, expenditures on computer equipment as a percentage of sales were less than half the national average.[19] Briefly, early signs were suggesting that New Brunswick, and for that matter all of Atlantic Canada, would not fare as well in the new economy as would the rest of the country.

The New Brunswick Government, Circa 1987

If the economic news was not all bright, Frank McKenna would discover that he was inheriting a first-rate public service. New Brunswick has had a professional, non-partisan and career public service for a long, long time. Indeed, its public service is arguably one of the best in the country.

Table 9
Provincial Distribution of R&D Expenditures, 1985 to 1987 (%)

PROVINCES	1985	1986	1987
Newfoundland	1	1	1
Prince Edward Island	—	—	—
Nova Scotia	2	2	2
New Brunswick	**1**	**1**	**1**
Quebec*	23	22	24
Ontario*	44	46	48
Manitoba	3	3	2
Saskatchewan	3	2	2
Alberta	9	8	7
British Columbia	7	7	6
Sub-total Canada[1]	93	93	94
National Capital Region	7	7	6
Total Canada	100	100	100
Canada – Total R&D expenditures ($ million)	6,901	7,460	7,866

[1] Includes the Yukon and Northwest Territories;
* Quebec and Ontario figures exclude federal government expenditures performed in the National Capital Region.
Source: Statistics Canada, *Science Statistics*, cat. 88-001, October 1996.

This is because since at least 1960, New Brunswick premiers have deliberately sought to build such a public service. Robichaud, as already noted, realized very quickly that he needed a first-rate public service to make his wide-ranging reforms work. He had inherited a career public service when he came to power in 1960. A Civil Service Act had been passed in New Brunswick in 1943 which established a three-person Civil Service Commission and gave "security of tenure" to the chairman by stipulating that he could be removed from office only by "an address in which two-thirds of the members of the Legislative Assembly concur."[20] The act also increased substantially the security of tenure of public servants and made it much "more difficult for clearly unqualified persons to enter the service"[21] so that after the act was passed there were no further wholesale firings in the civil service when a government changed. Accordingly, "when the Conservatives came in power in 1952, they retained all the deputy ministers except one who had reached retirement age."[22] From that moment on, wholesale firings in New Brunswick were limited to people not under the Civil Service Commission, mostly seasonal workers such as highway workers and game wardens.

Professional though this civil service was, it was small (2,908) and hardly qualified to manage a far greater role envisioned by Robichaud than it had in the past. Before the Robichaud era, nearly all its work had been administrative and clerical in nature and there was little need for a policy advisory capacity. Ministers, even though most worked on a part-time basis, assumed responsibility for broad policy issues, the details of policy, and even for the details of the day. Still, Robichaud, like his predecessor Hugh John Flemming, did not "fire" deputy ministers. He instead decided to work with them, but never hesitated to establish new units whenever needed and to staff them with the best talent available.

The fall of the CCF government in Saskatchewan to Ross Thatcher in 1964 proved to be a godsend to Robichaud. Thatcher decided to clear out a number of senior officials whom he felt had become too close to the CCF party and its philosophy. The CCF, it will be recalled, had been elected to power under T.C. Douglas twenty years earlier in 1944. Robichaud and his key advisors, meanwhile, recognized that, "What was needed was a working balance of professional, experienced civil servants, from within and outside of the Atlantic region, and local candidates anxious to learn to be professional bureaucrats. New Brunswick had, in fact, relatively few bureaucrats."[23] Robichaud made it clear that qualified people from outside New Brunswick would be welcome in his public service. He told one of his advisors, "No one is going to vote for me for appointing New Brunswickers. No, they vote on what I have done for the province. Therefore, find me the best man you can get from anywhere."[24] Thus, a number of Saskatchewan's best bureaucrats were lured to New Brunswick.

Throughout Robichaud's stay in office, the leaders of the public service had the full confidence of the government and, most notably, of the premier. It was a classic case of a sound working relationship where "Louis Robichaud himself, inspired, instituted and shaped policy, but his reliance upon the professional, indeed his enormous faith in the professional bureaucrat, made it virtually impossible for his successors to turn back the clock."[25] In brief, the Robichaud legacy was a modern public service with a strong policy planning capacity at the centre.

In leaving office, Hatfield could boast he had never removed a single deputy minister. Some members of the Saskatchewan "mafia" had already left for Ottawa while others chose to stay on in Fredericton until their retirement. Like Robichaud, Hatfield also looked outside the province for fresh talent. For example, he hired Marcel Massé from the federal government to be his Deputy Minister of Finance in the early 1970s and later appointed him Chairman of the Cabinet Secretariat, the first French Canadian ever to occupy the post. Massé, of course, later (1979) became Clerk of the Privy Council in Ottawa and subsequently Minister for Public Service Reform and President of the Treasury Board in the Chrétien government. Nor was Massé by any means the only outsider the Hatfield government was able to attract to New Brunswick's public service.[26]

Hatfield also promoted public servants who either had been hired by or came to prominence under Robichaud. Indeed, some of Hatfield's most senior and trusted public servants were inherited from Robichaud. Barry Toole, for one, had been strongly identified with the implementation of the Equal Opportunities Program and the Official Languages Act. Hatfield promoted him to the deputy minister level and made him his most senior advisor on federal-provincial relations. Patrice Blanchard had been a senior official in Robichaud's Community Improvement Corporation and an advisor on regional economic development policy. Hatfield made him a senior deputy minister in a revamped Department of Economic Development in the 1970s. He later promoted him to Head of the Cabinet Secretariat and de facto made him the province's most senior public servant in the 1980s. The list goes on.

With good reason then, very few have ever accused Hatfield of having politicized the public service or of having appointed political partisans to its senior ranks. Of course, not all of his appointments were non-partisan. But for these odd exceptions, Hatfield did not favour people with strong and publicly known ties to his own party. He admitted a self-serving reason for this. What he required from the public service, he reported, was "a degree of professionalism in administration and a willingness to provide objective advice that he would not necessarily obtain from a more partisan public service."[27]

78   Hatfield, like Robichaud, continued to reform the machinery of government by restructuring or reorganizing line departments in both the economic and social policy fields. He kept, and in time strengthened, the agencies Robichaud had put in place. He also added new central planning units in the Cabinet Secretariat to manage intergovernmental affairs and to provide advice on establishing government priorities. He strengthened the Treasury Board Secretariat in the area of personnel management, in the application of new information technology and in new management systems and designs. He also introduced new policy and decision-making processes. Underpinning all of the Hatfield changes was a strong confidence in the ability of senior public servants to provide objective advice and to manage change.

New Brunswick introduced a new budget system in the mid-1970s which became known as the Policy and Expenditure Management System (PEMS).[28] This was duplicated by the federal government when Marcel Massé was Clerk of the Privy Council and Secretary to the Cabinet. Yet, the Hatfield government never stopped experimenting with the budgetary process and government structures. When he came to power in 1970, Hatfield reorganized both the

Cabinet Secretariat and the Cabinet committee system. In the mid-1980s, he again completely overhauled them by establishing several Cabinet committees, including the Executive Committee, the Economic Development Policy Committee, the Social Policy Development Committee, the Management Board and the Financial and Internal Management Committee. Career public servants supported the work of all these committees.[29] In fact, the Hatfield government established several new deputy minister level positions in the Cabinet Secretariat and staffed all of them with career public servants.

All in all, Hatfield relied on the public service to the same extent as did Robichaud in establishing government priorities, planning new initiatives and implementing his government's policy agenda. Indeed, on this front, and on many others for that matter, there was little appreciable difference between the two leaders. As Hugh Mellon notes, "The government of both Robichaud and Hatfield displayed some truly significant similarities. Taken together, they bequeathed subsequent provincial leaders a heritage of modern, progressive reforms."[30] The size of the provincial public service grew substantially during the Hatfield years and in his last year in office it stood at 40,280 person years.[31]

There was, however, a downside to the admirable achievements of Robichaud and Hatfield. The New Brunswick government, by the mid-1980s had grown as dependent on federal transfer payments as had individual New Brunswickers. Though these transfers had given the province money to spend, there was a price to pay. The price, of course, was that, over time, it would become dependent on them and consequently vulnerable when spending cuts were threatened. Federal transfers had become a significant source of revenue for the government of New Brunswick and they were critical to the province as it sought to repair its balance sheet.

There is no denying the government of New Brunswick has long relied on federal transfers to sustain its expenditure budget. In 1960, when Robichaud came to power, fully half of provincial government revenues came from the federal government, a figure that remained relatively stable until the early 1980s. The cuts in federal transfers, beginning in the 1980s, were therefore deeply felt in New Brunswick, as they were in all the other slow-growth provinces.

Figure 2 below reports that as late as 1981 the New Brunswick government still relied on federal transfers for over 50 percent of its revenues. By 1987 and 1988, however, the figure had dropped to 40 percent. It was nearly as high for Nova Scotia during this period, while the governments of Prince Edward Island and Newfoundland and Labrador remained even more dependent on federal transfers for their revenues (46 and 47 percent, respectively, for 1987). Manitoba, meanwhile, saw a drop in federal transfers of 13 percent

79

Figure 2
Federal Transfers as a Percentage of Provincial Revenues
1981, 1987, 1988

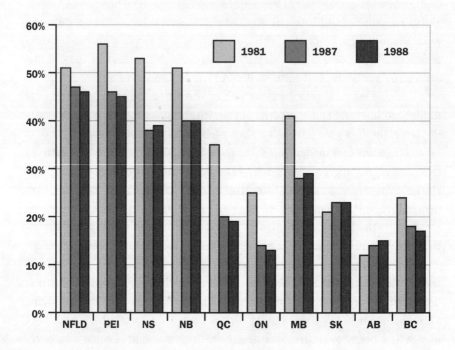

Source: Department of Finance Canada, *Fiscal Reference Tables*, 2000.

over the 1981-87 period, so that by 1987 it relied on Ottawa for only 28 percent of its revenues. This compared with 14 percent for Ontario, 20 percent for Quebec and 18 percent for British Columbia.

New Brunswick's annual deficit in 1986-87 was $368 million, which brought its net debt to $2.59 billion. The recession of the early 1980s had wrought havoc on New Brunswick's balance sheet, as it had on those of the other provincial governments. (In 1980-81, for example, New Brunswick's net debt stood at only $896 million.) In comparison, Nova Scotia's annual deficit in 1986-87 was $277 million and its net debt stood at $3.50 billion; Manitoba's annual deficit in 1986-87 was $1.25 billion and its net debt stood at $4.62 billion; while Newfoundland and Labrador's deficit in the same year was $231 million and its net debt was $3.15 billion.[32] The ratios of debt/GDP in 1986-87 for the four provinces mentioned here are New Brunswick, 28.5 percent; Nova Scotia, 29.5 percent; Manitoba, 26.7 percent; and Newfoundland/Labrador, 48.9 percent.

In this situation, the New Brunswick government, like other provincial governments, had no choice but to allocate more and more of its resources to service the debt. In the case of New Brunswick, debt charges amounted to $395 million in fiscal year 1986-87, up from $126 million in 1980-81. While in 1980-81, debt charges accounted for about only 7 percent of the province's total expenditure budget, by 1986-87 they amounted to over 12 percent.[33]

Statistics, the strength of an economic sector at a given point in time, the state of the provincial public service and public finance can never tell the whole story. Perceptions are also very important. In economic development, as in other matters, perceptions can all too often shape reality.

There is strong evidence to suggest that when McKenna came to power the perception of New Brunswick, by both outsiders and residents, was largely negative. Without putting too fine a point on it, the view was that New Brunswick was a backward province, hardly even worth a visit by tourists. One journalist wrote in 1987 that "the world's image of New Brunswick and New Brunswickers' image of themselves was lower than a snake's belly" and the perception was that "New Brunswick was the worst place to do business."[34]

Without question Frank McKenna inherited a mixed bag of goods when he became premier of New Brunswick in the fall of 1987. The province's key economic sectors were expanding, unemployment was coming down and the provincial public service had a solid track record of accomplishment and enjoyed a strong reputation as one of the best in the country. But there were problems. Both the provincial government and individual New Brunswickers were dependent on federal transfers of one kind or another as a source of revenue or income. The province was losing its better educated to migration and was faced with the perception that the province had little going for it – and precious little to induce investors. When one adds to this bleak picture the growing deficit and debt, the scope of the challenge taken on by McKenna was truly impressive.

81

Notes

1. Donald J. Savoie, *Establishing the Atlantic Canada Opportunities Agency* (Moncton: The Canadian Institute for Research on Regional Development, 1987), Executive Summary.

2. Savoie, *Establishing the Atlantic Canada Opportunities Agency.*

3. Alan C. Cairns, "The Nature of the Administrative State," *University of Toronto Law Journal*, no. 40 (1990), p. 345.

4. See, among others, S.H. Barnes et al., *Political Action: Mass Participation in Five Western Democracies* (London: Sage, 1979).

5. See Edmund A. Aunger, *In Search of Political Stability: A Comparative Study of New Brunswick and Northern Ireland* (Montreal: McGill-Queen's University Press, 1981), p. 16.

6. Hugh G. Thorburn, *Politics in New Brunswick* (Toronto: University of Toronto Press, 1961), p. 186.

7. R.K. Carty and David Stewart, "Parties and Party Systems," in Christopher Dunn (ed.), *Provinces* (Toronto: Broadview Press, 1996), p. 86.

8. Della M. Stanley, *Louis Robichaud: A Decade of Power* (Halifax: Nimbus Publishing, 1984), author's preface.

9. Quoted in John Edward Belliveau, *Little Louis and the Giant K.C.* (Hansport, NS: Lancelot Press, 1980), p. 71.

10. Stanley, *Louis Robichaud: A Decade of Power*, p. 227.

11. "Meech Lake foes pin hopes on McKenna," *Telegraph Journal*, Saint John, 18 April 1988, p. 1.

12. Fredericton, New Brunswick Information Service, statement by Premier Frank McKenna, *Canada-US Free Trade Agreement*, 16 December 1987, pp. 1-2.

13. Notes for remarks by the Hon. David Peterson to the Canadian Clerk and Empire Club, Toronto, 4 November 1987, pp. 13-14.

14. *The New Brunswick Economy – 1988*, a report to the Legislative Assembly, 1988, prepared by the New Brunswick Statistics Agency, Cabinet Secretariat, p. 3.

15. *The New Brunswick Economy – 1988*, p. 18.

16. *The New Brunswick Economy – 1988*, p. 26.

17. William J. Milne, *The McKenna Miracle: Myth or Reality* (Toronto: University of Toronto, Monograph series on public policy and public administration, 1996), p. 9.

18. Milne, *The McKenna Miracle: Myth or Reality*, pp. 17-19.

19. See, among others, Donald J. Savoie, *Rethinking Canada's Regional Development Policy* (Moncton: Canadian Institute for Research on Regional Development, 1997), pp. 38-43.

20. *The Civil Service Act, 1943*, in Revised Statutes of New Brunswick, chap. 29, s6.

21. Thorburn, *Politics in New Brunswick*, p. 160.

22. Thorburn, *Politics in New Brunswick*.

23. Quoted in Stanley, *Louis Robichaud: A Decade of Power*, p. 92.

24. Stanley, *Louis Robichaud: A Decade of Power*, p. 92.

25. Stanley, *Louis Robichaud: A Decade of Power*, p. 96.

26. Non-New Brunswickers were appointed at all levels of the public service during Hatfield's tenure, including deputy ministers (e.g., Health), the officer level in central agencies and in line departments.

27. Quoted in Donald J. Savoie, "New Brunswick: A Have Public Service in a Have-Less Province," in Evert Lindquist (ed.), *Government Restructuring and Career Public Service* (Toronto: Institute of Public Administration of Canada, 2000), p. 40.

28. See, for example, Savoie, "Governing a Have-Less Province."

29. Savoie, "Governing a Have-Less Province," pp. 34-35.

30. Hugh Mellon, "New Brunswick: The Politics of Reform," in Keith Brownsey and Michael Howlett (eds.), *The Provincial State: Politics in Canada's Provinces and Territories* (Mississauga, Ontario: Coop Clark Pitman, 1992), p. 100.

31. *The New Brunswick Economy – 1988*, p. 57.

32. See Canada, Department of Finance, *Provincial and Territorial Governments – Public Accounts 1998-99*, various dates.

33. Department of Finance, *Provincial and Territorial Governments – Public Accounts 1998-99*, various dates.

34. Don Cayo, "McKenna miracle demystified," *Telegraph Journal*, 23 October 1995, p. 2.

5

The McKenna Reforms: Taking Stock

Frank McKenna's rhetoric on economic development hardly changed during his ten years in office. He explained that he was employing the "term 'self-sufficiency' obsessively...constantly...in every speech" simply because that was his central purpose in political life. New Brunswickers, he insisted, "had to stand on their own two feet...shape their own destiny."[1] In his pursuit of this goal, he consistently called for economic diversification, a balanced budget, education reform, reductions in the size of the public service, a new approach to welfare – which, some argued, included "workfare" – and a better delivery of government services. How do McKenna's efforts and activities during his ten years in office square with these policy goals? In this chapter we seek to answer these and other related questions. Since our focus is on economic development, fiscal issues and government operations at the provincial level, we will not examine areas such as justice, health care or municipal government.

From the opening bell, Frank McKenna made it clear his government would be "business friendly" and he would have a firm hand on all the levers of power within the provincial government. Indeed, on the very day he was sworn into office, McKenna stressed to the private sector that "New Brunswick was open for business" and sent out clear signals to the public service that, in its case, it would no longer be business as usual. His aim was to bring an entrepreneurial style to government operations and in pursuing economic opportunities. In fact, he felt quite at ease being labeled (as he was) the "CEO of the province."[2]

85

Reforming the Public Service

The day after his government was sworn into office, McKenna dismissed Gordon Gregory, the deputy minister of Justice. The same fate befell two other deputy ministers – Frederick Arseneault, former deputy minister to Richard Hatfield and defeated Progressive Conservative in a federal election some fifteen years earlier, and Denis Haché, the deputy minister of Fisheries.[3] Within a few months, several other deputy ministers, on their own initiative, took early retirement packages. This was the extent of McKenna's "purge," despite the fact that there were concerns within his party and his newly elected caucus that the public service was still too closely identified with the Hatfield Conservatives and their seventeen-year rule.

Still, McKenna did dismiss three deputy ministers, something that both Hatfield and Robichaud had been able to avoid. But McKenna had an explanation. The premier, he pointed out, has the "exclusive authority with respect to the appointment or dismissal of deputy ministers."[4] However, he insisted that his decisions had nothing to do with political revenge. In the case of Haché, he explained it was widely known both inside government and in the fishing industry that there had been "total disunity" within the fisheries department for more than a year before he came to power. In the case of Gordon Gregory, McKenna suggested "Gregory was closely associated in the public mind with the creation and maintenance of the highway patrol. If he'd been asked to evaluate it, we'd have been the laughing stock of the province."[5] It was also revealed later in the media that Gregory had been involved in partisan activities, albeit on a very limited basis, on behalf of the Progressive Conservative party shortly before he was appointed deputy minister of Justice.[6] McKenna, however, had little to say about the reasons for letting Arseneault go. He did argue in an interview for the purpose of this study that "everyone knew that Arseneault was a deputy minister in name only, having been closely identified with the Progressive Conservative Party for years." In the same interview, I put this question to McKenna: "Any regrets for having dismissed three deputy ministers?" His answer, without any hesitation whatsoever, was to the point:

> No. The only regret I have is that I did not get rid of more of them. I say this not for partisan reasons. Running a government is in many ways like running a large business. You need competent and highly motivated people. Some of the senior people in the government had extremely poor work habits. In time, I was able to move them out. But I should have done it earlier.

McKenna added that Hatfield did not have to dismiss any deputy ministers because those that were expected to be dismissed (e.g., John Bryden, then deputy minister of Justice), had the good sense to resign on the day Hatfield was sworn into to office.[7]

This dismissal of three deputy ministers was the first of many signs that McKenna's management style would differ from that of his predecessors and that he would be less concerned with the finer points of public administration. Although encouraging advice from career public servants, he constantly challenged it. He would, from time to time, sing the praises of the public service but he also established new channels of advice in his own office and appointed close advisors, including some identified with the Liberal party, to key deputy ministerial positions.

McKenna's clear preference was for "responsive competence" rather than "neutral competence." The former is geared to the priorities of the political power of the day, while the latter speaks to the importance of unbiased advice, of speaking truth to power and of maintaining the more traditional values of public service. McKenna had a strong bias for action and he expected the public service to fall in step. He knew what he wanted to accomplish and had little patience with public servants who were trained to see all sides of an issue and took professional pride in having a proper sense of detachment and non-partisanship. McKenna himself set the tone he wished others to follow by putting in long hours and working hard to understand the workings of government and the budget process. The Secretary to the Cabinet under McKenna explains:

> Subtle and not so subtle changes in the pace of work confirmed that this was a government that meant business. Start times for all Cabinet and Cabinet Committee meetings were moved to 8 a.m. and rigorously held to. Budget Committee meetings went on late into the evening, as required, to finish the business of the day. Soon, the Centennial Building, site of most of the government operations in Fredericton, became known as Frank's Seven-Eleven.[8]

McKenna, in the tradition of Robichaud and Hatfield, for the most part promoted from within the public service when staffing senior positions, especially at the deputy minister level. A number of assistant deputy ministers were promoted to deputy minister and deputy ministers of small and medium-size departments were moved to larger departments. The government occasionally went outside the public service to staff senior appointments but many of the people chosen were, again, mostly non-partisan career professionals from other governments or from the private sector. McKenna also made a rule of turning to career New Brunswick public servants to fill key public service positions. For example, Max Lewis was appointed deputy minister of Finance, and Claire Morris secretary to the Cabinet and clerk of the Executive Council. Both were widely respected as career public servants and both had risen through the government ranks under Richard Hatfield.

But there were exceptions. Francis McGuire, who served on Lloyd Axworthy's staff in Ottawa and on his own staff when McKenna was leader of the Opposition, was appointed to head the Intergovernmental Affairs Department and later to the position of deputy minister of Economic Development and Tourism. McKenna also appointed Julian Walker as deputy minister in the Department of Environment. Walker had served on McKenna's staff while he was leader of the Opposition. Finally, he appointed Paul Lordon, a former chief of staff and candidate for the Liberal nomination in Miramichi, as deputy minister of Intergovernmental Affairs.

McGuire became a key player in implementing McKenna's plan for economic development. A leading New Brunswick journalist described McGuire as a "workaholic who believes anything is possible, even within the structures of a slow-moving public service."[9] McGuire, better than anyone in the public service, personified the image McKenna wanted for his government: "busy, lean, hard-working and enthusiastic."[10] In many ways, McGuire represented precisely what McKenna wanted in a public servant. Though strongly identified with the Liberal party, McGuire was not primarily motivated by partisan considerations. Rather, he was task oriented. He had no interest in becoming a career public servant – which would have been impossible in any event, given his close association with McKenna and the Liberal party. His objectives were McKenna's objectives and he showed no hesitation in saying so, within the public service or outside, and in pursuing them with abundant enthusiasm.

McKenna overhauled the centre of government within a year of coming to office. He abolished several Cabinet committees Hatfield had established, but created three new ones: Policy and Priorities, Management Board and the Budget Committee. The purpose of the Budget Committee was to send a message to Cabinet ministers and the public service that his "fiscal priorities" were as important to his government as were any social or economic policy proposals. Four years later, he abolished the Budget Committee, convinced that he was by then sufficiently knowledgeable and no longer needed a special committee to get a handle on the government budget.[11] McKenna also reorganized the Cabinet Secretariat by reducing the number of deputy ministers from five to one and by having all the units report to that one deputy minister.[12] He also removed the Intergovernmental Affairs unit from the Cabinet Secretariat Office and gave it independent agency status. And he merged the Management Board Secretariat and the Department of Finance into one department with the deputy minister of Finance serving as secretary to the Management Board Committee of Cabinet. At the same time, he established an Office of Economic Development in his own office to provide a new focus on economic developments at the centre of government.

McKenna's bias for action does not mean his government lacked a central policy, planning and coordination capacity. In fact, with McKenna at the helm, the centre lost very little in its ability to shape policy. McKenna was able to master the government decision-making process and acquire an intimate knowledge of government programs. As mentioned earlier, he regularly put in sixteen-hour days and he never hesitated to call on the relevant government officials, no matter what level in the hierarchy, to secure whatever information he needed.[13] It is also important to bear in mind that the machinery of the New Brunswick government is small. The entire executive early in the McKenna years was divided into sixteen departments (down from twenty-two under Hatfield) and several independent agencies with 10,233 employees. The entire New Brunswick government is only slightly bigger than an average federal department and is actually smaller than several of them.[14] Thus, given the small size of the government, a premier could, if he wished, dominate every facet of the policy-making process. There is no doubt this was McKenna's wish. There is also no doubt this is exactly what he did.

McKenna also sought to modernize the public service, but in a far different way than had Louis Robichaud. McKenna's purpose was not to build a modern policy advisory capacity or to enlarge the scope and size of his public service. Rather, he set out to make the public service far more efficient in delivering programs and services, to review what it ought to be doing, to determine what it is good at and to make it affordable. In brief, McKenna wanted the public service to be more businesslike.

In pursuing this objective, McKenna decided not to rule out any possible reform on ideological grounds. He embraced some of the ideas found in the New Public Management movement which was in fashion in government circles in Anglo-American democracies in the late 1980s; he often spoke the Osborne and Gaebler language of seeing government "steering" and not "rowing." He downsized a number of government units not only in the core public service, but also in school boards (from 42 down to 18 and later from 18 to 0) and hospital boards (from 37 to 8). About 2,500 positions were eliminated from the public service, from a total base of about 10,500 positions.[15] Some were eliminated altogether while others had their activities turned over to the private sector. Government departments were also restructured. In 1991, for example, the Department of Commerce, Technology and Tourism merged with the Department of Recreation and Heritage; Advanced Education and Training merged with Labour; and Municipal Affairs merged with Housing.

The "steering" rather than "rowing" criterion – again, not ideology – guided the McKenna government in deciding which activities ought to stay in government and which should be contracted out or privatized. No effort was made, for example, to privatize the policy advisory function or environment monitoring activities. However, many administrative support activities were candidates to be contracted out. For example, once it was discovered the government had an in-house capacity to rebuild starters for government-owned vehicles, it was decided that this activity should be contracted out. Similarly, the Language Training Program for public servants and all data-processing requirements were privatized.

The McKenna government also pushed back the privatization frontier on a few fronts. It contracted out the construction and continuing maintenance of a new school to the private sector through a twenty-five-year rental agreement. It also announced that the construction of two prisons would be undertaken by private firms. One of the new prisons was designed to replace the Kingsclear Youth Reform Centre which was closed down after an inquiry revealed widespread sexual abuse committed by some members of the centre's staff over a number of years during the 1960s and 1970s, and which was overlooked by management. McKenna often referred to this case to argue that government had no inherent or ideological right to run prisons or other operations traditionally associated with the public sector.

In addition, the Department of Income Assistance (subsequently changed to the Department of Human Resources Development) decided in 1992 to develop new programs and to restructure its operations. The department concluded that to introduce change and to make it stick it needed new investments and high-level technical resources. The department signed a $16 million contract with Andersen Consulting to secure "technology skills, change management skills and financing."[16] The first phase suggested that potential savings of $85 million could be realized which would substantially outweigh the cost of the contract. As a result, the department became confident the various proposed changes could not only repay Andersen's fees but also provide an important "fiscal dividend" to the government.[17] The changes included a "redefinition of regions, jobs redesigned, technology revitalized and work processes reengineered. Staff makeup was changed to provide more case managers and fewer managers and administrators."[18]

But the Andersen contract had a political cost. The new technologies would, for example, entail a job loss of 125 in the department. This, together with the fact that Andersen was a U.S.-based firm, dominated the New Brunswick media for several weeks. The provincial auditor general became highly critical of the contract, raising doubts about its cost and potential savings.[19] The McKenna government held firm, at least initially, explaining that Andersen had agreed to establish a multimedia centre in New Brunswick, creating 40 new jobs in addition to the 70 jobs they had already created to work on the Human Resources Development contract and other contracts it had secured with the provincial government.[20] The Andersen contract with Human Resources Development did, in the end, result in savings, but the relationship between Andersen and the provincial government soured over contracts in other departments. McKenna had little interest in debating the merits of who was doing the work or whether the consulting firm was American or local. His only interests were "results and getting the job done."[21]

While Andersen was restructuring the Human Resources Department, the McKenna government launched its own "reengineering exercise of the Human Resources Management (function) in the civil service."[22] The purpose was to redefine the relationship between the centre and line departments in this area. The thinking was that still more authority over such issues as staffing, classification and compensation could be decentralized to departments while ensuring that systems and processes were not duplicated. Again, the guiding principle here was that government departments and agencies should be run more like a business. It will be recalled that in the late 1980s empowerment was in fashion in the schools of management.

The review, however, did not prevent the government from experimenting with new approaches to human resources management. It again borrowed a page from the private sector in introducing a performance management system, including provision for bonuses for exceptional performance, and recognition and award programs with guidelines for "cash" and "non-cash" awards. It also put in place a new policy to deal with employee absenteeism. The policy emphasized non-disciplinary actions such as employee interviews, counseling and referral services to deal with problems. In addition, a flexible work time program, a public-service-wide Human Resources Information System and early retirement plans were introduced. In light of budget cuts, a committee made up of representatives from line departments, school districts and hospital corporations was established to share information to assist surplus public

91

sector employees in finding another job in government or the private sector. The redeployment success rate was approximately 80 percent.[23]

While the McKenna government was introducing spending cuts, it also decided to give line managers more flexibility in managing their financial resources. Departments were given the authority to transfer money from one vote to another without having to seek approval from the centre. They were also given greater flexibility within votes or in their program budgets to move financial resources around.[24] To ensure that senior line managers were "strong managers" and more businesslike, the McKenna government introduced a special assignment program to promote "systematic movement of senior managers between various line departments, and more importantly between central agencies and line departments."[25] In addition, the province put in place a corporate executive development program designed to encourage a "corporate view" and strong management skills.[26]

The McKenna government also established a "Service Quality Centre" within the Department of Finance. The centre led a major review of the mission and delivery models of "all programs, infrastructure, work processes and organizational structures within the public service, with the objective of creating a total client focus."[27] The centre, the government explained in its 1995 Speech from the Throne, was part of a broader strategy to promote "a competitive, quality-driven public service" which was believed to be "essential to our long-term strategy to position New Brunswick for the twenty-first century."[28]

The above came on the heels of two pilot projects in early 1992 by which two service centres were set up to test the delivery of government services with the same or fewer resources by bringing a variety of services under one roof and behind a single counter. The approach was designed to introduce a "fundamental change in the way government deals with citizens, in how it structures itself and in how public servants see themselves in their role as service providers."[29] The McKenna government was delighted with the success of the two pilot projects, and claimed they "reveal that the approach improves public access and customer satisfaction, and reduces the cost of providing government services."[30] It subsequently decided in 1996 to establish service centres throughout the province.[31] The objective of Service New Brunswick was to provide a one-stop delivery of services and to be the lead agency for mapping, registration and property valuation. The service delivery is carried primarily through eight service centres, employing about 600 people. Together, they provide 110 services from sixteen government departments, utilities and even some municipalities. Service New Brunswick now employs several delivery platforms including a call centre, IVR (Interactive Voice Response) applications,

92

Web applications and networked-based applications at the counter. The approach has caused wide interest, and governments both in Canada and abroad have come calling to see how they could incorporate the approach in their own operations.[32]

Lastly, the McKenna government introduced the "Special Operating Agency" concept to provide more flexibility and independence to line managers for selected activities. This is on top of special "sunset organizations" which were established for a designated period to focus on priority areas for policy development. Sunset organizations were introduced, for example, to review childhood services, family policy and the electronic information highway.

McKenna had no grand scheme or blueprint in mind when he set out to fix the public service. Still, an underlying theme can be detected: He wanted all government departments and agencies, no matter their mandate, to become more businesslike and to get a taste of what "competitive and quality-driven service" means. If New Brunswick was to become more self-sufficient, then the provincial public service had to play its part and, in defining that part, McKenna would look to the business community for inspiration.

Promoting Economic Development: Starting with New Brunswickers

For Frank McKenna, reforming the public service and government operations were a means to an end, not an end in itself. Economic development and job creation dominated his political agenda at all times. The central theme running through the three general elections he fought were "jobs," "more jobs" and "still more jobs," as well as the concomitant need for both the province and its citizens to move from "dependency to long-term self-sufficiency."[33] There is no indication that McKenna understood, let alone appreciated, the intrinsic value of public service. In fact, he offered public servants a leave of absence without pay if they wanted to start a new business. The initiative was not very successful; few public servants took up the offer. But it served to reveal what McKenna considered truly important. The New Brunswick economy is what counted and public servants could better serve the province by going out and starting a business rather than remaining in the bureaucracy.

In his efforts to fix the economy, McKenna started with New Brunswickers themselves. He asked an outside firm to assess New Brunswickers' views of themselves and their province and to get a feel for the perceptions other Canadians had of New Brunswick. The report card was not positive. It revealed that New Brunswickers' pride focused on their local community, their cultural heritage and on being Canadians. Pride in their province, meanwhile, trailed behind most everything else. Perceptions of New Brunswick in the rest of Canada were dominated by the "have-not" image. Except for Canadians who had a personal connection with the province, the rest of Canada, the wealthier provinces in particular, viewed New Brunswick as a place they had to subsidize.[34]

McKenna decided to attack this problem in many different ways. The government adopted a new visual public relations symbol for the province that it employed "widely, extensively and consistently."[35] It launched new publications such as *Trade Winds*, which was circulated widely to embassies and corporations around the world and reported on success stories in business and in university research in New Brunswick. McKenna himself accepted numerous speaking engagements outside the province to sell the assets of New Brunswick and to report on "the diversity and strength of its people and its successes."[36] He went to the major economic centres to promote the province and to "aggressively market New Brunswick to the world."[37]

At home, McKenna took a comprehensive approach to improve the image New Brunswickers had of their province and of themselves. For example, he turned to local firms to handle tourism promotion and other public relations work for the provincial government, rather than using Toronto-based companies, as had been done in the past. The thinking here was that, given a chance, New Brunswickers would, in the great majority of circumstances, be as creative and as productive as any out-of-province firm. He was proved right and today New Brunswick is home to several highly successful public relations and communications firms. Many of these firms have gone on to secure contracts in other parts of Canada and abroad and to win high profile work with leading New Brunswick firms, such as McCain and the Irvings.[38]

McKenna even linked highway construction to promoting pride in New Brunswickers, arguing that roads equal to national standards were necessary if they were to have a proper sense of pride in their province. A second-rate highway system would lead them to expect that other parts of their economy and its infrastructure would be second rate. It was, he felt, a vicious circle that required many initiatives to escape.

McKenna tabled a green paper on New Brunswick highways within months of coming to office. To underline its importance to economic development, the green paper was titled "Adequate Highways – A Key to Regional Economic Development." The paper proposed a fifteen-year $1.93 billion program (in 1988 dollars) to upgrade the province's arterial highways. The bulk of the budget, nearly $1.7 billion, would be spent upgrading the Trans-Canada highway to four lanes.[39] In tabling the green paper, McKenna made it clear that he expected the federal government to assume a significant share of the budget,

94

calling on Ottawa to assume between 70 to 90 percent of the cost. On the day he tabled the report, McKenna wrote to then Prime Minister Brian Mulroney asking for federal funding, arguing that "the current highway infrastructure is insufficient and puts our region at an immediate competitive disadvantage."[40] Ottawa was in no mood, given its fiscal problems, to commit $1.5 billion to highway construction in New Brunswick. Still, McKenna was not about to give up. He pressed the federal government repeatedly, even during his last months in office, to provide funding to build a four-lane Trans-Canada highway in New Brunswick. McKenna never hesitated to go to Ottawa when it came to highway construction and in the end he did meet with some success.[41] The provincial archives contain many letters McKenna wrote to prime ministers Mulroney and Chrétien, asking (at times pleading) for Ottawa to support the construction of a four-lane highway in New Brunswick. Some were handwritten, one simply asking Chrétien, "Will you help us?"[42]

McKenna's tenacity paid off. He was able to secure three federal-provincial highway agreements (two under Mulroney and one under Chrétien) providing over one billion dollars. McKenna's success was all the more remarkable given that Ottawa was clearly in a belt-tightening mode between 1987 and 1997. Given Ottawa's unwillingness to fully fund the four-lane Trans-Canada highway, McKenna tabled a white paper in 1993 called "Highways for the Next Century." The paper dealt with a number of technical issues such as truck weights and signage, but it focused on funding. The McKenna government pledged to continue to pursue new federal funding. However, McKenna announced that he would now consider partnership arrangements with private firms to build and finance sections of the four-lane highway. The government decided in 1995 to establish the New Brunswick Highway Corporation to accelerate highway construction. The corporation was designed to pursue an alternative approach to funding highway construction during a time of fiscal restraint in Ottawa and Fredericton. In December 1996, the government issued a Request for Qualifications to identify a private sector partner for the design, financing, construction, operation and maintenance of the new four-lane highway between Fredericton and Moncton. By March 1996, a Request for Proposal was issued to three short-listed firms.[43] One of these was subsequently selected – the Maritime Road Development Corporation – and New Brunswickers were introduced to a toll highway operated by a private firm. The government made the case that the toll charges would enable the province to complete the four-lane highway. But the toll highway became a heated political issue leading up to the 1999 general election and Bernard Lord pledged, if elected, to abolish it. The rest, as the story goes, is history.

donald j. savoie

The People Factor

McKenna attached a great deal of importance to education. His government announced new education initiatives in every year of its first mandate and in 1991 established a Commission on Excellence in Education to examine education from a broader perspective. The commission made a number of recommendations and the government responded positively to the great majority of them. It decided, for example, to introduce a comprehensive provincial testing program at key stages in the educational process. It also introduced early intervention measures, and placed more emphasis on science, math, literacy and stay-in-school programs, using summer and weekend camps. It implemented school-to-work transition programs, introduced entrepreneurship education throughout the school system and lengthened the school year.

The province's community colleges were also overhauled. The number of places in full-time programs was increased by 1,000 during McKenna's first term in office. The governance structure of the colleges was subsequently turned over to a special operating agency on 1 April 1996. This gave the colleges greater freedom to manage their programs and operations. The hope was that the community college system would become more creative, more entrepreneurial, more businesslike and, in the end, work more closely with the private sector.

The McKenna government also gained national media attention when it decided to link electronically every school in the province to every other and the Internet. It was the first provincial government to do so. It also decided to put in place the infrastructure required to enable all high school graduates to be computer literate. This was done through $22 million in new funding from the provincial, federal and private sectors.[44]

The government again gained a great deal of Canada-wide attention when it decided to reform its social assistance programming. McKenna argued repeatedly that the best form of social assistance was a job. He would often quote Félix Leclerc, who wrote, "the best way to kill a man is to pay him to do nothing" and insisted that "passive support programs are destroying our spirit and our soul. We are the only nation in the world providing such generous support with such inadequate reorientation toward training, education and work."[45] McKenna had cause for concern. In the throes of the economic recession of the early 1990s, and four years after coming to power, unemployment insurance recipients in New Brunswick reached 62,217, compared to 41,000 in 1980. Total unemployment insurance payments in 1991 "exceeded the total provincial revenue from personal income tax ($677 million) and from the provincial sales tax ($635 million)."[46]

In embarking on an ambitious overhaul of its income assistance program in the early 1990s, the McKenna government looked to Ottawa for some financial support. But the actual reforms were, for the most part, defined in Fredericton. The fundamental thinking was that governments had to move away from the traditional passive role of simply providing income support. The redesigned approach would provide for a much more active role on the part of government officials in assisting recipients to achieve self-sufficiency by helping them overcome barriers to employment, notably those related to education, skills and work experience. Additionally, the approach would seek to deal with built-in disincentives to taking up work. As is well known, some social assistance programs can impose a 100 percent tax on income from work because benefits are reduced dollar-for-dollar in response to any earned income. Though New Brunswick social assistance programs did not impose a 100 percent tax level, they did have some important disincentives to work.[47]

The government, as already noted, reorganized the Department of Income Assistance into the Department of Human Resources Development and initiated a comprehensive review of the province's Social Welfare Act. The new department declared that its mission was "client self-sufficiency." It also declared that in the future the department would devote 70 percent of its time to case management and client contact and only 30 percent to administrative tasks, rather than the reverse, as in the past.[48]

McKenna, however, was not content with simply reorganizing the machinery of government in the social assistance field. He wanted to deal directly with the disincentive factor, and he looked to "demonstration programs," to be financed in part through federal funding, to implement the necessary policy change.

In 1992, New Brunswick was chosen as one of two sites (the other was British Columbia) for the Self-Sufficiency Project. Some $155 million out of a total budget of $500 million was set aside for New Brunswick. This national research project was designed to discover whether temporarily increasing the income of social assistance recipients who leave welfare for work would help them achieve long-term self-sufficiency. The objective of the project was to generate credible findings to be used to guide future policy decisions in the income support sector. The project offered an earnings supplement to long-term, single-parent social assistance recipients if they left social assistance for work. Some 2,300 recipients volunteered to participate in the project. The target group was families that included children, receiving social assistance for 12 of the previous 13 months, and headed by single parents. The families were chosen by random sample and a control group was established. The participants had 12 months to find employment.

In the same year and again with Ottawa's support, New Brunswick launched a more ambitious demonstration project – NB Works. With a budget of $180 million over six years, this program also gained a high media profile. It was designed to provide education and training to welfare recipients to enable them to move into the labour market at a higher wage than otherwise would have been the case. Participants could take part in the program for up to 41 months.

The target population for NB Works had the following characteristics:
- between 18 and 45 years of age
- in receipt of benefits for at least six months and preferably for more than 12 months
- entitled to higher ranges of income support (e.g., single mothers and two-parent families)
- low educational attainment (less than a grade twelve but at least a grade seven education)
- little labour force attachment
- assessed as having the greatest potential for success in the program

NB Works had various phases: a five-month initial period of employment to reacquaint welfare recipients with the labour market; up to 24 months of literacy and other academic upgrading, provided by the New Brunswick community colleges, leading to a certified Adult High School Diploma; nine months of skills training; then three months of job search assistance. Finally, if necessary, the program ended with an optional eight months of subsidized private sector job placement. The program had three intakes of 1,000 participants, the last in May 1994, for a total intake of 3,000 people.

McKenna and provincial government officials claim the program was successful. Many graduates of NB Works have written extremely poignant comments explaining how the program gave them a new lease on life. Because of the program, many welfare recipients reported they were able to begin to climb the economic ladder. This is precisely what McKenna had in mind when he spoke about seeing New Brunswickers become more self-sufficient.

But NB Works also received criticism. Some observers and several evaluation reports pointed out that a $180 million price tag was too expensive. Given that the program had only 3,000 participants, it meant the cost per participant was about $60,000. Additionally, this figure assumes all participants successfully completed the program, which was not the case. From the first intake, for example, only 17 percent completed the program. But things got better for the second intake (45 percent) and the third (70 percent).[49]

In 1994, McKenna again turned to federal funding for yet another effort at reforming the province's social assistance programming. It established the NB Job Corps, a program for older workers. To become participants in the program, an individual had to be between 50 and 65, out of work, have no realistic chance for re-training, and the family income had to be less than $20,000. The objective was to assist 1,000 unemployed older workers find work. Funding was shared equally between the federal and provincial governments and the funds were put together by directing monies from passive social assistance measures. But the program itself was implemented by the provincial government.

Program participants worked in community-based projects and were guaranteed a work placement of 26 weeks each year. In return, they received taxable monthly benefits to a maximum of $12,000 per year. Typical jobs included silviculture, fish habitat enhancement, upgrading of tourist facilities and library automation, all undertaken by host organizations in the public, private and non-profit sectors. The program participants (and their families) were allowed to earn additional employment income without penalty.

McKenna summed up his approach to social assistance in a straightforward fashion: "to assist those able to work to make the transition to work."[50] He would look to Ottawa for cost sharing, and to the public service, his own staff and to his own experience and knowledge to come up with ideas on how this could be done. McKenna would not deny that NB Works was an expensive program but, he argued, the alternative of maintaining the status quo was in the long run more expensive and offered little hope to those who wanted to start climbing the economic ladder.

Some observers argued that McKenna was promoting a form of "workfare" through his various reform measures. But McKenna dismissed these charges out of hand, pointing out that at no time did his government impose the programs on anyone, since participation in them was always on a voluntary basis. McKenna reports that today no one would suggest that NB Works was a form of workfare. "But," he points out, "back then, NB Works was considered revolutionary and some were not happy with the message. They preferred the status quo, continuing to provide income assistance from a passive perspective."[51] But in the end, measures such as NB Works could be only one part of the equation. Actual jobs were the other part – and they had to be created.

Looking To NBTel and Bilingualism to Create Jobs

New Brunswick had two important comparative advantages in the mid-1980s: a top-flight local telephone company and a bilingual workforce. The McKenna government decided to exploit them to the fullest. NBTel, the provincial telephone company, had in place a digital network with the potential of attracting outside firms in the communications and information fields. Its digital switches could digitize and compress signals which, in turn, made multimedia possible. NBTel was the first telephone company in North America to offer a fully digital telephone network. It had installed fibre optic cables virtually everywhere in the province, which enabled it to provide a wide array of services not available elsewhere in Canada or, for that matter, in much of North America. Jonathan Rose points out that this communication infrastructure was of strong interest to telecommunications firms requiring a capacity to accommodate vast amounts of data reliably. He writes: "These features, unique in the country, were exploited by McKenna who saw a natural fit between the communications potential of the province and the changing demands of international businesses."[52]

McKenna was also able to sell the province's bilingual workforce to potential investors. Bilingualism, by the late 1980s, had become an economic asset for New Brunswick. Indeed, the days of Moncton Mayor Leonard Jones and the acrimonious debate over the merits of bilingualism (putting aside CoR's rather brief and marginal existence) were long gone. Bilingualism was now as much an economic issue as a political one and a great number of English-speaking New Brunswickers had come to see merit in bilingualism, at least from a practical perspective. In brief, bilingualism could mean new jobs and economic opportunities for New Brunswick, something English New Brunswickers could easily support, if not applaud.

McKenna put his considerable energy and sales ability to work selling New Brunswick to outside investors. His sales trips to Toronto and various major urban centres in the United States were well reported in the media. The Globe and Mail, in Report on Business, ran an article on his exploits, labeling him "The Energizer Premier," and concluding that "in a relentless search for jobs, industry and self-respect for his province, New Brunswick's Frank McKenna just keeps going and going and going...."[53] McKenna made on average 20 trips a year across Canada and around the world to meet with CEOs and sell New Brunswick as a place to invest. He placed a 1-800-McKenna ad in leading newspapers inviting businesses to contact him personally to discuss a possible location for their activities. Atlantic Business magazine summed up McKenna's role in economic development by observing that "Frank McKenna...was very much the star player."[54]

There were other factors working in McKenna's favour apart from a bilingual workforce and having one of North America's leading telephone companies in his own backyard. The provincial government was able to establish a strong collaboration with NBTel in pursuing new investors. To be sure, this was in NBTel's interest since it would also gain large-scale users tapping into its established infrastructure – NBTel executives were always at the ready to support McKenna's job hunting forays with facts, figures and whatever else they could put together to attract investors to the province.

Even Ontario's 1990 election of Bob Rae's NDP government provided a boost to McKenna's job hunting expeditions to Toronto. It gave McKenna the opportunity to contrast his business-friendly agenda with Rae's left-leaning platform. There is a protocol among provincial premiers that a car and driver are made available to premiers visiting one another's provincial capital. The media made much of the fact that McKenna made full use of Rae's hospitality when visiting Toronto-based corporations to entice them to move some of their activities to New Brunswick.

McKenna made certain that someone had already done the necessary homework before he went knocking on the doors of major corporations. He claimed he was just "sitting on the tractor," meaning his advisors did "most of the (background) work while [he] is the one who must perform the major selling job...."[55] His officials would prepare a cost-benefit analysis demonstrating that a New Brunswick location for the firm in question would not be a political move; instead, it made good business sense. They would also put together packages outlining possible incentives to locate in the province, including loan guarantees, grants, tax breaks, power rate reductions and low telephone rates.[56]

All this was on top of a very aggressive public relations effort designed to showcase New Brunswick as a place to invest and to shake off the image of a have-not province. When the provincial government purchased advertisements in Toronto's *The Globe and Mail*, a key McKenna advisor explained that "The national press, *The Globe and Mail* in particular, was a tough nut to crack. It habitually ignored developments in this province, so the government began buying ads to state its case. There was just one target for those ads...the editor of *The Globe and Mail*. We know he read his paper, and we wanted him to see what was happening here. The ads were followed up by telephone calls to the editor. The province began advertising in other papers and dropping ads in papers that did not write about the New Brunswick business scene. They got the message, and news coverage soon followed."[57]

McKenna would meet with any Chief Executive Officer willing to look to New Brunswick as a place to invest. One of his advisors again explains:

These guys [CEOs] all have big egos and like to meet with a Premier. The idea...[was] to use this personal relationship with the man in charge [to have] a cost analysis of such things as establishing a call centre in New Brunswick...they'd be astonished at the savings the study would invariably find...the recession of the early 1990s made big business truly cost conscious.[58]

McKenna agreed to focus his efforts on opportunities that made solid business sense, such as call centres that could benefit from NBTel technology and the province's bilingual workforce. But he did not tie his efforts to one area, or one niche. For example, when he heard that COM DEV, a leader in satellite and communications technology was looking to expand its manufacturing capacity, McKenna called on the company's CEO. COM DEV subsequently decided to set up shop in Moncton, employing 50 people in its initial phase. The reason for choosing Moncton, a senior COM DEV official explained, was that "Frank McKenna sold the province to Val O'Donovan, the company's CEO, and Keith Ainsworth, COM DEV's president."[59] McKenna also proved to be creative on the financing front. True to David Peterson's observation that McKenna goes to meetings with solutions, not problems, a special package was put together to entice COM DEV to locate in Moncton. New Brunswick purchased $1.45 million of COM DEV Atlantic preferred shares through its Provincial Holdings Ltd.

The McKenna government proved to be particularly adroit at attracting call centres to the province. This is where NBTel's infrastructure and the province's bilingual workforce came into their own. By the mid-1990s, New Brunswick was being called the call centre capital of North America and by the time McKenna left office over sixty call centres had moved or had set up their operations in New Brunswick, creating more than 9,000 jobs providing a variety of services. Some of the major call centres to locate in the province included Purolator, Royal Bank, United Parcel Services (UPS), Federal Express, Xerox, Camco, Canada Trust, Nortel, IBM, Sun Life, CP Hotels, Unisys and Canada Post. By the year 2000, New Brunswick was home to 89 call centres creating 12,000 jobs with a $250 million annual payroll.[60]

New Brunswick did not rely solely on its bilingual workforce and NBTel to lure call centres. It will be recalled that several premiers voiced strong concern over McKenna's activities, arguing that he was "poaching" jobs, not creating them, and even accusing him of violating interprovincial trade agreements.[61] They were particularly incensed over the UPS decision to relocate 900 jobs to New Brunswick, from Ontario, British Columbia and Manitoba, after it received $6 million from the province in forgivable loans. The provincial government also provided, in many instances, $10,000 per job for employee training for new call centre jobs. Its promotional literature claimed New

Brunswick was able to offer "the lowest legislated fringe benefit costs in North America for call centre operations,"[62] citing as evidence that the provincial tax on all 1-800 numbers had been abolished, that the province had no corporate capital or payroll tax and that it had overhauled the Workers Compensation Act, removing stress as a legitimate claim, thus reducing the amount of money firms paid to the Workers' Compensation Fund.

McKenna took advantage of every opportunity to promote New Brunswick as a place to invest. When the province and the federal government agreed to harmonize their goods and services taxes and sales tax, McKenna would meet with business leaders from other provinces to explain the advantages the new harmonized tax would have for their firms if they located or relocated some of their activities in New Brunswick. He annoyed more than one of his fellow premiers when he made a pitch to Quebec and Ontario business leaders on a Team Canada trade mission to Asia to move some of their operations to New Brunswick and take "the advantage of harmonizing the sales tax with the GST."[63] For McKenna, everything was fair game in promoting his province. If another premier could "out-hustle" him in selling his province, that was fine. That was the way things worked in the private sector and, for McKenna, that was also the way things should work when running a government. But when it came to hustling on behalf of his province, McKenna was no easy match. It was no coincidence that *MacLean's* magazine labeled him "Fast Frank," comedians on *This Hour Has 22 Minutes* parodied him as "The Hustler," and Michael Tutton wrote about McKenna's "image as a hustler."[64]

McKenna was the first premier to appoint a minister responsible for the information highway and his government was the first in Canada to put information about its programs on the Internet.[65] One observer reports that "McKenna's drive along the information highway began in September 1993 when he appointed a steering committee of deputy ministers to develop a strategy for government to accelerate evaluation of the information highway in New Brunswick."[66] The objective was to put the province at the leading edge of Internet developments. The steering committee tabled a report establishing four guiding principles: ensure provincial availability and affordability; open and shared access; respect for privacy and security; and establish standards-based products and services.[67]

The provincial government did deliver on its commitment to make the information highway widely accessible throughout the province. As already noted, all schools in the province were linked to each other through the Internet. In addition, through TeleEducation NB, college and university courses were offered at 50 sites across the province. Teachers and students in the province began to communicate through "teleconferencing." Thanks to fibre optics and broadband technology, sound and pictures were transmitted across telephone lines, something that could not be done elsewhere in Canada.

McKenna also wanted to put the information highway to use as an economic development tool. He made it clear the information highway would be accessible to anyone "with a good idea for a product or a service to sell and willing to pay a fair price to the communication service provider."[68] The information highway became an important part of McKenna's tool kit in selling the province to potential investors. It provided access to opportunities in software development, advanced training technologies, content development, communications networks and technologies, remote application centres and on-line services. The potential paid off. In 1994 McKenna was able to unveil a NBTel-Nortel initiative labeled "Call Mall," which was designed to deliver a variety of services to people's home. Later, he announced the development of medically related artificial intelligence applications, processing tools for the year 2000 problem and a new resource information system. New firms, tied to the Internet, notably Perform and First Class Systems, were also born in the province or decided to locate there, and new high profile and successful Internet activities such as Scholars.com were launched in the province.[69]

The Traditional Economic Sectors

104   The McKenna government was also very active in the more traditional economic sectors. For example, it added an aquaculture division to the Department of Fisheries and a new marketing section to promote fishery products outside the province, and it launched new initiatives to develop underutilized species. In the mining sector, it exempted sales tax on spending on machinery and equipment for ventilation shafts in order to improve the industry's competitiveness. It also initiated a series of airborne geophysical surveys and measures to promote the transformation of minerals in the province. McKenna would later argue that "New Brunswick may not have the most mining resources in Canada but, at least, it has the best mining policy."[70] In the forestry sector, it invested a considerable amount of new money in silviculture. And in 1995 in agriculture, the department's name was changed from Agriculture to Agriculture and Rural Development. A new Rural Development Branch was added a year later to promote the economic development of artisans, craftspeople and small-scale projects in rural areas. It also promoted agro-tourism, farmers' markets and encouraged, with some success, cranberry and blueberry growing projects.[71]

McKenna was also particularly interested in the tourism sector. He reorganized the departments of Commerce and Technology and the Tourism components of the Department of Tourism Recreation and Heritage into the Department of Economic Development and Tourism. McKenna believed tourism had more to do with economic development than with recreation and heritage. His goal was to make New Brunswick a major Maritime destination rather than just a place one had to drive through on the way to Prince Edward Island or Nova Scotia.

McKenna's focus on tourism was directly tied to his intention to strengthen the image New Brunswickers and others had of the province. An attractive logo featuring a ship soon graced all government publications and promotions and the province decided to promote tourism in all four seasons and to join forces with the other Atlantic provinces to market the region. Two new provincial parks were established, Fundy Escarpment and the St. Croix River Park. Seventeen ecological and conservation areas were designated in support of the province's eco-tourism strategy. In addition, a provincial trails system was developed and promoted.[72]

McKenna, perhaps more than any of his predecessors, was willing to stroke the local business community, speak its language and acknowledge its contributions to the provincial economy. In his speeches, both at home and elsewhere, he often referred to the "renaissance of the province's entrepreneurial spirit." He made time for anyone contemplating opening a new business, plant or office anywhere in the province. He never shrank from being seen as a friend of the local business community and was always willing to defend its interests. The columnist Dalton Camp, a well-known Tory partisan, observed that "in New Brunswick people will tell you that Frank McKenna is the best leader the Conservative party never had."[73]

The provincial government's Small Business Directorate introduced a "Self-Start Program," which provided funds to aspiring or first-time entrepreneurs up to a maximum of $10,000 for start-up equity. A variety of initiatives were undertaken to reduce red tape for small businesses, eliminate overlap and duplication in government programs, and encourage local firms to tap into foreign markets. As already noted, the Workers' Compensation Board was restructured to bring its unfunded liability under control and reduce premiums. The government passed legislation in late 1992 to reduce benefits from 90 percent to 80 percent of net earnings for the first 39 weeks and 75 percent thereafter, to restrict the ability to top-up benefits, and to discontinue pension benefits beyond age 65. These and other changes resulted in reducing the province's workers compensation premiums to some of the lowest in Canada.[74] McKenna did not stop

105

there, however. He also tried to repair the province's balance sheet, another action the local business community and outside investors widely applauded.

Repairing New Brunswick's Fiscal House

As newly elected governments are now commonly wont to do, the McKenna government called for an external review of the province's books shortly after it assumed power. The Doane Raymond report issued a stern warning: Get the fiscal house in order or New Brunswick would soon hit a debt wall. The report revealed that over the previous ten years New Brunswick had seen its net debt grow by an average of $177 million a year.[75] Also, that the province had substantial amounts of unfunded liability in its pension plans. All in all, the Doane Raymond report painted a bleak portrait of New Brunswick's public finances and suggested that a strong wrench of the wheel was needed to reorient the ship of state.

Of course, by the mid-1980s, all the provinces and the federal government shared this problem. Indeed, this issue, together with constitutional reforms, dominated Canada's public policy agenda for much of the 1980s and well into the 1990s. The problem in a nutshell was the all too apparent inability of governments to balance expenditures and revenues. The fact that past deficits had not been attended to made matters worse simply because the cost of servicing the accumulated debt added new spending year after year even before it was time to plan the next budget.

New Brunswick and the other slow-growth provinces had an added problem. They had traditionally counted on federal transfer payments as an important source of revenue. However, the federal government – also faced with the need to cut its expenditure budget – now looked to transfers to the provinces as an inviting target. Slow-growth provinces argued that when Ottawa cut transfers it was simply downloading the fiscal problem to them. This argument had little impact.

Still, McKenna left no doubt in the minds of his ministers and senior public servants that he wanted to place the government of New Brunswick on a more solid financial footing. Further, he made it clear that his goal was to cut taxes while he was repairing the province's balance sheet. His government's widely read *Economic Development Strategy in the Nineties* stated, "Our strategy must be based on sound public finances and less tax burden to provide a climate of confidence and to permit a more attractive tax environment."[76] The solution clearly then was to cut spending.

McKenna took a direct interest in budget making and invested a great deal of his time in reviewing, in considerable detail, departmental spending plans.

In late 1988, he decided to introduce zero-based budgeting in his government, on a pilot basis. Without putting too fine a point on it, the approach forced program managers, senior departmental officials and the premier and his ministers to think about why something was actually being done. In other words, departments and agencies had to justify their ongoing programs and activities and not just new activities. McKenna saw a great deal of merit in this kind of discipline and by 1989 zero-based budgeting was utilized in some form by all departments.

The McKenna government also made a commitment in 1988 to limit growth in ordinary expenditures to growth in revenues. This required a great number of difficult decisions but none proved too trivial for McKenna, if it meant saving money. For instance, he and his Cabinet colleagues agreed to voluntary salary restraint and non-essential government offices were shut down between Christmas and New Year's Day to reduce energy costs.

McKenna delivered on his commitment in the sense that total program spending was consistently lower than total revenues by the late 1980s and beyond. However, the cost of servicing the debt became such that the province was still running a deficit in the late 1980s and, when the recession hit in the early 1990s, its fiscal situation took a turn for the worse. For example, there was a $355 million shortfall in 1991-92 between total expenditures (including debt charges) and total revenues.[77] One reason for the shortfall was a sudden drop in federal equalization payments in that year.[78]

McKenna made a commitment in the 1992 election campaign to introduce legislation that would require balancing the Ordinary Account over a five-year period, beginning in fiscal year 1992-93. In the following year, the province's Legislative Assembly enacted an "Act Respecting the Balancing of the Ordinary Expenditure and Ordinary Revenues of the Province." The act directed the provincial government to balance the ordinary account budget over a three-year period, from 1993-94 to 1995-96. The legislation was innovative, at least for Canada, but it also had flaws that soon became all too obvious:

- the capital account was excluded, which meant that an important expenditure item was excluded
- changes in federal transfer payments to the province were excluded
- there was no guarantee that some items would not be taken "off budget"
- the legislation had no teeth – that is, there was no penalty for not balancing the budget
- the legislation called for a balanced budget over the political cycle rather than over the business cycle

McKenna decided to amend his original balanced budget legislation to deal with the above shortcomings and, in particular, to require that "all" the province's books be balanced over a four-year period, beginning in 1996-97. That is, beginning in 1996-97 total revenues had to balance or exceed all spending including ordinary, capital, debt charges, special purpose expenditures and Special Operating Agency account spending. The objective was to ensure that provincial debt levels would not increase during the remainder of the decade and beyond.

Alan Maher, McKenna's minister of finance, rose in the Legislative Assembly on 21 February 1995 to table what he called his "watershed budget." He explained that the budget "incorporates a bold and achievable vision of the future – a future where New Brunswick becomes a pay-as-you-go province, a future where the province's debt does not grow." He added, "for the first time since 1979-80, this budget will enable a New Brunswick finance minister to make a payment against the Province's debt."[79]

The merits of balanced budget legislation have been debated for some time.[80] Some observers argue that such legislation raises more questions than it answers. For example, how binding is the legislation? What happens if the objective is not met, and what is the consequence? How can legislation ever control creative accounting procedures? The list goes on. Still, the legislation at least served notice that the McKenna government was serious about repairing the province's balance sheet. In addition, McKenna could already point to some tangible accomplishments. By the time the "watershed budget" was tabled, McKenna could tell New Brunswickers and out-of-province investors,

- New Brunswick was the only province to receive an upgrade in its credit rating in the 1990s (a year later, however, Quebec and Alberta were also able to make the same claim).
- Several banks and investment firms had issued highly positive reports on New Brunswick. For example, Nesbitt Burns observed that New Brunswick "deserves high marks for its restraint measures...only a few other provinces have managed to cut outlays in back-to-back years," and the Dominion Board Rating Service commented that "the province has been one of the most fiscally responsible provinces in Canada and has contained its deficits mainly by restricting expenditure since 1990."[81]
- Strong progress was also being made in dealing with unfunded pension liabilities so that by 1995 total unfunded liability was reduced by $600 million from a total of $1.7 billion when McKenna took office. A New

Brunswick Crown Investment Management Corporation had also been established to act as trustee for major public sector pension funds. It was argued that the corporation would assist in the development of a New Brunswick-based financial services industry.

The McKenna government could also boast that it had been able to cut taxes while it brought order to the province's public finances. It reduced small business corporate income tax that applied to the first $200,000 of active business income for Canadian controlled private corporations to seven from nine percent. As already noted, the sales tax on 1-800 toll charges was eliminated in 1992-93. In that same year, the cost of conducting research and development was reduced by an exemption from sales tax for R&D expenditures. A year later, a ten percent corporate income tax credit for R&D was introduced, as well as an income tax credit for investment in prescribed labour-sponsored venture capital funds.

The New Brunswick government, along with two other Atlantic provinces, signed an agreement to harmonize its sales tax with the federal GST in 1996. The new tax, the harmonized sales tax (HST), came into effect 1 April 1997. The New Brunswick sales tax rate dropped to 8 percent from 11 percent and the combined sales tax rate dropped to 15 percent from an effective rate of 18.77 percent. The new tax applied to all goods and services previously covered by the GST. This change involved a major restructuring of the New Brunswick sales tax system and harmonization with the GST reduced the amount of total revenue from the New Brunswick sales tax by approximately $170 million annually, despite the broadening of the tax base. The federal government, it will be recalled, provided adjustment assistance – based on a set formula – to ease the transition between the two tax systems. Under this formula, New Brunswick received $364 million. This amount together with interest was meant to allow the province to adjust to the new tax structure over a four-year transition period.

The 1997-98 budget, the last McKenna budget, also announced a number of important tax changes. The personal income tax rate was to fall to 57.5 percent from 64 percent of basic federal tax by 1999. On 1 January 1997 the rate was reduced to 63 percent from 64 percent of basic federal tax, on 1 January 1998 it was reduced to 61 percent of basic federal tax and, finally, on 1 January 1999 the rate was to be reduced further to 57.5 percent of federal basic tax. However, Camille Thériault, who became premier of New Brunswick after winning the Liberal leadership convention called after McKenna stepped down, decided to cancel this last scheduled tax cut.

Dealing with Ottawa

McKenna was front and centre in his government's dealings with the federal government. He played the lead role for the province in both the Meech Lake and Charlottetown constitutional reform attempts. He was also able to establish a strong personal relationship with prime ministers Mulroney and Chrétien. McKenna, like Mulroney, had a personal link to the Miramichi region of New Brunswick and was a graduate of St. Francis Xavier University. Chrétien and McKenna, meanwhile, were both Liberals and McKenna gave Chrétien a helping hand in the 1993 general election. McKenna never hesitated to make full use of his relationship with both prime ministers to seek support from Ottawa for his government's agenda (NB Works is just one of many examples) and to secure federal funding for special projects. Yet, McKenna did not hesitate to confront either Mulroney or Chrétien, even on issues that were personally important to them and to their governments. McKenna, as is well known, challenged Mulroney on the proposed Meech Lake agreement, an initiative to which Mulroney personally attached a great deal of importance. McKenna challenged Chrétien on his government's proposed gun control legislation and on his approach to reforming the unemployment insurance program, writing to Chrétien to oppose elements of his government's reform plan. McKenna wrote,

> I do not believe that there is a full appreciation of the consequences of the [proposed] changes. I would note that as of May this year [1995], 23 percent of all the new social assistance cases in the Province of New Brunswick were U.I. exhaustees...it does not make sense to penalize seasonal workers who have absolutely no chance of other employment but who are otherwise valuable contributors to the economy.... For New Brunswick alone, the impact of the changes will remove approximately $175 million per year from the economy. This is little short of devastating.... Prime Minister, I beg of you to take the time to examine the ramifications of this legislation.[82]

To be sure, McKenna was always personally quick to intervene in Ottawa on behalf of a New Brunswick initiative or to speak in the interest of the province. His papers in the provincial archives reveal a constant stream of letters, more often than not to the prime minister, but with copies to all relevant ministers, dealing with a host of issues both large and small. Some letters deal with constitutional reform, the state of the Canadian economy and the problem of youth unemployment, but others are concerned with relatively minor issues

Table 10
Budget Data, the McKenna Years ($ million)

YEAR	Own-source revenues	Federal cash transfers	Total revenues	Total program expenditures	Debt charges	Total expenditures	Deficit (-) or surplus	Total financial	Net debt balance
1987-88	1,918	1,261	3,179	3,100	415	3,515	-336	-465	2,919
1988-89	2,167	1,360	3,527	3,179	427	3,606	-79	-250	2,993
1989-90	2,213	1,459	3,672	3,260	437	3,697	-25	-227	3,013
1990-91	2,297	1,504	3,801	3,500	482	3,982	-181	-394	3,236
1991-92	2,352	1,455	3,807	3,686	476	4,162	-355	-569	3,603
1992-93	2,268	1,742	4,010	3,737	538	4,275	-265	-514	5,297
1993-94	2,507	1,517	4,024	3,695	585	4,280	-256	-473	5,552
1994-95	2,672	1,626	4,298	3,721	645	4,366	-68	-304	5,621
1995-96	2,803	1,623	4,426	3,780	595	4,375	51	-384	5,569
1996-97	2,950	1,521	4,471	3,791	564	4,356	115	-108	5,734
1997-98	2,821	1,653	4,474	3,865	574	4,439	35	-446	5,748

Source: Department of Finance Canada, *Fiscal Reference Tables*, Table 20, 2000, p. 30.

donald j. savoie

ranging from possible layoffs in selected communities to a special appeal that the prime minister intervene so that the federal government would provide additional groundfish quota to New Brunswick from the 2J3KL zone.[83]

McKenna and his advisors also kept a watchful eye on how Ottawa was dealing with other provinces, if only to ensure that New Brunswick was not being shortchanged. For example, he wrote to several federal ministers on 16 August 1988 to express concern over possible federal financing for a major gypsum project for Cape Breton, Nova Scotia, while a similar project in McAdam, New Brunswick, had recently received federal funding. McKenna wrote to R. Robert de Cotret, the then minister of Regional Industrial Expansion, with copies to three of his colleagues, to say, "I would like your clear assurance that the Cape Breton project will not be prejudicial to the viability of the Eastern Gypsum initiative for McAdam. This is an extremely sensitive and serious situation and an immediate reply would be appreciated."[84] Two months later, he wrote to Gerald Merithew, New Brunswick's representative in the federal cabinet, about the newly established Atlantic Canada Opportunities Agency (ACOA) and its track record in New Brunswick relative to the other Atlantic provinces. He wrote,

> We are extremely concerned with the implementation of the ACOA program in the Province of New Brunswick. At the present time, 44 percent of all applications in Newfoundland have been processed, 42 percent of applications in Nova Scotia, and 50 percent of applications in Prince Edward Island. In New Brunswick, only 31 percent of applications have been processed and we have received an allocation of $62.5 million as compared to $89.2 million in the Province of Nova Scotia. In spite of an agreement signed with the Province of New Brunswick, we have only received 103 applications for processing out of a total of 1,814 received by ACOA.[85]

McKenna's ten years as premier of New Brunswick coincided with Ottawa's attempt to repair its own balance sheet. Given that New Brunswick is so dependent on federal transfers as a source of revenue, McKenna could not in this sense have picked a worse time to serve as premier. Things have improved on this front since he left office, in that the federal government has recently been laying down plans to deal with a growing surplus. Before McKenna came to power, Ottawa's attempts at deficit reduction were, at best, tentative.[86] The Mulroney government was somewhat more committed by its second mandate, beginning in 1988 but, as history now reveals, Chrétien left no doubt that he was deeply serious about cutting federal government spending.

Ottawa undertook an ambitious program review in the 1994 budget. That same year, the peso went into free-fall as Mexico experienced a major downturn in its economic fortunes following a twenty-year period of progress. Given its high accumulated government debt, Canada then became the focus of scrutiny by international financial markets. In early January 1995, the *Wall Street Journal* described the Canadian dollar as a "basket case." The Journal ran an editorial on 12 January 1995 titled "Bankrupt Canada?" and declared that "Mexico isn't the only US neighbour flirting with the financial abyss." It went on to argue that "if dramatic action isn't taken in the next month's federal budget, it's not inconceivable that Canada could hit the debt wall and have to call in the International Monetary Fund to stabilize its falling currency." This editorial had a major effect on those in Ottawa still hesitant to accept the argument made by the minister of finance that he had no choice but to introduce deep spending cuts. The impact was such that Deputy Minister of Finance David Dodge later described it as a "seminal event" in the politics of the 1995 budget.[87]

The "seminal event" in Ottawa had a seminal impact on New Brunswick and other slow-growth provinces in Atlantic Canada. The result of the program review and spending cuts contained in the 1995 Martin budget are well known. Suffice it to note that 50,000 public service and military positions were eliminated, as were long-established programs like Freight Rate Assistance and transportation subsidies for Atlantic Canada, and major reductions were made in various agricultural and industrial subsidies. A further $1 billion in spending cuts were made in defence and $500 million in foreign aid. New cuts affected the unemployment insurance program and federal-provincial transfers in the social policy area. Seventy-three boards, commissions and advisory bodies were shut down. In total, $29 billion in cuts were announced. By 1996-97, program spending would be reduced to 13.1 percent of GDP, the lowest level since 1951.[88]

The impact on New Brunswick was immediate and is still being felt today. Some federal regional development programs, for example, were transformed from providing "contributions" and "grants" to "loan guarantees" or "interest buy-down" programs. There was also less federal money for regional development agreements. In the 1970s and early 1980s, virtually all provincial departments responsible for an economic sector had their own federal-provincial agreements to support every conceivable economic development project. From 1974 to 1987, Ottawa signed forty economic development agreements worth $1.2 billion with New Brunswick in sectors such as industrial development, fishery, forestry, agriculture, tourism and minerals. By the time McKenna came

113

to office, Ottawa was in a much less generous mood. When it first began to sign such agreements in 1974, Ottawa would typically assume 75 to 90 percent of the cost, on occasions paying even 100 percent of all costs. By 1981-82, it had scaled back its share to 62 percent and by 1989 it tried, albeit not always successfully, to introduce a 50-50 cost-sharing formula.[89]

Some provinces, such as Nova Scotia, agreed to a 60-40 cost sharing formula and signed agreements on this basis. McKenna, however, resisted, holding out for a 70-30 formula, not just for New Brunswick but for the other Atlantic provinces as well, in the area of economic development. He stated bluntly that they simply did not have the resources for anything more. How could they, he asked, given the constant stream of federal spending cuts in the region? The economic development agreements, he insisted, were key to future growth in the region and Ottawa should assume a larger share of the cost. His arguments, according to officials with the Atlantic Canada Opportunities Agency, had an impact, and in many cases the federal government agreed to pay 70 percent of the cost.

But McKenna could not turn back the clock to the free-spending 1970s and early 1980s when, for example, the DREE spent nearly $70 million in 1979-80 in New Brunswick alone (in 1979-80 dollars).[90] During the McKenna years, ACOA spent on average about $75 million a year (in 1992-93 dollars in the province).[91] Appendix 1 provides a complete list of all federal-provincial agreements for New Brunswick signed while McKenna was premier. The federal government signed fewer agreements covering fewer sectors between 1987 and 1997 than it did in the previous ten years or even between 1974 and 1977, and federal government cost sharing was considerably less generous, mostly in the 70-30 range.[92] Moreover, Ottawa decided that it would no longer cost-share federal-provincial agreements in the resources sector, which meant that the four Atlantic provinces had no choice but to take on new expenditures to promote further development in this sector.

Martin's 1995 budget also had a profound impact on the province's seasonal workers, given its cuts to the unemployment insurance program. In addition, the budget introduced significant cuts to federal-provincial agreements under Ottawa's Established Program Financing (EPF) and the Canada Assistance Plan (CAP). These two programs were replaced by the Canada Health and Social Transfer (CHST) program which provided funding to the provinces in the form of a block grant. The bad news for the provinces, however, was that the changes entailed a reduction of federal transfers of $2.5 billion in 1996-97 and $4.5 billion in 1997-98. The reduction in transfer payments to all provinces represented a 33 percent cut over two years. Cash transfers to New Brunswick under these two programs and then under the new CHST were reduced as follows: 1993-94 ($510 million); 1994-95 ($501 million); 1995-96 ($493 million); 1996-97 ($401 million); 1997-98 ($337 million); and, finally, 1998-99 ($333 million).

McKenna was thus getting a helping hand from Ottawa in his effort to make New Brunswick more self-sufficient, although perhaps not the kind he was looking for. The 1995 Martin budget meant fewer federal jobs in New Brunswick, less funding for the provincial government and, as already mentioned, it had a serious impact on seasonal rural workers because of the cuts to the unemployment insurance program. All in all, New Brunswick had no choice but to become more self-sufficient. Moreover, the 1995 Martin budget also personified a new mindset that was beginning to percolate through society: Governments can not always be counted on to assist those in danger of falling off the economic ladder. This applied to both individuals and regions. Deficit or not, government intervention in the economy was falling out of favour and the implications for a province like New Brunswick were all too obvious. There were precious few credible voices anywhere being heard in favour of new government interventions in the economy. Even John Kenneth Galbraith, the leading figure of the twentieth century to advocate the benefits of a greater role for government in society, was starting to express caution. He had observed, as early as 1986, that "it's more than the Liberal task now to defend the system.... It is far more important now to improve the operations than enlarge and increase its scope. This must be the direction of our major efforts."[93]

Despite its impact on New Brunswick, McKenna supported Ottawa's program review and the resulting spending cuts and said so publicly. The 1995-96 New Brunswick budget stated, "Clearly, there is little support for tax increases, and a strong current of opinion suggests that the federal government should meet its deficit targets solely on the expenditure side of its budget." However, although McKenna supported the Martin budget, he warned that he would strongly advance "concerns to the federal government, with respect to treatment of seasonal workers under federal unemployment insurance proposals." He also called on the federal government to put in place "a well-managed implementation process, a reasonable period of transition, and for appropriate compensation if there are instances where the province must assume some of the off-loaded program responsibilities." The budget papers concluded with the statement that the government "must be ready for change, be nimble in (its) responses and, above all, continue to be responsible in our stewardship of public finances."[94]

McKenna's energy, enthusiasm and "can do" attitude became well known right across Canada. He enjoyed a strong relationship with both Prime Minister Mulroney and Prime Minister Chrétien, in part because of the credibility he was given by the media and in financial and business circles. In addition, with the sweeping mandate New Brunswickers gave him in the three general elections he fought, one could assume he would have a free hand to reform all facets of the province's public sector if he so desired.

However, there were two major public sector organizations he left virtually unchallenged during his ten years in office: the province's universities and the provincial electrical power utility. Both were, and remain, extremely important to New Brunswick's economic development. In the case of universities, they are generally considered the "engines" of the new economy. They not only develop knowledge workers but also are at the leading edge of much research and development. In the energy sector, much of the industrialized world was embarking on deregulation and privatization while McKenna was premier. This was also true in Canada where New Brunswick's neighbour, Nova Scotia, decided to sell all of its electrical power assets to the private sector. The government of Ontario announced in its document *Direction for Change* that it also fully intended to make the "move to a competitive electricity market."[95] New England had already done so by the time McKenna left office. These decisions in other jurisdictions were all designed to reduce the cost of energy and the most successful would be in a stronger position to expand and create new jobs. The cost of energy is extremely important in a number of sectors, including forestry, mining and manufacturing, sectors that have played a vital part in the province's economic development.

In the case of the universities, it is surprising that McKenna did nothing. He neither challenged them to increase their research and development nor did he ask university administrators to alter the status quo in their own institutions. In addition, he never initiated a debate, let alone take concrete action, on possible changes to the governance structure of New Brunswick universities.

McKenna did more in the energy field, but his efforts here too cannot be described as bold or innovative. His government supported the construction of a new thermal generating unit at Belledune in northern New Brunswick and made investments in the reduction of airborne emissions. It also launched a major energy efficiency program in 1995. Under this program, provincial government buildings were upgraded with funds from private sector firms, funds which were repaid from the resulting energy cost-savings. In November

1994, the McKenna government approved a co-generation policy for NB Power. The policy stated that, prior to building new capacity for in-province needs, NB Power would solicit co-generation options from industry through a request for proposals. This initiative was expected to foster further modernization and promote NB Power's overall least-cost resource plan. But in the end, the policy had a modest impact. It led to the development of a new 38-megawatt co-generation facility at the Frasers paper mill in Edmundston, which was completed in December 1996. The facility supplies process steam for Frasers and electricity for purchase by NB Power.

The McKenna government also sought to bring a more private sector culture to NB Power. It appointed the first non-elected or non-politician chairman of the board of directors. It also called for the development of a five-year business plan to be updated annually and reviewed by the Crown Corporation Committee of the Legislature.

But that was the extent to which McKenna sought to prepare NB Power to deal with significant changes in the industry, even though NB Power was a publicly owned company and McKenna had a free hand in reshaping its destiny. There were also some serious problems at the Point Lepreau nuclear power plant which, according to a provincial government discussion paper, "resulted in the plant operating below planned levels." The paper went on to reveal that "NB Power has been unable to meet its revenue requirements, including an appropriate rate of return and also has not been able to make appropriate progress toward retiring its debt."[96] A task force report produced about a year after McKenna left office and while the province was still under Liberal rule concluded that "the maintenance of the status quo – NB Power operating as a monopoly provider of electricity in New Brunswick – is possible, [but it is] problematic. The energy world, particularly electricity, is changing all around New Brunswick...it is not in the interest of New Brunswickers to try to build a protective wall around the province."[97]

McKenna thus left office without leaving much of a trace on the electrical sector and the universities, though both were important economic development tools. I asked McKenna why he decided to leave these two sectors largely unreformed. He said that if he could turn back the clock, he would certainly put them on his reform agenda. But he added,

I was brought up to believe that universities function best when they are independent and when they are free to chart their own course. This view may no longer hold, given the pace of change in society, but in 1987 it still held true. In hindsight, I should have done more with NB Power. But we were pioneers in many, many areas and there is a risk in overloading your agenda for change. We were always pushing the envelope.[98]

In the case of NB Power, however, McKenna added that he saw little merit in privatizing NB Power if it were simply to become a "private sector monopoly." He also insisted that NB Power was, at least in his day, an efficient public sector monopoly. He was quick to produce fact sheets showing that electricity was a great deal cheaper in New Brunswick than in other North American jurisdictions, including Alberta, Ontario and New England.[99]

This chapter documents that the government of New Brunswick was indeed an activist government and that it undertook sweeping reforms in many sectors. It also documents how McKenna became a highly effective salesman for New Brunswick and reports on his willingness to undertake sweeping reforms in many sectors. Significant changes were also introduced in sectors such as health care and more modest ones in electoral reform (e.g., it reduced the number of electoral districts in the province from 58 to 55); these are not dealt with here, however. McKenna was tireless in his pursuit of job creation and in repairing the province's balance sheet. This was done at a particularly difficult time when Ottawa was making serious spending cuts to its own programs and to transfers to the provinces and individuals. In the next chapter, we will assess the impact of these changes.

118

Appendix 1
Cooperation Program Initiatives
Signed from October 1987 to February 1998

PROGRAM	Date Signed	Termination Date	Total Cost ($ million)	Federal Share	Cost-sharing Ratio
New Brunswick					
Amendment # 1	01/11/90	32/03/92	5.0	5.0	100/0
Amendment # 2	28/07/92	31/03/96	37.9	26.3	69/31
Amendment # 3 (1)	10/06/93	31/03/97	40.0 (1)	20.0 (1)	50/50
Amendment # 4 (1)	30/06/94	31/03/97	2.857 (1)	2.0 (1)	70/30
Amendment # 5 (1)	31/05/95	31/03/97	8.57 (1)	6.0 (1)	70/30
Amendment # 6 (1)	25/07/95	31/03/98	98.0 (1)	49.0 (1)	50/50
Agri-Food Development	06/10/89	31/03/94	32.0	20.0	62/38
Amendment # 1	01/10/93	31/03/95	0.67	0.45	80/20
Fisheries Development	03/11/89	31/03/94	19.6	11.7	60/40
Forestry Development	15/12/89	31/03/94	91.0	50.0	55/45
Planning	06/02/90	31/03/94	2.0	1.0	50/50
Amendment # 1	23/07/92	31/03/97	3.0	1.5	50/50
Economic Diversification	16/08/90	31/03/95	36.2	23.5	65/35
Amendment # 1	04/08/92	31/03/97	29.6	19.2	65/35
Amendment # 2	05/08/94	31/03/98	24.3	17.4	64/36
Amendment # 3					
(TAGS-CED)	01/09/95	31/03/98	1.0	1.0	100/0
1995 Budget cuts			(-7.795)	(-5.25)	—
Urban Economic Development	12/09/90	31/03/95	46.0	23.0	50/50
Amendment # 1	30/09/93	31/03/95	4.3	2.2	50/50
Entrepreneurship & HRD	23/07/92	31/03/97	25.8	17.0	66/34
Economic Development	23/07/92	31/03/97	38.0	25.0	66/34
Amendment # 1	05/08/94	31/03/98	30.0	20.475	68/32
Amendment # 2 (2)	27/05/94	31/03/98	(-1.095)	(-0.765)	—
1995 Budget cuts			(-7.75)	(-5.25)	—
Special Response	10/05/90	31/03/91	2.3	1.5	65/35
Bi-Capital	10/08/90	31/03/95	8.3	8.3	100/0
Cultural Development	11/10/90	31/03/95	5.0	2.5	50/50
Mineral Development	12/09/90	31/03/95	10.0	6.0	60/40
Industrial Development	12/09/90	31/03/92	10.0	5.0	50/50
ALFI (Extension)	06/12/91	30/09/92	2.25	1.8	80/20
Recreational Fishery	07/08/92	31/03/96	15.0	15.0	100/0
Tourism - Travel Generators	23/07/92	31/03/94	5.7	4.0	70/30
Regional Economic Development	31/07/96	31/03/01	53.714	37.6	70/30
Total New Brunswick			816.42	512.16	

(1) Not Cooperation Program funding
(2) Funds transferred to the Pan-Atlantic International Business Development agreement

Notes

1. Frank McKenna, "The Path to Self-Sufficiency," speech to the Greater Moncton Chamber of Commerce, 101st annual banquet, 6 May 1992.

2. "Getting Down to Business in New Brunswick: An Interview with Premier Frank McKenna," *Canadian Business Review*, Toronto (Winter 1994), p. 7.

3. "Premier Made Decision to Oust Deputy Ministers," *Daily Gleanor*, Fredericton, 4 March 1989.

4. "Premier Made Decision to Oust Deputy Ministers," *Daily Gleanor*.

5. "Public perception reason for firing deputy ministers: premier," *Telegraph Journal*, Saint John, 16 March 1989, p. 4.

6. "Premier Made Decision to Oust Deputy Ministers," *Daily Gleanor*.

7. Interview with Frank McKenna, Moncton, New Brunswick, 2 March 2000.

8. "The New Brunswick Experience," remarks by Claire Morris before the Ontario Management Forum, Toronto, June 1995, p. 8.

9. "Top bureaucratic changes signal new McKenna drive," *Telegraph Journal*, St. John, 1 August 1989, p. 4.

10. "Top bureaucratic changes signal new McKenna drive," *Telegraph Journal*, p. 4.

11. Consultation with Claire Morris, Secretary to the Cabinet, Government of New Brunswick, 8 September 1995.

12. The Cabinet Secretariat was a central agency serving as a secretariat to the Cabinet, much like the Privy Council Office functions as a secretariat to the federal Cabinet in Ottawa.

13. "McKenna hunts jobs worldwide," *The Globe and Mail*, 9 September 1995, p. A6. See also Gilles Bouchard, "Les sous-ministres du Nouveau-Brunswick: de l'ère des techniciens à l'ère des gestionnaires," *Canadian Public Administration*, Vol. 42, no. 1 (Spring 1999), p. 104.

14. See Government of New Brunswick, *New Brunswick Report to the 1995 Annual Civil Service Commissioners' Conference at Aylmer*, Quebec, 25-27 June 1995.

15. This number, according to Statistics Canada, stood at about 50,000 positions but it included all public sector employees such as those employed by hospitals and school boards.

16. New Brunswick, Department of Human Resources Development, *Annual Report: Partners in Change* (July 1995), p. 1.

17. Department of Human Resources Development, *Annual Report: Partners in Change*, p. 1.

18. Department of Human Resources Development, *Annual Report: Partners in Change*, p. 2.

19. Department of Human Resources Development, *Annual Report: Partners in Change*, p. 2.

20. See letter to the editor from Hon. Ann Breault, minister of Human Resources Development – New Brunswick, in response to Jackie Webster's article, undated, copy in the New Brunswick archives.

21. Consultations with Frank McKenna, Moncton, April 2000.

22. See Government of New Brunswick, *New Brunswick Report to the 1995 Annual Civil Service Commissioners' Conference at Aylmer*.

23. See Government of New Brunswick, *New Brunswick Report to the 1995 Annual Civil Service Commissioners' Conference at Aylmer*.

24. Consultation with Sylvestre McLaughlin, former deputy minister of Fisheries, Government of New Brunswick, 20 June 2000.

25. "The New Brunswick Experience," p. 27.

26. "The New Brunswick Experience," p. 26.

27. New Brunswick, *Speech from the Throne*, Fourth Session of the 52nd Legislative Assembly of New Brunswick, 7 February 1995, p. 19.

28. New Brunswick, *Speech from the Throne*, p. 19.

29. See *Moving Together: The Platform of the New Brunswick Liberal Party for the 1995 Provincial General Election*, Fredericton (August 1995), p. 28.

30. *Moving Together*, p. 28.

31. *Moving Together*, p. 28.

32. See, among others, Gyslain Chiasson and Kafi Nzeya-Wéva, "Service New Brunswick — An Illustration," a paper presented to the Atlantic Conference on the Future of Public Administration, 11-12 February 2000, Université de Moncton and Dalhousie University, Memramcook, New Brunswick.

33. See, for example, *Moving Together*, pp. 1 and 19.

120

34. See, among others, "The New Brunswick Experience," pp. 11-12.

35. "The New Brunswick Experience," p. 12.

36. "The New Brunswick Experience," p. 13.

37. Quoted in "Looking back and looking ahead," The New Brunswick Business Journal, Vol. 8, no. 1 (January 1991), p. 1.

38. Examples include Hawk Communications and Communications Plus, both in Moncton, and together employing about 40 people.

39. The $1.69 billion would also serve to carry out the appropriate upgrading on the connecting links to St. John. See speech for delivery by the Hon. Frank McKenna, "Discussion Paper: Adequate Highways – A Key to Regional Economic Development," 24 August 1988, p. 6.

40. Letter from Premier Frank McKenna to Prime Minister Brian Mulroney, 24 August 1988, provincial archives, p. 1.

41. Only a few months before leaving office, McKenna secured a multi-year highway construction agreement with the federal government during a golf game with the prime minister. See Donald J. Savoie, Governing from the Centre: The Concentration of Power in Canadian Politics (Toronto: University of Toronto Press, 1999), p. 75.

42. Letter from Premier Frank McKenna to Prime Minister Jean Chrétien, 29 January 1997, provincial archives.

43. See, among many others, Speech from the Throne, 7 February 1995, the Hon. Margaret Norrie McCain, Lieutenant-Governor, p. 19.

44. "The New Brunswick Experience," p. 23.

45. McKenna, "The Path to Self-Sufficiency," p. 4.

46. Economic Development Strategy in the Nineties, Government of New Brunswick, Policy Secretariat, 1992, p. 4.

47. See, for example, William J. Milne, The McKenna Miracle: Myth or Reality (Toronto: University of Toronto Press, monograph series on public policy and public administration, 1996), p. 72.

48. Communication Toolkit NRD – NB Transformation – Partners in Change, Fredericton, July 1995, p. 1.

49. Milne, The McKenna Miracle, p. 76.

50. Quoted from "Building New Brunswick Together," document prepared for the 1995 election campaign, Fredericton, undated, p. 6.

51. Interview with Frank McKenna, Moncton, New Brunswick, 3 March 2000.

52. See Jonathan W. Rose, "The Selling of New Brunswick: Fibre Optics or Optical Illusion?", in Douglas M. Brown and Jonathan W. Rose (eds.), Canada: The State of the Federation, 1995 (Kingston: Institute for Intergovernmental Relations, 1995), p. 174.

53. "The Energizer Premier," Report on Business, Toronto (March 1993), p. 20.

54. "Bernard Lord: Beyond 200 days," Atlantic Business, Vol. 11, no. 1 (2000), p. 13.

55. "Bernard Lord: Beyond 200 days," Atlantic Business, p. 22.

56. Milne, The McKenna Miracle, p. 39.

57. "The secret of success: Economic official tells what's behind the McKenna miracle revealed by McKenna aide," Telegraph Journal, Saint John, 23 October 1995, p. 1.

58. "The secret of success" Telegraph Journal, p. 2.

59. "COM DEV: Atlantic," Atlantic Business (January 1995), p. 17.

60. Based on information provided by a senior Government of New Brunswick official, November 2000.

61. See, among many others, "UPS Agreement with NB called 'Theft of Jobs'," The Globe and Mail, 12 January 1995, p. A4.

62. New Brunswick: More than a Location (Fredericton: Government of New Brunswick, Department of Economic Development, 1995), p. 1.

63. See, among many others, Canada, Hansard, House of Commons debates, 10 February 1997, www.parl.gc.ca

64. See "Fast Frank's failure in rural areas," in Michael Tutton, "Atlantic Connections," Telegraph Journal, 22 April 1997, p. D1.

65. See, among others, Rose, "The Selling of New Brunswick," p. 175.

66. Rose, "The Selling of New Brunswick," p. 178.

67. Driving the Information Highway: The Report of the New Brunswick Task Force on the Electronic Information Highway (Fredericton: Information Highway Secretariat, 1994), p. 10.

68. See Rose, "The Selling of New Brunswick," p. 185.

69. Scholars.com is now "Smart Force" and it is one of the world's largest and most successful on-line training firms.

70. Interview with Frank McKenna, September 1999.

71. Based on information gathered through various documents from the Frank McKenna papers deposited at the provincial archives, January 2000.

72. Based on information gathered through various documents from the Frank McKenna papers deposited at the provincial archives, January 2000.

73. Quoted in "The Energizer Premier," p. 25.

74. Milne, The McKenna Miracle, pp. 87-90.

75. Claire Morris, "The New Brunswick Experience," p. 6.

76. Economic Development Strategy in the Nineties, p. 6.

77. See Public Accounts of New Brunswick, information for 1998-99 budget.

78. One provincial government reports that the drop in federal transfer payments was over $100 million in fiscal year 1991-92.

79. Budget 1995-1996, Government of New Brunswick, Department of Finance, 21 February 1995, pp. 5-6.

80. See, among others, Donald J. Savoie, The Politics of Public Spending in Canada (Toronto: University of Toronto Press, 1990).

81. Quoted in Budget 1995-1996, p. 11.

82. Letter from Premier Frank McKenna to Prime Minister Jean Chrétien, 23 November 1995, provincial archives, pp. 1-3.

83. See, for example, letter to Prime Minister Brian Mulroney from Premier Frank McKenna, dated 22 July 1988, provincial archives.

84. Memorandum from Frank McKenna to R. Robert de Cotret, minister of Regional Industrial Expansion with copies to senators Lowell Murray, Gerald Merithew, and Bernard Valcourt, 16 August 1988, provincial archives.

85. Letter to Gerald Merithew from Frank McKenna, 21 October 1988, provincial archives, p. 2.

86. See, among many others, Savoie, The Politics of Public Spending in Canada.

87. See Edward Greenspon and Anthony Wilson-Smith, Double Vision: The Inside Story of the Liberals in Power (Toronto: Doubleday, 1996), p. 236.

88. See, for example, Armelita Armit and Jacques Bourgault (eds.), Hard Choices or No Choices: Assessing Program Review (Toronto: Institute of Public Administration, 1996).

89. See Donald J. Savoie, Regional Economic Development: Canada's Search for Solutions (Toronto: University of Toronto Press, 1992), Appendices B and C.

90. Canada, Annual Report 1979-80, Department of Regional Economic Expansion, p. 51.

91. Consultations with senior officials with the Atlantic Canada Opportunities Agency, Moncton, February 2000.

92. See Appendix 1 at the end of this chapter and Appendices B and C in Savoie, Regional Economic Development.

93. Quoted in Dimensions (Winter 1986), p. 13.

94. Budget 1995-1996, pp. 17-19.

95. Government of Ontario, Direction for Change: Charting a Course for Competitive Electricity and Jobs in Ontario, November 1997, p. 1.

96. Electricity in New Brunswick Beyond 2000: Discussion Paper (Fredericton: Government of New Brunswick, February 1998), pp. 5-6.

97. Electricity in New Brunswick and Options for Its Future (Fredericton: Special Task Force Report, July 1998), p. 53.

98. Interview with Frank McKenna, Moncton, New Brunswick, 3 March 2000.

99. The material McKenna provided me was produced by "The Competitive Alternatives – A Comparison of Business Costs in North America, Europe and Japan," KPMG, 1999.

THE DENOUEMENT

6

New Brunswick in 1997

Two years after he left office, McKenna claimed in an interview that he had never really rejoiced in winning an election. Even when he won every seat in his first general election, he reports he experienced no great feeling of exhilaration. The thrill in politics for him, he insisted, was not in winning but in knowing he had the chance to change things for the better, help his fellow New Brunswickers climb the economic ladder and make the province stronger. The phrase often heard in Quebec – *un projet de société* – captures very well for him the essence of politics, speaking as it does to the importance of articulating a sense of purpose and collective action.[1]

127

There is no denying McKenna had a vision, a purpose, a *projet de société*, in mind when he became premier of New Brunswick. Simply put, his vision was to make New Brunswick and New Brunswickers more economically self-reliant. The question then is what impact did his *projet de société* have? How did it affect the public service and the state of the province's public finances? What about employment and income levels?

This chapter takes stock of the McKenna years. We also compare economic circumstances in New Brunswick, as outlined in Chapter 5, with those existing in the province in 1997 and beyond from data produced by Statistics Canada and others. We again compare its economic circumstances with that of other provinces of similar size. This comparative perspective will enable us to produce a more objective assessment of the McKenna years.

The New Brunswick of 1997 was in many ways not much different, population-wise, from the New Brunswick of 1987. Immigration had no appreciable impact during the McKenna years. There are still only three main or dominating cultural groups in the province, as described in Chapter 4.

Charts 1 and 2 below provide a breakdown of "landings by province of intended destination" of new Canadians for all ten provinces and territories during the ten years McKenna held office. They show in the most telling way the economic pull that Ontario and British Columbia, and to a lesser extent Quebec and Alberta, hold for new Canadians. The charts also show, in equally revealing terms, that Atlantic Canada is scarcely present in the minds of new Canadians as they search for a home in Canada. For example, in 1997, McKenna's last year in office, New Brunswick was able to attract just 0.3 percent of new Canadians, while Ontario became home to 54.6 percent of immigrants.

On this issue, McKenna observed,

> In the Province of British Columbia, some 54 percent of all immigrant investors end up going there, as opposed to some 2 percent for the Maritime provinces. That has allowed that part of Canada to enjoy an enormous amount of benefit through that rich fuel of entrepreneurship and that dynamic quality that entrepreneurs bring.[2]

The point here is that entrepreneurship or any economic dynamism in New Brunswick must be, by definition, homegrown. In brief, it underscores the lesson that there would be no "giant silver bird arriving" in the form of new Canadians "bearing all manner of gifts and things" to New Brunswick. This was as true in 1997 as it was in 1987.

The above is not to suggest the McKenna government or other Maritime governments were or are unaware of the problem. In the case of McKenna, for example, he gave numerous speeches abroad encouraging potential new Canadians to move to New Brunswick. He launched a national campaign and organized special sessions in Toronto, Ottawa and Montreal to encourage former New Brunswickers to move back to the province. He also established a committee of the Legislative Assembly, chaired by Joan Kingston, a member of the Legislative Assembly, to review the situation.

Though these efforts met with some success, the charts below make it clear that the success was hardly resounding. For his part, McKenna argues that he never received a helping hand from Ottawa in his efforts to promote New

Chart 1
Landings by Province of Intended Destination of International Immigrants — **1987**

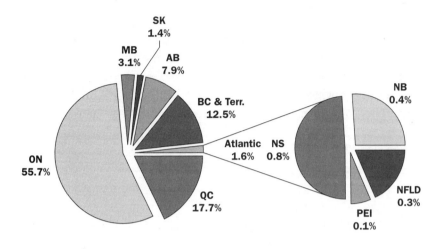

Source: WFDSS LANDSPPR, 27 January 2000.

Chart 2
Landings by Province of Intended Destination of International Immigrants — **1997**

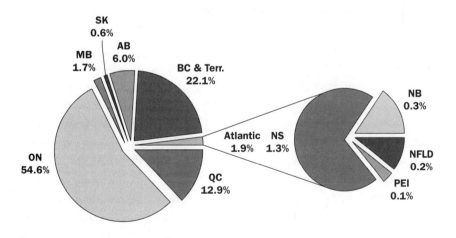

Source: WFDSS LANDSPPR, 27 January 2000.

Brunswick as a destination of choice for new Canadians. Ottawa's attitude, he explains, was to do nothing, and "clearly, unless encouraged to do otherwise, new Canadians will look to such places as Toronto, Vancouver and Ottawa to locate." The problem, he added, "is that federal government policy, in a passive way, discourages immigration to this region."[3]

The lack of immigration has not been felt only at the economic level; it probably also explains the province's continued political conservatism. There has been, for example, limited public support for such concepts as the political union of the three Maritime provinces. Political stability still rules in New Brunswick and radical politics has yet to make much inroad in its society. In fact, the anti-bilingual party, CoR, as noted in Chapter 4, has now disappeared altogether from the electoral map. The provincial New Democratic Party still elects only one member to the Legislative Assembly – its party leader, Elizabeth Weir. By electing Bernard Lord and his Progressive Conservative Party to power in 1999, New Brunswickers again demonstrated their loyalty to the two traditional political parties.

At the federal level, the Reform Party never became a political force in New Brunswick politics during the McKenna years. The federal New Democratic Party had somewhat of a breakthrough in the 1997 election, winning two seats. Both victories, however, were in rural ridings with a high number of seasonal workers. It is now widely accepted that Ottawa's cuts to its employment insurance program cost the federal Liberals these two seats. In electing two NDP federal members, New Brunswickers were not embracing radical politics. Rather, voters in both ridings were protesting the cuts in the employment insurance program.

New Brunswick's population remained stable during the McKenna years. Indeed, the province lost ground when compared with the national average (see Chart 3). It had a total population of 727,877 in 1987 compared with 753,304 in 1997 when McKenna left office. A growth of 25,427 (3.5 percent) over a ten-year period is modest by national standards. The Canadian population grew by 3,565,784 over the same period, to 29,968,054 from 26,402,270 for a growth of nearly 14 percent. However, Newfoundland and Labrador fared even worse than New Brunswick, actually losing 20,564 people. Its population dropped to 554,602 from 575,166 in the same period. Nova Scotia, meanwhile, saw its population grow to 934,097 from 892,881 for an increase of 41,216 or about 4.6 percent, while Manitoba's population grew to 1,134,121 from 1,096,976, an increase of 39,195 or about 3.6 percent.[4] Chart 4 reports on the net interprovincial migration over a 22-year period and reveals the kind of challenges confronting smaller provinces.

Though political stability remains constant, it appears the McKenna years did have an impact on how New Brunswickers now view their province. I have heard people remark time and again in recent years (the business community

Chart 3
1987–1997 Population Change, Selected Provinces

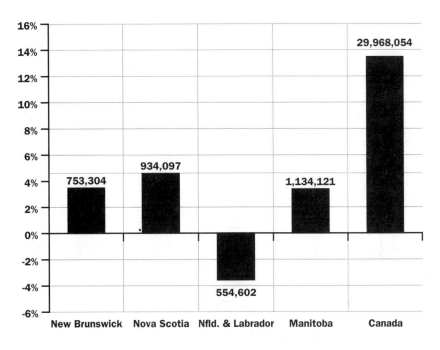

Source: Statistics Canada, *Report of the Demographic Situation in Canada*, cat. 91-209.

in particular) that McKenna was able to turn things around and instill a "can do" attitude in many areas of New Brunswick society. Indeed, many believe this was perhaps McKenna's greatest accomplishment. One business leader explained, "What McKenna did was raise the bar for New Brunswickers and then tell us that we could jump over it. Many of us believed him and many of us learned to do just that."[5] Another claims McKenna was able to instill in New Brunswickers a renewed sense of confidence in themselves and in their province. He added, "We no longer need to take a backseat to anyone in Canada about what we can do in business. We can compete with the best of them because McKenna showed us that he could compete and win for his province."[6] Public opinion surveys also reveal that McKenna had an important impact on this front.[7] And McKenna himself considers this one of his greatest accomplishment.[8]

One does not have to look very far in New Brunswick to read articles about this psychological turnaround. Rory McGreal, executive director of TeleEducation NB, told a US journalist that before McKenna came to power "we had a notion of ourselves as backward and isolated."[9] Don Desserud, who teaches political

Chart 4

Net Interprovincial Migration, Selected Provinces

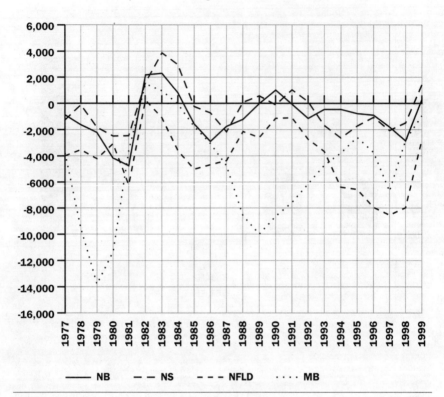

Source: Department of Finance, *Economic Reference Tables*, 1995, p. 31; CANSIM, Serios D31236 and D31248.

science at the University of New Brunswick in Saint John, observed that McKenna's "main achievement has been his ability to convince the rest of the country and the investment community that New Brunswick is under capable hands, that it is attractive for business and that he is doing something about all the things the other provinces only seem to complain about."[10] There are many other similar published comments from both inside New Brunswick and elsewhere. Two years after McKenna left office, the *Ottawa Citizen* ran an editorial stating,

> [He] attracted a lot of jobs, among other things, almost single-handedly creating a vast new call-centre industry in the Maritimes. And, most important, he ended the image of New Brunswick as a poor, backward and dependent place...he remains this decade's Miracle Man, the most popular premier Ontario never had...[11]

David Adams Richards, an internationally acclaimed novelist, wrote,

> [McKenna] has managed to do something better than any New
> Brunswick politician this century. He has managed to sell New
> Brunswick to the outside. Gone are the days (at least for now) when
> the egotistical, self-important CBC can show tarpaper shacks.... He
> has sold N.B. and because of this they want him up there with them
> closer to the center of things.

But he added quickly,

> [I will] never understand why we...ever needed a consulting firm
> from New York to tell us what our identity should be.[12]

But the report from the consulting firm, no matter its origin, did serve a
purpose – it confirmed the problem and pointed the way to some solutions.
Within days of coming to power, McKenna started to "beat the bushes" to
promote New Brunswick. He explained, "I've got to try, amongst other things,
to create a mood of confidence both for the business community and for the
public of New Brunswick."[13] His efforts did not stop there. His government
launched a series of high profile ads to sell the province. Michael Tutton,
arguably Atlantic Canada's leading business journalist, contrasted New
Brunswick's ad campaigns with those of Nova Scotia. He wrote,   133

> There are two images. One an eagle, staring fiercely at you. The other
> is an angler, casting leisurely out to the sea. Each tells a tale about
> the economic strategy of the two provinces. One (New Brunswick)
> has found pinpoint focus, the other (Nova Scotia) fires its marketing
> blunderbuss into the sky in the hope something will fall out.[14]

We now know McKenna also paid close attention to the people factor in economic development. He set about selling New Brunswick to New Brunswickers
and to others. He even linked, as we saw, highway construction to the pride
New Brunswickers would feel if a four-lane highway ran through their province,
as in Ontario and Quebec. Since he could not rely on the arrival of new
Canadians to inject a sense of optimism about economic development in the
province, McKenna reformed a number of human resources development
policies and introduced new initiatives to encourage New Brunswickers to
"jump" over the bar. He also made a point of praising the local business

community, often waxing eloquent about its important contribution to the province's economy, and he made every effort to show that his government was pursuing a business-friendly agenda.

McKenna decided to overhaul the province's approach to social assistance, convinced that a job, not a handout, was not only the most effective but also the kindest form of welfare. Initiatives such as NB Works were, in their day, highly innovative. To be sure, he came in for some criticism from certain quarters. Claude Snow, a former government official, for example, wrote a brief polemic arguing,

> In social development, New Brunswick witnessed nothing less than a calamity when McKenna was in power.... McKenna's credo...was...to create jobs, and private business.... [McKenna] only spoke about the need to be frugal, effective, and the pursuit of excellence. He was able to convince a majority of the citizens that government should not be there to provide social assistance.[15]

McKenna, in fact, saw nothing wrong with his critics' descriptions of his approach and probably actually agreed with most of it. In any event, it is true that New Brunswick made sharper cuts in social spending as a share of total provincial expenditures under McKenna than, for example, either Nova Scotia or Newfoundland and Labrador during the same period (see Table 11 below). For McKenna the important challenge was to reduce welfare rolls, not 134 increase spending. Again, McKenna believed that the kindest form of social assistance was a job, convinced it was the only way to restore personal dignity for those capable of working but unable to find employment.

Chart 5 is quite revealing and shows that McKenna did make progress in reducing New Brunswick's welfare dependency ratio. The progress in New Brunswick is, as the chart reveals, in contrast to the experience in other provinces and Canada as a whole. Moreover, as Chart 4 shows, New Brunswick

Table 11
Social Expenditures as a Percentage of Total Expenditures

Province	1985	1995
Newfoundland	52.0	54.6
Nova Scotia	55.4	56.5
New Brunswick	55.0	52.7

Source: Conference of Atlantic Premiers, 8 June 1998.

experienced this decline while witnessing less severe outmigration during the McKenna years than either Manitoba, Newfoundland and Labrador or even Nova Scotia.

Chart 5
Welfare Dependency Ratios
Canada and Selected Provinces

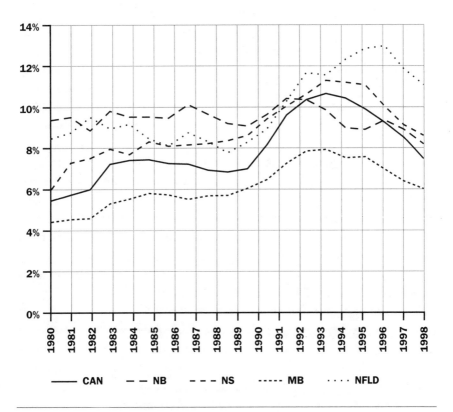

Note: The Welfare Dependency Ratio is defined as the number of welfare recipients divided by the total population.
Source: National Council of Welfare, *Profiles of Welfare: Myths and Realities*, 1998; Statistics Canada, *Provincial Economic Accounts: Annual Estimates 1981-1999*, cat. 13-213, 2000

McKenna also sought to improve things for the province's linguistic and ethnic minorities. His government took a major step to ensure strong linguistic rights for French-speaking New Brunswickers. McKenna requested the Canadian Parliament through Prime Minister Brian Mulroney to entrench in the Constitution the principle of New Brunswick's Act recognizing the equality of the province's two official linguistic communities. The purpose was to establish the requirement that future amendments of the province's language act would require the approval of both Parliament and the New Brunswick legislature. His efforts proved successful.[16]

The McKenna government also broke new ground when it agreed in 1994 to establish, with Ottawa and the province's Native communities, a Joint Economic Development Initiative (JEDI). It is not much of an exaggeration to say that provincial governments, by and large, have long regarded Aboriginal affairs to be a matter for the federal government, having limited provincial relevance. Things subsequently changed, if only because court decisions are forcing the provinces to get involved. The JEDI process has been given wide approval in recent years by government officials and, more importantly, by Native communities, because it has provided a forum where all relevant policy actors can meet to discuss Aboriginal issues and consider a wide array of economic development initiatives.[17] Former Supreme Court Justice Gérald La Forest and Justice Graydon Nicholas praised the JEDI initiative in their recent *Report of the Task Force on Aboriginal Issues* in New Brunswick.[18] The McKenna government also hired Noah Augustine, a high-profile Aboriginal, to work on developing tourism-related projects for Native communities. It is revealing to note that Mr. Augustine was the first Aboriginal ever hired by the government of New Brunswick in this department. Mr. Augustine's work met with success and there are now several Aboriginal packages and attractions included in the province's promotional tourism campaigns.[19]

Many observers acknowledge all of the above but at the same time argue it does not in the end add up to much in the way of real economic progress. Indeed, some suggest that apart from a few specific initiatives much of it was illusion, the work of "spin doctors," a charge often directed at McKenna and his advisors. They would point out, for example, that JEDI, however innovative in its day, is just a government process and, further, that a constitutional amendment to strengthen the language rights of French-speaking New Brunswickers does not create jobs. Only hard economic evidence, they insist, can truly assess McKenna's impact. The *Ottawa Citizen* may have been right that McKenna was able to end "the image of New Brunswick as a poor, backward and dependent place." But this must be asked: Was "image" the only thing that changed or was there "real" change?

The Public Service

The New Brunswick public service remains non-partisan and professional and it still enjoys the support and confidence of the province's political elite. In the televised leaders' debate leading up to the September 11, 1995, general election, the leaders of all four parties expressed their confidence in the public service. Premier McKenna concluded the exchange by saying, "All the leaders here tonight have defended our public servants. It is true that our public servants are the best in all of Canada."[20] This all-party support continues precisely because the provincial public service is non-partisan and professional. It is important to note that no premier in New Brunswick, at least since the 1950s, has or would appoint a politically partisan person to lead the public service or to occupy its most senior position, as some of the other provinces have done and continue to do.[21] McKenna continued in this tradition when he appointed Claire Morris secretary to the Cabinet and *de facto* head of the public service. Ms. Morris, a career public servant, was first appointed deputy minister by Richard Hatfield.

But what about its size? What about its capacity to remain one of Canada's top public services? The danger in comparing the size of the public service and the total number of government employees is, of course, that one may not be comparing oranges with oranges and apples with apples. Some jurisdictions, for example, will include Crown corporation employees, others will not, while some may include them in one decade, but not in the next. How a government accounts for "casual workers" can also play havoc with attempts to assess the size of its workforce. Many governments do not include casual workers, even those who work 10 to 12 months of the year, when providing a head count. But others do. The McKenna government decided to include long-term casual workers when calculating the size of its workforce and this, we are informed by provincial government officials, served to add about 1,500 employees to the size of government. Still other governments have recently introduced FTEs (Full-Time Equivalent) when giving some kind of head count of their public service. Many claim this provides a more accurate count, since it includes all employees but prorates the number on a twelve-month basis. New Brunswick is now in the process of following this trend.

The total number of provincial government employees in 1987, when McKenna took office, was, according to Statistics Canada, 26,568. The number stood at 26,823 ten years later when he left office.[22] It is important to note that this number includes provincial public sector employees outside of the provincial public service, notably those employed in schools and public enterprises. There was thus a gain of 255 positions in a decade. But this does not give the complete picture. Indeed, the above-mentioned reclassification of casual workers to permanent status alone suggests that the public service was substantially reduced during the McKenna years.

It is also difficult to provide a comparative perspective on the size of the public sector, again because it is extremely difficult, if at all possible, to compare oranges with apples. Statistics Canada, for instance, reveals that the size of the Nova Scotia public service grew to 13,855 from 13,117 (an increase of 738) between 1987 and 1997, that of Manitoba's was reduced to 20,756 from 20,856 (-100), and Newfoundland and Labrador went to 9,941 from 12,481 (-2,540) during the same period.[23] It is important to remember, however, that, as a result of the Robichaud reforms of the 1960s, the provincial government occupies jurisdictions that in other provinces belong to local or municipal governments. It explains why New Brunswick's public service is considerably larger than, say, that of Nova Scotia or Manitoba, two provinces with larger populations.

The above data suggest that McKenna was able to arrest growth in the public sector, broadly defined. Still, we need to add a few additional points of clarification. First, consultations with provincial government officials suggest that the New Brunswick public service, narrowly defined, actually shrank by about 2,500 during the McKenna years. A narrowly defined public service includes only those public servants who work in government departments, are part of the executive branch and report to a minister in one fashion or another. They estimate that in 1987 this core public service employed about 10,500, but by 1997 the number had fallen to a little over 8,000.

A significant factor determining the size of a public sector is growth in population. If there is some growth, it only stands to reason that new positions will be created to serve the increased number of citizens, assuming no productivity improvement is realized in the delivery of public services. This is true even if no new programs are created because additional staff is needed simply to maintain current levels of services in existing programs. New Brunswick's population, as already noted, grew slightly between 1987 and 1997.[24]

Though McKenna's interest did not lie in questions of government machinery or the public service, he did in the end sign on to the need for a non-partisan professional public service, but perhaps more out of convenience than conviction. One senses that although McKenna did not fully appreciate the intrinsic value of public service, he did appreciate the public service for its ability to provide advice on programs and to stabilize the ship of state. But when it came to doing things close to his heart, or at the top of his policy agenda, he often looked elsewhere for advice. For example, he used US public relations firms to advise on the overhaul of the operations of the Department of Income Assistance and to rebuild New Brunswick's tarnished image. He also turned to partisan advisors in his own office and to non-career public servants (Francis McGuire et al.) to lure out-of-province investors to New Brunswick and to promote jobs.

In what shape did McKenna leave the New Brunswick public service? The numbers reveal that he left it not much different from the way it was when he

138

came to power, except that it is now smaller. The core service is smaller by about 2,500. McKenna did break new ground, however, in government organization when Service New Brunswick was introduced. It was an innovative approach to service delivery and, as already noted, other provincial governments as well as governments from abroad have come knocking to see how it works. McKenna looked to the private sector for inspiration in reforming government operations, convinced that government departments should be managed, to the extent possible, like private businesses. Still, one could easily recognize the New Brunswick public service, its basic form (leaving aside Service NB), its culture, and even some of its key actors in 1997, even if one had not seen it for ten years. But reforming the public service was not at the top of McKenna's agenda. Repairing the province's balance sheet and creating jobs were.

The Balance Sheet

McKenna confronted two formidable challenges in 1987 when he decided to attack the province's balance sheet: the declining federal cash transfers and the increasing cost of servicing the debt. The province's debt, as McKenna made a point of saying frequently throughout his ten years in office, had risen to some $2.6 billion, or almost 30 percent of provincial GDP in 1987, from $800 million, or less than 20 percent of GDP, in 1977 (see Chart 6).

How did McKenna do on the public finance front? Here again we need to be careful and compare oranges with oranges, not with apples. In 1987-88, New Brunswick's net debt stood at $2.92 billion. By 1997-98, it had nearly doubled to $5.67 billion. It is important, however, to recall that the McKenna government finally agreed to add unfunded pension liability to the province's net debt in fiscal year 1992-93: the auditor general, for one, had long argued it should be done. That decision alone added $1.6 billion to the debt, which explains in large part why it jumped from $3.6 billion in 1991-92 to $5.3 billion in 1992-93. Leaving the $1.6 billion outside of the equation, the province's net debt still increased by $1.16 billion during the McKenna years.

Looking at New Brunswick during the McKenna's years in isolation can tell only part of the story because the federal government made significant cuts to its transfer payments to the provinces at that time. For this reason, we need to compare New Brunswick's performance with other provinces of similar size to establish how well McKenna did (see Table 12). Chart 6 shows that under McKenna New Brunswick did a great deal better than Nova Scotia on the debt front when one measures net debt as a percentage of GDP. Manitoba did better than New Brunswick. However, if one takes the $1.6 billion of unfunded

Chart 6
Net Debt as Percentage of GDP
Federal Government and Selected Provinces

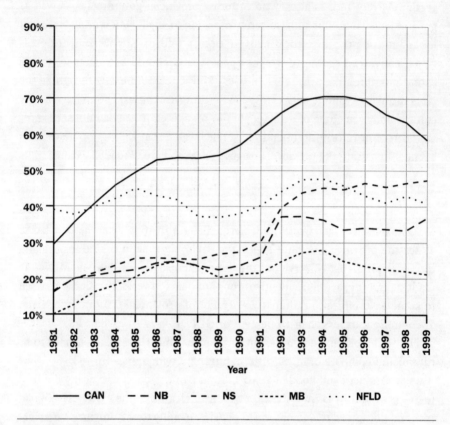

Source: Department of Finance, *Fiscal Reference Tables*, 2000; Statistics Canada, *Provincial Economic Accounts: Annual Estimates 1981-1999*, cat. 13-213, 2000.

pension liabilities out of the equation, then New Brunswick's performance is similar to Manitoba's.

McKenna got his wish on the fiscal front: his government became less dependent on federal transfers. In fiscal year 1987-88, nearly 40 percent of provincial government revenues came from federal transfers. By fiscal year 1997-98, the figure dropped to 34 percent, or by six percentage points. The drop is significant and it is the largest drop of any province of its size. Figure 3 below provides a breakdown for all ten provinces and reveals that, in the case of Nova Scotia, federal transfers as a percentage of provincial revenues actually increased by one percent between 1987 and 1997, Manitoba's increased by three percent, and Newfoundland and Labrador's dropped by three percent. All

pulling against gravity

Table 12
Comparative Provincial Public Finances

PROVINCE	Net Debt ($ million)		Net Increase
	1987-88	**1997-98**	
New Brunswick	2,919	5,672 (-1,600)	1,153
Newfoundland and Labrador	3,150	4,351	1,201
Nova Scotia	3,756	8,369	4,613
Manitoba	5,162	6,773	1,611

Source: Department of Finance Canada, *Fiscal Reference Tables.*

this is to say that New Brunswick made the greatest progress of any province in lessening its dependence on federal transfers as a source of revenue for the provincial government.

The McKenna government left the province's tax structure pretty well intact until its last years in office. As we saw, it reformed the province's Workers Compensation Board, removed the sales tax on 1-800 numbers to encourage the location of new call centres in the province, and made a number of relatively modest adjustments to several taxes. But it did not lower any of the major revenue-generating taxes, such as the sales tax and the corporate and personal income tax until late 1996. The need to make up for cuts in federal transfers and to deal with the provincial deficit kept McKenna and his finance minister focused on implementing spending cuts.

However, the province's 1996 budget provided for nearly $600 million in new tax cuts. These included a 10.2 percent reduction in income tax over three years and a drop of $118 million in sales tax revenues due to the introduction of a blended federal and provincial sales tax.[25] At the same time, the budget projected a $25.6 million surplus by the end of the 1997-98 fiscal year and a payment on the province's debt. McKenna argued that the 1996 budget was designed to "set an example for other provinces that are trying to boost consumer and business confidence and get their economies rolling after a decade of tight-fisted restraint."[26]

McKenna reported in an interview given for this book that he attached a great deal of importance to tax cuts. Indeed, he reveals that if he could do it all over again, he would be much more aggressive and would certainly not have allowed his successors to cancel his scheduled tax cuts, as Thériault did in 1999 to the last phase of the 10.2 percent reduction in income tax. For McKenna, tax cuts were a vital part of his economic development strategy. He contended that they would attract outside investors and encourage New Brunswickers to invest and become more entrepreneurial. Table 13 below reports

141

Figure 3
Federal Transfers as a Percentage of Provincial Revenues
1981, 1987, 1997

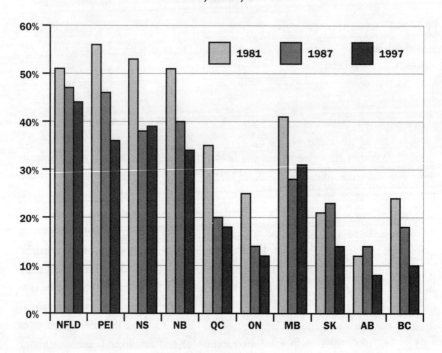

Source: Department of Finance Canada, *Fiscal Reference Tables*, 2000.

on New Brunswick's tax burden from a comparative perspective for the year 1994-95. It shows that New Brunswick ranked 6 out of 10 (with "1" representing the highest average tax burden) representing a slightly lower burden than Prince Edward Island, but a higher one than Newfoundland, Nova Scotia or British Columbia. McKenna sought to improve the province's position in this area. Provincial officials report that by the time he left office in 1997, this had been accomplished: New Brunswick now ranks 7 out of 10.[27]

The New Brunswick Economy, Circa 1997

We ask the same questions here as in Chapter 4, but as they apply ten years later. What were economic circumstances like when McKenna left office? What were the province's strengths and weaknesses? Had they changed appreciably in the ten years since McKenna took office? How did New Brunswick's performance compare with other provinces of similar size?

Table 13
Personal Tax Burden, 1994-95

PROVINCES	Personal taxes as a share of personal income	Rank*
Newfoundland	16.63	9
Prince Edward Island	17.85	5
Nova Scotia	16.85	8
New Brunswick	17.41	6
Quebec	18.45	3
Ontario	18.82	2
Manitoba	18.43	4
Saskatchewan	21.87	1
Alberta	15.27	10
British Columbia	16.95	7
Average	18.10	

* Rank of 1 = highest tax burden; 10 = lowest burden.
Source: 1994-95 (3) *Estimate of Equalization*, February 1995.

By 1997 the Canadian economy was performing well, following the recession of the early 1990s, much as it had done ten years earlier as it came out of the recession of the early 1980s. New Brunswick had again enjoyed several years of growth. Indeed, at the time, the Conference Board of Canada was reporting in its *Provincial Outlook* that "a broadly based recovery in New Brunswick's primary sectors will allow the province to lead in the Atlantic region in 1997."[28] It is worth delving deeper into this performance in order to evaluate its source, its impact on the province's position within Canada and its sustainability. I will do so here by summarizing trends in employment, output and incomes, and productivity and trade.

Employment
As we have seen, McKenna made job creation a key objective of his government. He relentlessly pursued it, in particular by touting the province as an attractive location for call centres and for the information technology (IT) sector. In 1997 alone, there were over 1,000 new call centre jobs established in the province,[29] while about 600 new jobs were created in the province's IT industry. The list of those companies involved in this expansion includes Cendant Canada, with 190 new call centre jobs, Nortel, consolidating its operations in Saint John, a new SAP office in Moncton and AT&T Long Distance Services in Edmundston.

On the IT front, Scholars.com created more than 100 jobs, and Bombardier opened an office in Fredericton, employing 20 people, with plans to hire another 45 over the following three years.

But all was not well on other fronts and there were significant job losses in several sectors. In particular, the downsizing of the public sector had at least one evident drawback – a loss of once stable and well-paying jobs. The provincial public sector, as we have already seen, even broadly defined, saw no growth in employment and, with term and casual employees given permanent status, there is no doubt that there was a net job loss. Things were even worse for federal employees in the province. All regions and all provinces were severely affected by cuts in the operations of federal departments and agencies. But some suffered more than others, and New Brunswick was one of them (see Table 14). Additionally, job losses in rail transportation, accompanying the restructuring of Canadian National Railways, were staggering. It is interesting to note that while the federal payroll dropped by 14.8 percent between 1987 and 1997, it actually rose by one percent in Ontario during the same period.

In spite of these difficulties in key sectors, New Brunswick's record of job creation during the McKenna years is noteworthy. At 11.1 percent, employment growth in New Brunswick was only slightly lower than the national average of 11.8 percent, and superior to that of Nova Scotia (7 percent) or Newfoundland and Labrador (no growth). It is true that this strong performance on the employment creation front translated into only modest progress in terms of reducing levels of unemployment from 1987 to 1997 (see Table 15). However, this is due to the fact that there was an increase in the labour force participation rate (share

144

Table 14
Federal Employees and Payroll, 1987 and 1997

| | Number of Federal Employees | | | Federal Payroll | | |
| | ('000s) | | | ($ millions) | | |
	1987	1997	% change	1987	1997	% change
New Brunswick	28.3	19.8	-30.0	66.8	56.9	-14.8
Nova Scotia	55.4	43.4	-21.7	89.9	81.8	-9.0
Newfoundland	15.8	10.9	-31.0	37.4	33.2	-11.2
Ontario	251.7	200.7	-20.3	674.1	680.9	+1.0
Manitoba	39.1	24.4	-37.6	100.5	87.0	-13.4

Note: The privatization of Air Canada contributed to Manitoba's drop in federal employment.
Source: New Brunswick Department of Finance, *The New Brunswick Economy, 1999: A Report to the Legislative Assembly*, Fredericton, 1999, p. 53.

of the working-age population that is either working or looking for work) in New Brunswick during those years. This, in itself, is a sign of increased vitality, given that the participation rate fell significantly in Canada as a whole during the same period. In what appears to be a major structural shift, New Brunswick's labour force participation rate even caught up to that of Nova Scotia in the final year of the McKenna administration (see Chart 7).

Much of that good performance on the employment creation front can be attributed to the above-mentioned efforts to attract jobs in call centres, IT, and

Table 15
Unemployment Rates (%)

	1987	1992	1997
Canada	8.9	11.3	9.2
Newfoundland	18.1	20.2	18.8
Prince Edward Island	13.3	18.1	14.9
Nova Scotia	12.4	13.2	12.2
New Brunswick	13.2	12.8	12.8
Quebec	10.3	12.8	11.4
Ontario	6.1	10.9	8.5
Manitoba	7.5	9.7	6.6
Saskatchewan	7.4	8.2	6.0
Alberta	9.7	9.5	6.0
British Columbia	12.0	10.5	8.7

Source: Statistics Canada, *Historical Labour Force Statistics*, cat. 71-201-XPB, 1999.

communications-related activities in general. Indeed, while New Brunswick's employment growth far outstripped the national average in management, administrative and other support services (a category which includes call centres, among many other activities), and in professional, scientific and technical services (albeit growth in New Brunswick occurred from a very small base), the province also registered a much stronger performance than the national average in the primary sector, a traditional mainstay of its economy (see Table 16a). Furthermore, comparisons with other provinces of similar size and economic diversity, in this case Nova Scotia and Manitoba, suggest that New Brunswick was certainly not unique in experiencing fast employment growth in business services. But on the manufacturing side, New Brunswick's job creation performance was considerably inferior to that of Manitoba.

An important difference between the employment performance of New Brunswick and that of Nova Scotia or Manitoba occurred in utilities. The latter

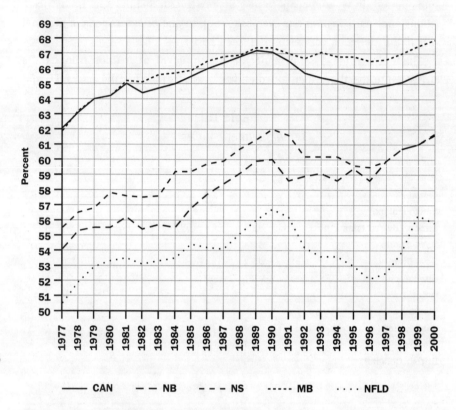

Chart 7

Labour Force Participation Rates

Canada and Selected Provinces

Y-axis: Percent (50 to 69)

X-axis: 1977 to 2000

Legend: CAN — NB — — NS ----- MB ···· NFLD

Source: Statistics Canada, *Historical Labour Force Statistics*, cat. 71-201-XPB, 1999.

two provinces experienced declines in these industries, whereas data on hours worked suggest that New Brunswick benefited from a major shift toward the communications sector. In particular, New Brunswick registered phenomenal employment growth in the postal and courier services industries as well as strong growth in telecommunications carriers. To see how New Brunswick fared sector by sector in relation to the Canadian average, see Table 16b.

Those looking for a "McKenna Effect" in the New Brunswick employment data can thus derive a certain degree of satisfaction, insofar as the "action" does seem to have been taking place in many areas where the premier did indeed concentrate his administration's energies. While the province remains dependent on a traditional resource base and has made few inroads in manufacturing and suffered from the loss of well-paid public-sector jobs, it has

Table 16a

Employment by Sector, NB, NS and MB

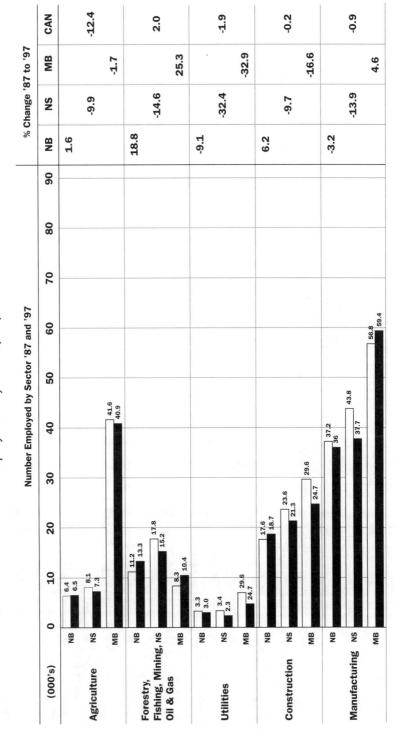

147

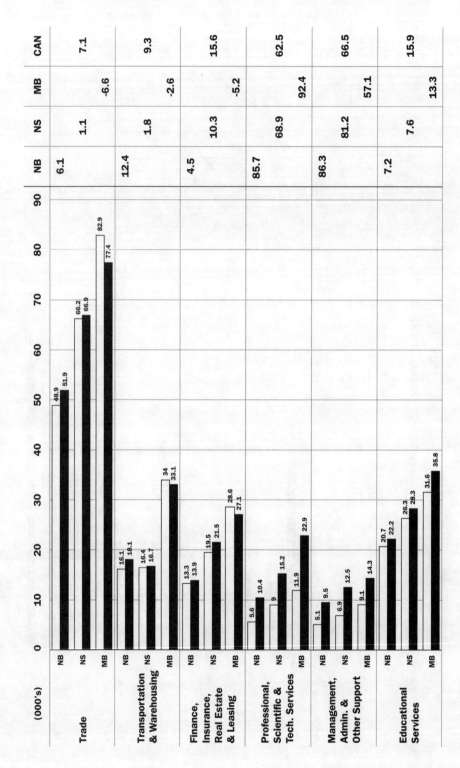

	NB	NS	MB	CAN
Trade	6.1	1.1	-6.6	7.1
Transportation & Warehousing	12.4	1.8	-2.6	9.3
Finance, Insurance, Real Estate & Leasing	4.5	10.3	-5.2	15.6
Professional, Scientific & Tech. Services	85.7	68.9	92.4	62.5
Management, Admin. & Other Support	86.3	81.2	57.1	66.5
Educational Services	7.2	7.6	13.3	15.9

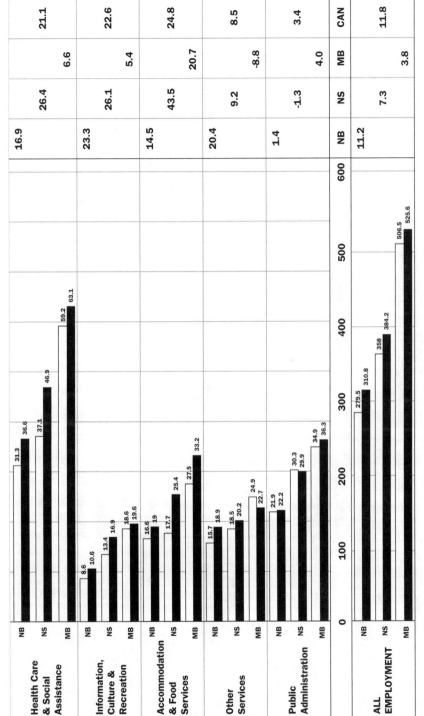

Source: Statistics Canada, Historical Labour Force Statistics, cat. 71-201-XPB, 2000.

149

donald j. savoie

Table 16b

New Brunswick Sectoral Employment Shares as a Percentage of Canadian Average

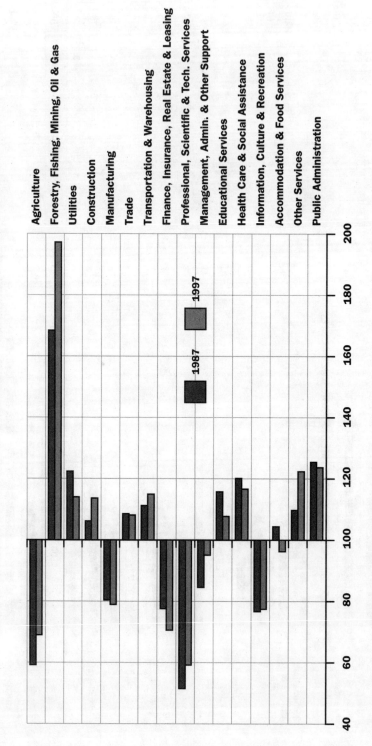

Source: Statistics Canada, *Historical Labour Force Statistics*, cat. 71-201-XPB, 1999 and author's calculations.

nevertheless been able to swim against the tide, at least when looked at strictly in terms of job creation.

Output and Incomes

If economists agree on one thing, it is that an economy's Gross Domestic Product (GDP) is a key sign of its health or weakness. During the McKenna years, the New Brunswick economy made significant progress on its GDP both in relation to other provinces and in relation to the national average. Table 17 below reveals that its GDP per capita rose nearly five percentage points in relation to the national average during this period. New Brunswick also did better on this front than other provinces of similar size, notably Nova Scotia and Manitoba. In fact, Nova Scotia lost ground while Manitoba registered a gain of four percentage points. Only Newfoundland and Labrador did better than New Brunswick, registering a gain of six percentage points between 1987 and 1997.

Table 17
GDP Per Capita as % of National Average

	1987	1992	1996	1997
Canada	100.0	100.0	100.0	100.0
Newfoundland	62.4	66.9	68.4	68.5
Prince Edward Island	60.7	72.8	76.4	76.0
Nova Scotia	76.4	80.2	76.2	75.9
New Brunswick	**74.8**	**77.2**	**80.2**	**79.3**
Quebec	90.8	90.0	88.4	88.2
Ontario	112.7	109.3	107.3	107.5
Manitoba	86.5	88.9	91.0	90.6
Saskatchewan	83.0	86.0	100.8	97.8
Alberta	115.1	115.0	122.7	125.8
British Columbia	97.5	102.8	100.6	98.6
Yukon Territory	153.3	156.2	139.0	125.0
Northwest Territories	134.6	153.0	157.6	153.9

Source: Statistics Canada, *National Income and Expenditure Accounts*, cat. 13-201, various issues.

Again, it is noteworthy that this progress was accomplished despite substantial cuts in federal government purchases of goods and services (i.e., to be distinguished from transfers to persons, businesses and other levels of government and from capital expenditures) in New Brunswick. Federal government purchases in 1987 accounted for 8.2 percent of New Brunswick's GDP, but the figure dropped to 5.8 percent by 1997, a drop of 2.4 percent. This compares with a drop of only one percent at the national level, with similar declines being registered in Newfoundland and Labrador, and Manitoba, among the provinces of comparable size. Nova Scotia fared worse than New Brunswick on this front, with federal spending on goods and services dropping by the equivalent of 3.9 percent of provincial GDP.[30]

New Brunswick also continued to make progress in reducing disparities in per capita income between 1987 and 1997. Despite cuts in transfer payments, especially to Ottawa's employment insurance program, New Brunswick's per capita income rose by seven percentage points relative to the national average between 1987 and 1997. By comparison, Nova Scotia registered a gain of .9 percent, Manitoba saw an improvement of five percent, and Newfoundland and Labrador improved its position by five percent relative to the national average (see Table 18).

Table 18

Personal Income Per Capita, by Province and Territory
Selected Years, 1987-97: relationship to national average
(Canada = 100)

	1987	1992	1996	1997
Canada	100.0	100.0	100.0	100.0
Newfoundland	70.7	74.2	76.1	75.3
Prince Edward Island	72.5	81.2	83.6	81.5
Nova Scotia	83.4	86.2	84.2	84.3
New Brunswick	**77.4**	**81.7**	**83.9**	**84.4**
Quebec	94.8	91.8	92.2	92.5
Ontario	111.8	110.1	107.5	107.6
Manitoba	88.8	90.8	94.0	93.3
Saskatchewan	83.4	81.4	90.0	85.2
Alberta	101.8	102.1	103.9	105.0
British Columbia	99.6	104.1	105.0	104.3
Yukon Territory	102.5	116.9	122.6	121.4
Northwest Territories	87.3	97.8	104.6	105.0

Source: Statistics Canada, *National Income and Expenditure Accounts*, cat. 13-201, various issues.

There is no denying, however, that despite the cutbacks, employment insurance benefits and other transfer payments are still an important component of personal income, particularly for Atlantic Canadians, as Table 19 below reveals. Atlantic Canada, given its traditional dependence on federal transfers, registered the biggest loss of any region. New Brunswickers received

$766 per capita in employment insurance benefits in 1987 and the figure dropped to $754 by 1997, for a loss of $11 per capita. The figure for Newfoundland and Labrador also dropped, while Nova Scotia saw a drop of only $1, and during the same period Manitoba registered a small decline. The figure for both Newfoundland and Labrador and, albeit to a lesser extent, Nova Scotia, may well be understated because of other federal transfer payments to fishing communities resulting from the collapse of the groundfish. New Brunswick had a very limited number of its fishers employed in the groundfish sector and federal government programs, such as TAGS (The Atlantic Groundfish Strategy), had only a modest impact in the province.

Table 19
Unemployment Insurance/Employment Insurance Benefits Per Capita, Dollars

	1987	1992	1995	1996	1997
Canada	391	654	430	407	347
Newfoundland	1,121	1,825	1,114	1,121	1,052
Prince Edward Island	946	1,603	1,218	1,153	1,155
Nova Scotia	552	897	661	615	551
New Brunswick	**766**	**1,148**	**920**	**861**	**754**
Quebec	458	792	554	523	446
Ontario	245	528	314	301	259
Manitoba	299	439	303	293	235
Saskatchewan	275	391	261	252	192
Alberta	387	499	336	295	212
British Columbia	476	611	397	377	328
Yukon Territory	769	967	806	750	776
Northwest Territories	357	571	433	478	600

Source: Statistics Canada, *Provincial Economic Accounts*, cat. 13-213.

153

Table 20 below reports on the shift to greater self-sufficiency on the part of New Brunswickers. In 1987, 22 percent of New Brunswick's per capita income came from transfer payments, but by 1997 the figure had dropped to 19.8 percent, a drop of 2.2 percent. In contrast, the figure for Nova Scotia went up by 1.4 percent and that for Manitoba went up by 1.9 percent. The figure for Newfoundland and Labrador dropped by 3.6 percent. It is interesting to note that while New Brunswickers were becoming increasingly self-sufficient, other Canadians, notably residents of Ontario, Quebec, Saskatchewan and Nova Scotia were becoming more dependent on government transfers.

Table 20
Government Transfers as a Percentage of Personal Income

	1987	1992	1996	1997
Canada	14.4	16.0	15.6	15.4
Newfoundland	28.8	27.2	25.9	25.2
Prince Edward Island	23.9	24.8	22.8	23.0
Nova Scotia	18.8	19.8	20.4	20.2
New Brunswick	**22.0**	**21.3**	**20.1**	**19.8**
Quebec	16.6	17.7	17.9	17.9
Ontario	11.2	15.0	14.5	14.2
Manitoba	15.1	16.7	16.9	17.0
Saskatchewan	17.9	18.5	17.5	18.6
Alberta	14.0	13.3	11.4	11.1
British Columbia	15.1	14.5	14.1	14.1
Yukon Territory	12.5	16.0	17.1	16.6
Northwest Territories	11.9	13.2	15.1	15.1

Source: Statistics Canada, *Provincial Economic Accounts*, cat. 13-213.

Earned per capita income, as already noted, is a much better indicator of a region's economic vitality than is per capita income. Here again, New Brunswick made important gains during the McKenna years. Between 1987 and 1997, earned income per capita in the province rose 7.5 percentage points in relation to the national average. As Table 21 below reveals, New Brunswick outperformed by a considerable margin not only the national average but also other provinces of similar size. Newfoundland and Labrador saw a gain of 3.5 percentage points, Nova Scotia shows a loss of 2.7 percentage points, and Manitoba a gain of 2.1 percentage points.

All told, the story here is certainly one of output growth and greater self-reliance on the income side, in spite of adversity, surely a story from which the premier of New Brunswick during those years can draw some measure of satisfaction. However, questions remain: How durable is this progress? Is the changing economic structure of New Brunswick sufficient to ensure even greater dynamism in the future?

Productivity and Trade Structure

If economists agree on another thing, it is that productivity – output per hour worked – is an important determinant of standards of living. Here, it must be said that the story of New Brunswick during the McKenna years is troubling on a number of fronts. New Brunswick witnessed an important drop

Table 21

Earned Income Per Capita as a Percentage of the National Average

	1987	1992	1996	1997
Canada	100.0	100.0	100.0	100.0
Newfoundland	65.4	68.2	70.0	68.9
Prince Edward Island	64.4	68.9	71.6	66.9
Nova Scotia	81.0	82.3	78.5	78.3
New Brunswick	**74.3**	**79.4**	**81.5**	**81.8**
Quebec	93.8	91.7	91.5	91.3
Ontario	115.3	110.8	108.3	108.4
Manitoba	86.7	87.0	89.2	88.8
Saskatchewan	72.0	74.2	78.3	79.1
Alberta	101.2	105.9	109.8	111.7
British Columbia	96.0	104.6	106.5	105.1
Yukon Territory	114.8	127.8	130.5	129.0
Northwest Territories	103.6	116.8	120.5	119.4

Source: Statistics Canada, *Provincial Economic Accounts*, cat. 13-213.

in its aggregate productivity performance measured as constant dollar value added per person-hour relative to Canada (see Figure 4).

The transport industry was one of the few bright spots for New Brunswick during the 1987 to 1997 period in terms of productivity performance, no doubt due to cutbacks on the railroad side. There were two other success stories on the productivity front: the mining and quarrying industry and the accommodation, food and beverage industry. Again, in the case of mining and quarrying, increased output was achieved alongside a sharp reduction in hours worked. In the hospitality industry, New Brunswick was able to achieve both higher output growth and slower growth in hours worked than counterparts in the rest of Canada, hence its stronger productivity performance.

It is important to highlight a number of productivity developments that relate to the policy priorities or non-priorities of the McKenna government. First, it appears the productivity of government operations and services (as far as one can calculate it) improved during the McKenna years relative to the Canadian average. However, this was not the case for the broader public service (i.e., education and health and social services). Second, in spite of cutbacks in hours worked, the "other utilities" sector (see our discussion on New Brunswick Power) – already one of the sectors in which New Brunswick was the furthest behind – actually fell further relative to the Canadian average during the McKenna years. For example, the productivity of Nova Scotia's electric utilities

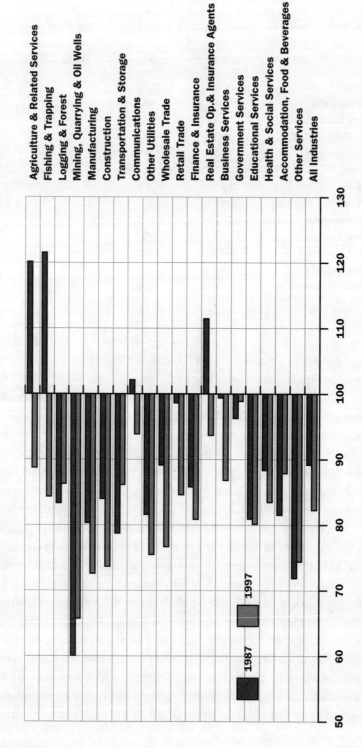

Figure 4

New Brunswick Productivity by Sector, 1987 and 1997 (Canada=100)

Source: Statistics Canada, *Provincial Economic Accounts: Annual Estimates 1981-1999*, cat. 13-213, 2000.

pulling against gravity

actually increased by 80 percent, while it shrank in New Brunswick. Third, productivity in New Brunswick's "business services" sector also dropped relative to the Canadian average during the McKenna years. This is true despite McKenna's successful efforts to attract call centre jobs to New Brunswick.

These observations actually illustrate what may well be New Brunswick's long-term economic dilemma: To remain competitive in some high-paying sectors, it has had to cut jobs, whereas it has been able to expand employment but only in relatively low-paying sectors of its economy. Certainly, New Brunswick is more plugged into the "New Economy" than ever before, but the new economy consists of both low value-added and high value-added activities. New Brunswick has been able to capture jobs under both activities, but the productivity data suggest that the province has not been able to replace traditional high-end jobs (e.g., government and CN jobs) with as many high-paying new economy jobs.

New Brunswick is also not helped on the productivity front by the structure of its economy – the weight of history as it were. For example, Manitoba outperformed New Brunswick at the aggregate productivity level between 1987 and 1997 due in part to the composition of its industry. New Brunswick's relative productivity gains tended to be concentrated in smaller sectors of its economy, and productivity losses in somewhat more prominent sectors. The reverse tended to be true for Manitoba. For example, the gain in agricultural productivity loomed very large in that province's overall performance, much larger than the even more impressive gains in mining and quarrying sector in New Brunswick. There were productivity declines in fishing and trapping and in logging in both provinces, but they hurt New Brunswick far more because these industries constitute a larger share of that province's economy.

What about exports and trade specialization patterns? McKenna, it will be recalled, attached a great deal of importance to establishing and exploiting new markets and new trade opportunities, thinking they pointed the way toward greater economic self-sufficiency. He even went against the leadership of his own political party at the national level to support the free-trade agreement with the United States.

That said, New Brunswick's performance in export and domestic markets between 1986 and 1996 was mixed. New Brunswick's growth in international exports did not keep pace with the Canadian average during that period (see Table 22). New Brunswick did better than Nova Scotia during the same period, but not as well as Manitoba. In fact, Manitoba outperformed Canada in the growth of international exports between 1986 and 1996 while New Brunswick's contributions dropped as a percentage of Canada's total exports, as did Nova

157

Scotia's. But New Brunswick did perform better in the Canadian domestic market than either Manitoba or Nova Scotia (see Table 23).

A closer look at the trade specialization data (see Appendix 2 at the end of this chapter) reveals that New Brunswick was not very successful in making a transition away from resource-based activities. It was able to strengthen its position in the Canadian market in pulp and paper products, lumber, sawmill and other wood products, machinery and equipment and in non-metallic mineral products. But it lost ground in retail services, forestry products, wholesale services and personal and miscellaneous services. In comparison, Nova Scotia was able to strengthen its position in communications services, personal and other miscellaneous services, and textile products, while Manitoba improved its position in retail services, machinery and equipment, printing and publishing and agricultural products.

What about the future? How well did the McKenna government position the province to capture future economic opportunities? We observed in Chapter 4 that knowledge industries and research and development activities would fuel future economic activities worldwide. We also noted that in 1987 New Brunswick was ill prepared in this area and that it trailed every province except Prince Edward Island and Newfoundland and Labrador in R&D spending. Things did not improve greatly during the McKenna years. Canada's R&D activities are still largely concentrated in Ontario and Quebec. In addition, there has been little change for New Brunswick in its provincial ranking except that the province now trails every province except Prince Edward Island (see Table 24). Still, it is important to note that New Brunswick does not have a medical school. Medical schools, as is well known, generate a great deal of R&D activities. In addition, there was no federal NRC (National Research Council of Canada) presence in New Brunswick during or before the McKenna years.

The information highway has, in recent years, made its presence felt in Atlantic Canada, as it has elsewhere. As early as 1995, the software development and computer service industry employed 2,500 people in the region. By January 1997, there were 448 firms offering these services in Atlantic Canada. New Brunswick accounted for 141 of the firms, compared with 85 in Newfoundland and Labrador, 21 in Prince Edward Island and 201 in Nova Scotia.[31] Though there are important exceptions, for the most part, software and computer firms in Atlantic Canada are small and have limited R&D capacity.

Service industries in Atlantic Canada still also lag other regions in Canada in the use of computers, trailing by as much as 10 to 15 percent, the only exception being computerized financial systems, inventory control and property management systems. In manufacturing, the food and beverage, wood, primary and fabricated metal, machinery, transportation equipment,

Table 22
Trade, Percent of Canadian International Exports

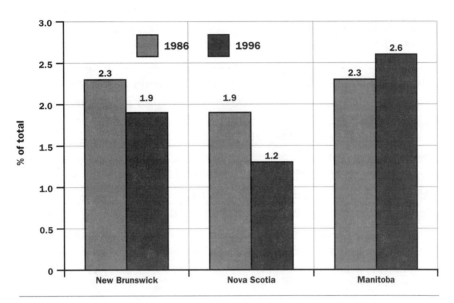

Source: Statistics Canada, *Interprovincial Trade in Canada 1984-1996*, cat. 15-546-XPE, 1998.

Table 23
Trade, Percent of Canadian Domestic Market

159

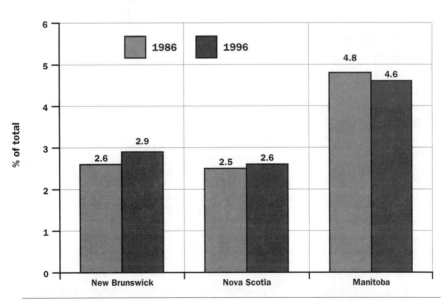

Source: Statistics Canada, *Interprovincial Trade in Canada 1984-1996*, cat. 15-546-XPE, 1998.

donald j. savoie

petroleum and chemical industries all lag the national average in the use of advanced technologies.[32]

As we demonstrated in Chapter 2, the Maritimes "missed the boat" in the old economy – the development of Canada's manufacturing sector. There is now every indication to suggest this situation could well repeat itself as the North American economy shifts to a knowledge-based economy.

Statistics Canada defines R&D, which underpins the development of the knowledge-based economy, as creative work undertaken on a systematic basis to increase the stock of scientific and technical knowledge and to use this knowledge in new applications. Expenditures on R&D are thus an important indicator of the effort devoted to creative activity in science and technology. Given the findings in Table 24 below, there is certainly cause for concern in New Brunswick, and Atlantic Canada generally. We know that in provinces with strong R&D performance (Ontario, Quebec, Alberta and British Columbia), the business sector and governments are both very active on the R&D front.

The private sector in New Brunswick and the other three Atlantic provinces do not invest nearly as much, even in per capita terms, in R&D activities as

Table 24
Provincial Distribution of Federal R&D Expenditures, 1987-97 (%)

PROVINCES	1987	1997
Newfoundland	1	2
Prince Edward Island	0	0
Nova Scotia	2	2
New Brunswick	1	1
Quebec*	24	27
Ontario*	48	46
Manitoba	2	2
Saskatchewan	2	2
Alberta	7	7
British Columbia	6	7
Sub-total Canada[1]	94	94
National Capital Region	6	6
Total Canada	100	100
Canada - Total R&D expenditures ($ million)	7,866	14,100

[1] Includes the Yukon and Northwest Territories;
* Quebec and Ontario figures exclude federal government expenditures performed in the National Capital Region.
Source: Statistics Canada and consultations with federal government officials, Moncton and Ottawa, February-March 2000.

do private firms in Ontario and Quebec. This is also true for the federal government which, while being a major player in R&D in Ontario and Quebec, is hardly present in this sector in Atlantic Canada. It may well be that one influences the other and that federal programs designed to encourage R&D activities are tied to private sector participation. This would explain at least in part why federal R&D programs have had so little impact in Atlantic Canada. In other words, we may well be dealing with a Catch-22, a kind of vicious circle from which the region cannot escape.

Whatever the reason, one thing is clear: Federal presence in the R&D field is not much evident in Atlantic Canada, including New Brunswick. For instance, the Department of Industry's high-profile Technology Partnerships program has been largely insignificant to Atlantic Canada. Minister of Industry John Manley described the program as a "key element of the government's Science and Technology and its Jobs and Growth Agenda."[33] It will be recalled that two government backbenchers and two Liberal senators from Atlantic Canada, taking dead aim at this program, signed a report on economic development in Atlantic Canada. The report stated,

> The program's objective is to foster investment in innovation through science and technology. To date, it has invested in environmental technologies; aerospace and defence; and enabling technologies, which include applications of information technologies, biotechnology, advanced manufacturing and advanced materials – in other words, the knowledge-based industries of the future. *However, only 2 per cent of the money invested by Technology Partnerships Canada in 1997 and 1998 has gone to Atlantic Canada – $17 million out of a total of $972 million spent.*[34] [Emphasis added]

161

It will also be recalled that the report, adding insult to injury, made the point that "one of the very few Atlantic Canadian projects to benefit from this program was engaged in research to control the spread of zebra mussels infesting the Great Lakes water system." [something that benefits central Canada][35] New Brunswick, meanwhile, has received less than $1 million (out of $972 million) from the Technology Partnerships program.[36] More recent data suggests, if anything, the program has become even less relevant to Atlantic Canada. We are informed,

> Although the bulk of that money [under the TPC program] has been used to finance aerospace and defense initiatives, almost $340 million has been invested in enabling technologies. From September

1999 to April 2000, biopharmaceutical projects alone received $140 million from the fund. These projects, however, were earmarked for firms in Quebec and Ontario. TPC investments in Atlantic Canada have been limited to 1.5 percent of total funding and have supported the creation of about 330 jobs in the region (in contrast to the more than 23,230 jobs created or maintained by the program elsewhere in the country).[37]

The Atlantic Canada Opportunities Agency, a federal government agency, in a review of the Department of Industry's R&D activities, concluded that the "Industry portfolio could be contributing to Atlantic Canada's innovation, R&D and productivity gaps."[38] These are strong words coming from a sister department, given the usually carefully crafted and cautious phrasing of government departments. There is no denying that Atlantic Canada does not account for much in virtually any of the department's R&D programs. The region, for example, received less than two percent of the funding under Ottawa's "Network of Centres of Excellence" program, at least in part, we are informed, because the "networks appear to be in areas with limited Atlantic research strength."[39] ACOA officials report that these programs are essentially designed to meet the economic circumstances of central Canada. A columnist with *The Globe and Mail* recently summed up the impact of Ottawa's Technology Partnership program (TPC) in this fashion:

162

> TPC...is best known for lavishing hundreds of millions of dollars on big-name companies including Pratt & Whitney (the world's third largest aerospace group) and Bombardier. In the past three years, Pratt & Whitney alone has received $301 million...[and] every few days another TPC news release goes out 'On behalf of John Manley, Minister of Industry....' A few million here and a few million there have gone to various companies in the name of creating jobs...most are small and unproven and many can be found in the Ottawa-Kanata-Hull region.[40]

It will also be recalled that Paul Martin, the Minister of Finance, in the mid-1990s unveiled with considerable fanfare a new $850 million Foundation for Innovation. Martin's department has produced a series of budget papers and economic and fiscal updates making the case for the new foundation. They argued that the key to job creation in the future and to "Canada's economic success is...to accelerate the adoption of innovative technologies in all sectors of the economy."[41] Again, however, Atlantic Canada and New Brunswick have not benefited much from the foundation and its programs. Ontario and Quebec account for nearly 65 percent of total funding invested by the foundation in R&D infrastructure. Atlantic Canada, meanwhile, has been allocated less than four percent of the funding. New Brunswick has been awarded $4.6 million in funding from the foundation, or about one percent of its total funding to date.[42] There are only two possible explanations for this turn of events: Either the measures did not correspond to New Brunswick's economic circumstances or the province did not have the required capacity to respond.

McKenna, or for that matter other Atlantic premiers, can hardly be held fully responsible for the level of federal investment in R&D. Yet, it matters a great deal to the economic development field. The federal government is a dominant player in R&D activities in the public sector in Canada. For example, in the case of Ontario and Quebec, two of the country's strongest provinces with the fiscal capacity to support R&D on their own, Ottawa spends on average about four to five times more in R&D activities than do either the Ontario or Quebec government. Much as it did in the case of the National Policy and in planning the war effort, Ottawa is again carving out a role for itself in the development of the next important wave of economic development. Once again, the focus is on central Canada even though both Ontario and Quebec are strong enough to fly on their own in the new economy.

McKenna did put pressure on the federal government to invest in the new economy in Atlantic Canada. He wrote on numerous occasions to the prime minister calling for Ottawa to support a new economic plan for the region. He asked for help in expanding "computer capabilities in all our schools and in our teachers; creating content for the new digital world; enhancing and enriching the Community Access initiative; training and retooling company personnel; growing co-op training and expanding our centres of excellence in information technology; providing seed capital for regional information technology firms," and he requested that the "Export Financing Regime" be adjusted to take into account Atlantic Canada's economic circumstances and "particularly to cover industries which are badly understood elsewhere in the country, industries such as aquaculture, fisheries, shipbuilding and information technology."[43] In another of his numerous letters, McKenna told the prime minister that the federal government should respond urgently to these issues because if "we cannot provide these opportunities, our future is bleak indeed. Our population base is in relative decline and no echo boom has been identified. The depletion of our well-educated youth will have a major impact in years to come."[44]

The McKenna Years: A Report Card on Economic Development

New Brunswick outperformed provinces of similar size and even the national average on some key economic indicators during the McKenna years. While it is not possible to establish definitively that the McKenna government is responsible for this performance, one can easily assume it had an impact. It is hardly possible to isolate one or even several factors explaining economic development in any region. Any number of forces can explain the levels of economic development in a province over which its government has no control – interest rates, for example, or the performance of the United States economy.

Still, we do know the McKenna government was highly activist and it concentrated much of its efforts on economic development and job creation. This chapter reveals that the McKenna government led the way in repairing the province's balance sheet (for example, it had the lowest increase in net debt when compared with provinces of similar size); in reducing or at least arresting growth in the public service; in reducing taxes; and in becoming less dependent on federal transfers as a source of revenue. This chapter also reveals that McKenna jumped at every opportunity to hustle jobs on behalf of his province, often to the annoyance of other premiers.

We saw earlier in this chapter that data from Statistics Canada and other public agencies demonstrate that New Brunswick also led the way in a number of key indicators of economic development between 1987 and 1997. In this sense, the following observations are based on "hard" economic data or on standard and widely employed indicators of economic well being.

New Brunswick's growth in GDP per capita outperformed the national average and two provinces of comparable size, Nova Scotia and Manitoba. The same is true for per capita income and earned income per capita. In addition, New Brunswickers did better than Nova Scotians and Manitobans in lessening their dependence on government transfers as a percentage of their personal income. Between 1987 and 1997 New Brunswick also outperformed the national average and both Nova Scotia and Manitoba in lowering unemployment rates. This at a time when the province's participation rate was increasing and the federal government was implementing significant job cuts to its New Brunswick operations. During his time as premier, McKenna had a direct impact in creating call centre jobs in New Brunswick. That said, we also saw in this chapter that New Brunswick had a very modest population growth during the McKenna years. While it was greater than that of Newfoundland and Labrador, it badly trailed the national average and even the growth rate of Nova Scotia and Manitoba, albeit by a very slim margin in both cases.

New Brunswick, however, underperformed in several areas, not only in relation to the Canadian average but also when compared to Manitoba and Nova Scotia. New Brunswick was not as successful as either Manitoba or Nova Scotia in making the transition away from resource-based activities in the Canadian and international marketplaces. Also during the McKenna years, the Manitoba economy outperformed New Brunswick both in capturing a larger share of Canadian exports and in strengthening its productivity. Moreover, Manitoba did better in the international marketplace, capturing a larger share of Canada's total exports.

However, there is plenty of evidence to suggest McKenna had a substantial impact on how New Brunswickers perceive themselves and their province. "Raising the bar" and then convincing people "they can jump over it" can make all the difference in economic development, and many New Brunswickers, especially members of the business community, claim this is something McKenna did for his province. He also had a direct hand in attracting over 6,000 call centre jobs to the province. As already noted, it is clear he "out-hustled" his fellow premiers in the pursuit of outside investors. And there is little doubt McKenna had a direct hand in the development of the province's information technology sector, which grew from a handful of companies in 1987 to over 237 by the time he left office in 1997. Many of these firms are very small but a few are not, including, for example, Scholars.com (now Smart force), which by 1997 had become the world's largest online trainer.[45] As noted, McKenna was the first premier to appoint a minister responsible for the information highway and New Brunswick was the first province to put information about its programs online.

To be sure, McKenna was pulling against gravity to develop the province's information technology (IT) sector. The federal Department of Industry, at the risk of sounding repetitive, was and remains largely preoccupied with developments in the IT sector in central Canada and has hardly been visible in New Brunswick. In addition, the province has had for years a weak track record in the R&D sector.

Still, McKenna could point to the following accomplishments in the IT sector at the end of his 10 years in power:

- The government subsidized the purchase of personal computers for individual citizens, paying between $200 and $300 per unit. Approximately 20,000 computers were purchased during the first six months of this program.
- The government made computer literacy a provincial standard for high school graduation.

- The government also used IT to increase their 911 emergency services, aiming for 24-hour-a-day coverage throughout the province.
- By the end of 1998, New Brunswick had 266 IT firms employing 3,295 people. There was also an important variety in the type of IT firms, as Table 25 below reveals.

McKenna is best known for the 6,000-plus new call centre jobs created in the province during his period in office. He worked with the provincial telephone company and stressed the province's bilingual workforce to induce outside firms to locate their call centres in New Brunswick. Though the centres did create "jobs" and "more jobs," they were criticized from several quarters for being little more than "electronic sweatshops."[46] There is no denying call centre jobs are low paying jobs. But they *are* jobs and many New Brunswickers are happy to have them. McKenna would argue, "better to have call centre jobs than welfare," and he would be right.

The McKenna years did make a difference in New Brunswick, so Three Cheers! They encouraged greater self-reliance, led New Brunswick to outperform provinces of similar size on several fronts in the economic development field and gave rise to important new economic activities. McKenna came to office with a *projet de société*, a sense of purpose and a vision. He stayed the course. If McKenna had not been premier for those ten years, New Brunswick would likely be worse off today. Conversely, had McKenna been Nova Scotia's premier at that time, its public finance and job creation record would have been better than it was. But McKenna's success can hardly be described as complete. This chapter reveals that Manitoba and Nova Scotia outperformed New Brunswick in some important areas.

Additionally, it is clear the New Brunswick economy has not been transformed. It looks much as it did in 1987. Though improvements have been made, they are at the margins. The province's stagnant population growth and the fact that new Canadians are going elsewhere speaks eloquently to this fact. Furthermore, there is cause for concern over the province's participation in the new economy. Call centres and other developments in the province's information technology sector have enjoyed a high profile in the media. But New Brunswick, like the rest of Atlantic Canada, lags in research and development activities, which is the key factor that gives life to the new economy. David Amirault, an economist with the Atlantic Provinces Economic Council, put his finger on the challenge ahead when he observed in October 1997, or as McKenna was leaving the premier's office, that "Only 11 to 13 percent of the New Brunswick economy is knowledge-based. Low-tech

Table 25
New Brunswick Information Technology Companies
December 1998

BY SECTOR	Total Companies
Advanced Training/Multimedia	74
Communications/On-Line Services/Internet	8
Computer System Design	50
Consulting Engineering/Artificial Intelligence	15
Industry Associations	29
Software (Excluding Training)	67
Telecommunication/Electronic Equipment	10
Telecommunications Carrier	3
Other (Sector not defined)	10
BY SECTOR	**Employees – Total 3,295**
Advanced Training/Multimedia	353
Communications/On-Line Services/Internet	12
Computer System Design	1,321
Consulting Engineering/Artificial Intelligence	208
Industry Associations	312
Software (Excluding Training)	561
Telecommunication/Electronic Equipment	285
Telecommunications Carrier	201
Other (Sector not defined)	33

Source: Based on information provided by government of New Brunswick officials, January-April 2000.

industries still are producing 53 percent of economic activity and many of them aren't modernizing."[47]

This suggests McKenna's job creation initiatives may, in time, run out of steam. The Boyd Company carried out a "major geographically-variable operating costs" study and ranked New Brunswick at the top of the 60 communities or jurisdictions surveyed in terms of "annual cost rankings" for locating call centres.[48] But things appear to be changing. Jim Carroll, a noted Internet expert, recently observed, "New Brunswick could lose its buzz if the new (provincial) government does not keep up the province's reputation as the most wired place in North America."[49] He explained that "New Brunswick's information technology industry profile in the rest of North America has been eroded by competitors.... As a result, New Brunswick is now in danger of missing out on much of the growth expected in the information technology sector."[50]

donald j. savoie

Call centre jobs constitute the first step on the economic success ladder, but it is not at all clear that the required foundation has been put in place for New Brunswickers to climb up to the next step. In fairness to McKenna, however, it may well be that the forces shaping the new economy were largely beyond his influence and that he did not have access to the proper levers to influence development on this front. But even on this point, the McKenna years present New Brunswick and the other Atlantic provinces with important lessons to learn.

168

Appendix 2

Industry Trade Data and Interprovincial Revealed Comparative Advantage (RCA) Index

Provincial Trade ($ million)

Sector	NB Interprov. 1986 value	1986 % of total	1986 RCA index	NB Interprov. 1996 value	1996 % of total	1996 RCA index	NB Internat. 1986 value	1986 % of total	1986 RCA index	NB Internat. 1996 value	1996 % of total	1996 RCA index	Interprov. share pct. pt. change 1986-1996	Internat. share pct. pt. change 1986-1996
Fruit, Veg., Feed, Misc. Food Prod.	290.8	10.1	1.96	466.6	9.9	1.95	60.2	2.0	1.79	110.5	1.9	1.25	-0.2	0.0
Transportation Services	289.6	10.1	1.02	405.8	8.6	1.01	250.3	8.3	1.26	465.6	8.2	1.63	-1.4	-0.1
Meat, Fish & Dairy Products	129.3	4.5	1.12	245.7	5.2	1.24	225.6	7.4	3.07	464.6	8.1	4.80	0.7	0.7
Financial Services	141.0	4.9	0.71	239.2	5.1	0.60	4.4	0.1	0.17	14.8	0.3	0.26	0.2	0.1
Wholesale Services	201.6	7.0	0.92	229.9	4.9	0.47	144.0	4.7	1.52	218.7	3.8	1.04	-2.1	-0.9
Paper & Paper Products	125.3	4.4	1.24	216.2	4.6	2.14	947.7	31.3	3.95	1,306.5	22.9	3.61	0.3	-8.3
Communication Services	94.7	3.3	0.97	198.9	4.2	1.00	6.3	0.2	0.74	19.3	0.3	0.87	0.9	0.1
Lumber, Sawmill, Other Wood Prod.	93.7	3.3	2.14	164.7	3.5	2.62	161.8	5.3	1.24	581.1	10.2	1.99	0.3	4.9
Personal & Other Misc. Services	101.5	3.5	0.79	140.1	3.0	0.59	86.0	2.8	0.89	197.4	3.5	1.00	-0.5	0.6
Business Services	26.9	0.9	0.30	116.9	2.5	0.51	9.1	0.3	0.19	79.8	1.4	0.55	1.6	1.1
Chemicals & Chemical Products	80.6	2.8	0.48	97.1	2.1	0.41	49.7	1.6	0.52	164.3	2.9	0.66	-0.7	1.2
Utilities, incl. electricity, water, gas	30.0	1.0	2.40	82.6	1.8	3.43	281.1	9.3	11.34	137.1	2.4	6.87	0.7	-6.9
Retail Services	45.2	1.6	1.12	69.3	1.5	0.82	N/A		—	N/A		—	-0.1	—
Metal Fabricated Products	29.5	1.0	0.34	63.9	1.4	0.55	6.1	0.2	0.13	44.5	0.8	0.40	0.3	0.6
Primary Metal Products	24.0	0.8	0.27	60.8	1.3	0.39	74.6	2.5	0.42	96.6	1.7	0.32	0.5	-0.8
Machinery & Equipment	16.8	0.6	0.37	45.7	1.0	0.97	28.8	0.9	0.24	50.5	0.9	0.16	0.4	-0.1
Beverages	51.5	1.8	3.01	43.6	0.9	1.62	39.5	1.3	2.36	55.6	1.0	1.68	-0.9	-0.3
Non-metallic Mineral Products	27.9	1.0	0.92	38.1	0.8	1.33	2.2	0.1	0.10	11.6	0.2	0.29	-0.2	0.1
Misc. Manufactured Products	15.4	0.5	0.45	34.4	0.7	0.97	9.1	0.3	0.16	31.3	0.5	0.28	0.2	0.2
Fishing & Trapping Products	9.6	0.3	2.91	28.3	0.6	4.22	56.9	1.9	5.08	80.5	1.4	10.38	0.3	-0.5
Forestry Products	15.9	0.6	3.37	17.4	0.4	0.62	10.8	0.4	2.21	7.9	0.1	3.14	-0.2	-0.2
Printing & Publishing	9.8	0.3	0.17	14.9	0.3	0.17	0.4	0.0	0.03	1.3	0.0	0.06	0.0	0.0
Knitted Products & Clothing	10.7	0.4	0.15	10.7	0.2	0.14	0.5	0.0	0.04	0.9	0.0	0.03	-0.1	0.0
Furniture & Fixtures	10.1	0.4	0.32	7.1	0.2	0.19	0.4	0.0	0.02	8.1	0.1	0.18	-0.2	0.1
Electrical & Communication Prod.	16.3	0.6	0.16	4.6	0.1	0.05	4.9	0.2	0.05	2.5	0.0	0.01	-0.5	-0.1
Grains	1.0	0.0	0.06	1.2	0.0	0.04	1.7	0.1	0.03	2.1	0.0	0.03	0.0	0.0
Tobacco & Tobacco Products	N/A		—	N/A		—	0.0	0.0	0.00	0.0	0.0	0.00		0.0
Mineral Fuels	N/A		—	N/A		—	1.1	0.0	0.0	0.0	0.0	0.0		0.0
Autos, Trucks, other Transp. Equip.	N/A		—	N/A		—	100.6	3.3	0.1	16.8	0.3	0.0		-3.0
Petroleum & Coal Products	N/A		—	N/A		—	313.9	10.4	5.9	1,151.7	20.2	9.7		9.8
Metallic Ores & Concentrates	N/A		—	N/A		—	46.9	1.5	0.4	126.2	2.2	1.1		0.7
Agricultural Products excl. Grains	N/A		—	N/A		—	27.5	0.9	0.9	43.5	0.8	0.5		-0.1
Rubber, Leather, Plastic Fab. Prod.	N/A		—	N/A		—	3.9	0.1	0.1	17.7	0.3	0.2		0.2
Textile Products	N/A		—	N/A		—	1.7	0.1	0.1	11.0	0.2	0.2		0.1
Non-metallic Minerals	N/A		—	N/A		—	26.3	0.9	0.9	66.0	1.2	4.2		0.1
Residual	990.0	34.4	—	35.2	0.7	—	48.0	1.6	—	116.0	2.0	—	0.8	0.3
Total	**2,878.7**	**65.6**	**1.00**	**4,695.5**	**64.8**	**1.00**	**3,032.0**	**98.4**	**1.00**	**5,702.0**	**98.0**	**1.00**		**0.5**

169

donald j. savoie

| Provincial Trade ($ million) | Nova Scotia Interprovincial Exports | | | | | | Nova Scotia International Exports | | | | | | percentage point change in interprovincial share 1986-1996 | percentage point change in international share 1986-1996 |
| | 1986 | | | 1996 | | | 1986 | | | 1996 | | | | |
Sector	value	% of total	RCA index	value	% of total	RCA index	value	% of total	RCA index	value	% of total	RCA index		
Fruit, Veg., Feed, Misc. Food Prod.	204.2	7.2	1.40	243.6	5.9	1.17	32.3	1.3	1.15	61.2	1.7	1.08	-1.3	0.4
Transportation Services	331.9	11.7	1.18	436.1	10.6	1.24	150.8	6.0	0.91	265.5	7.3	1.45	-1.1	1.3
Meat, Fish & Dairy Products	92.6	3.3	0.81	229.8	5.6	1.33	428.5	16.9	6.97	595.7	16.3	9.62	2.3	-0.6
Financial Services	130.6	4.6	0.67	284.2	6.9	0.82	3.3	0.1	0.15	17.2	0.5	0.48	2.3	0.3
Wholesale Services	176.4	6.2	0.82	314.9	7.7	0.73	165.9	6.5	2.09	382.0	10.5	2.84	1.4	3.9
Paper & Paper Products	127.4	4.5	1.28	121.1	2.9	1.37	367.0	14.5	1.83	475.6	13.0	2.05	-1.5	-1.5
Communication Services	125.1	4.4	1.31	273.4	6.7	1.57	7.1	0.3	0.99	23.1	0.6	1.63	2.2	0.4
Lumber, Sawmill, Other Wood Prod.	27.1	1.0	0.63	22.4	0.5	0.41	46.8	1.8	0.43	159.3	4.4	0.85	-0.4	2.5
Personal & Other Misc. Services	130.1	4.6	1.03	257.6	6.3	1.23	84.1	3.3	1.05	208.1	5.7	1.65	1.7	2.4
Business Services	70.2	2.5	0.80	125.5	3.1	0.62	5.7	0.2	0.14	54.9	1.5	0.59	0.6	1.3
Chemicals & Chemical Products	18.0	0.6	0.11	44.6	1.1	0.22	7.8	0.3	0.10	29.2	0.8	0.18	0.5	0.5
Utilities, incl. electricity, water, gas	0.3	0.0	0.02	0.2	0.0	0.01	0.2	0.0	0.01	0.4	0.0	0.03	0.0	0.0
Retail Services	62.0	2.2	1.56	105.2	2.6	1.42	N/A	–	–	N/A	–	–	0.4	–
Metal Fabricated Products	30.4	1.1	0.35	75.4	1.8	0.75	11.0	0.4	0.29	37.6	1.0	0.53	0.8	0.6
Primary Metal Products	65.4	2.3	0.75	78.1	1.9	0.57	28.7	1.1	0.20	68.1	1.9	0.36	-0.4	0.7
Machinery & Equipment	4.7	0.2	0.11	2.4	0.1	0.06	25.6	1.0	0.26	18.7	0.5	0.09	-0.1	-0.5
Beverages	14.7	0.5	0.87	28.1	0.7	1.19	6.2	0.2	0.44	12.0	0.3	0.57	0.2	0.1
Non-metallic Mineral Products	10.8	0.4	0.36	31.2	0.8	1.25	7.9	0.3	0.45	9.0	0.2	0.35	0.4	-0.1
Misc. Manufactured Products	6.2	0.2	0.18	14.3	0.3	0.46	4.7	0.2	0.10	10.0	0.3	0.14	0.1	0.1
Fishing & Trapping Products	70.4	2.5	21.70	74.6	1.8	12.70	207.1	8.2	22.14	63.0	1.7	12.69	-0.7	-6.4
Forestry Products	1.5	0.1	0.32	9.8	0.2	0.40	9.3	0.4	2.28	2.1	0.1	1.31	0.2	-0.3
Printing & Publishing	14.1	0.5	0.25	30.0	0.7	0.39	1.3	0.1	0.12	0.7	0.0	0.05	0.2	0.0
Knitted Products & Clothing	36.4	1.3	0.51	39.2	1.0	0.58	4.6	0.2	0.39	6.8	0.2	0.32	-0.3	0.0
Furniture & Fixtures	5.1	0.2	0.16	9.0	0.2	0.28	1.2	0.0	0.08	2.7	0.1	0.09	0.0	0.0
Electrical & Communication Prod.	22.3	0.8	0.22	43.0	1.0	0.50	22.6	0.9	0.29	23.3	0.6	0.13	0.3	-0.3
Grains	0.2	0.0	0.01	0.2	0.0	0.01	0.1	0.0	0.00	0.3	0.0	0.01	0.0	0.0
Tobacco & Tobacco Products	0.0	0.0	0.00	0.0	0.0	0.00	0.1	0.0	0.03	0.0	0.0	0.00	0.0	0.0
Mineral Fuels	18.0	0.6	0.1	8.8	0.2	0.0	97.8	3.9	0.7	34.9	1.0	0.2	-0.4	-2.9
Autos, Trucks, other Transp. Equip.	122.7	4.3	1.0	353.3	8.6	1.4	206.6	8.2	0.3	297.7	8.2	0.3	4.3	0.0
Petroleum & Coal Products	N/A	–	–	N/A	–	–	96.4	3.8	2.2	83.7	2.3	1.1	–	-1.5
Metallic Ores & Concentrates	N/A	–	–	N/A	–	–	10.0	0.4	0.1	0.0	0.0	0.0	–	-0.4
Agricultural Products excl. Grains	N/A	–	–	N/A	–	–	18.2	0.7	0.7	20.7	0.6	0.4	–	-0.2
Rubber, Leather, Plastic Fab. Prod.	N/A	–	–	N/A	–	–	368.1	14.5	12.5	457.8	12.5	7.1	–	-2.0
Textile Products	86.8	3.1	1.5	111.5	2.7	2.1	14.0	0.6	1.2	11.1	0.3	0.4	-0.3	-0.2
Non-metallic Minerals	N/A	–	–	N/A	–	–	50.8	2.0	2.0	57.8	1.6	5.7	–	-0.4
Services Incidental to Mining	2.8	0.1	0.3	79.3	1.9	5.2	N/A	–	–	N/A	–	–	1.8	–
Residual	826.2	29.1	–	661.3	16.1	–	41.6	1.6	–	160.2	4.4	–	-13.0	2.7
Total	2,834.6	70.9	1.00	4,108.1	83.9	1.00	2,533.3	98.4	1.00	3,650.4	95.6	1.00		

pulling against gravity

Provincial Trade ($ million)

Sector	Interprovincial 1986 value	1986 % of total	1986 RCA index	1996 value	1996 % of total	1996 RCA index	International 1986 value	1986 % of total	1986 RCA index	1996 value	1996 % of total	1996 RCA index	percentage point change in interprovincial share 1986-1996	percentage point change in international share 1986-1996
Fruit, Veg., Feed, Misc. Food Prod.	317.8	5.9	1.14	391.2	5.4	1.05	72.5	2.4	2.12	308.5	4.0	2.58	-0.5	1.6
Transportation Services	893.0	16.5	1.66	1,055.3	14.4	1.69	532.7	17.3	2.64	853.0	11.0	2.20	-2.0	-6.3
Meat, Fish & Dairy Products	405.8	7.5	1.86	398.9	5.5	1.29	170.9	5.5	2.29	135.3	1.7	1.03	-2.0	-3.8
Financial Services	234.8	4.3	0.63	312.7	4.3	0.50	21.4	0.7	0.81	44.4	0.6	0.58	-0.1	-0.1
Wholesale Services	630.2	11.6	1.52	969.1	13.3	1.27	152.5	5.0	1.58	304.3	3.9	1.07	1.6	-1.0
Paper & Paper Products	112.8	2.1	0.59	78.9	1.1	0.50	88.4	2.9	0.36	213.3	2.8	0.43	-1.0	-0.1
Communication Services	149.3	2.8	0.81	289.6	4.0	0.94	9.4	0.3	1.08	25.4	0.3	0.84	1.2	0.0
Lumber, Sawmill, Other Wood Prod.	56.6	1.0	0.69	129.3	1.8	1.32	24.0	0.8	0.18	157.6	2.0	0.40	0.7	1.3
Personal & Other Misc. Services	218.0	4.0	0.90	441.9	6.0	1.19	95.7	3.1	0.98	222.2	2.9	0.83	2.0	-0.2
Business Services	64.8	1.2	0.39	223.2	3.1	0.62	23.6	0.8	0.49	141.9	1.8	0.72	1.9	1.1
Chemicals & Chemical Products	125.2	2.3	0.40	185.2	2.5	0.51	71.1	2.3	0.73	310.2	4.0	0.91	0.2	1.7
Utilities, incl. electricity, water, gas	13.2	0.2	0.56	20.8	0.3	0.55	73.2	2.4	2.91	208.3	2.7	7.70	0.0	0.3
Retail Services	119.9	2.2	1.57	239.7	3.3	1.82	N/A	—	—	N/A	—	—	1.1	—
Metal Fabricated Products	176.2	3.2	1.07	167.1	2.3	0.93	33.4	1.1	0.72	93.0	1.2	0.62	-1.0	0.1
Primary Metal Products	123.5	2.3	0.75	175.4	2.4	0.72	217.8	7.1	1.22	537.0	6.9	1.33	0.1	-0.1
Machinery & Equipment	116.0	2.1	1.36	145.5	2.0	1.99	199.4	6.5	1.67	1,158.7	15.0	2.65	-0.1	8.5
Beverages	38.3	0.7	1.19	85.7	1.2	2.04	31.1	1.0	1.83	6.9	0.1	0.15	0.5	-0.9
Non-metallic Mineral Products	18.3	0.3	0.32	25.5	0.3	0.57	14.8	0.5	0.69	18.7	0.2	0.35	0.0	-0.2
Misc. Manufactured Products	19.2	0.4	0.30	32.3	0.4	0.58	44.3	1.4	0.75	111.2	1.4	0.73	0.0	0.0
Fishing & Trapping Products	0.2	0.0	0.03	0.9	0.1	0.09	17.4	0.6	1.53	11.2	0.1	1.07	0.1	-0.4
Forestry Products	10.3	0.2	1.16	7.5	0.1	0.17	2.8	0.1	0.56	0.3	0.0	0.09	-0.1	-0.1
Printing & Publishing	127.1	2.3	1.19	226.7	3.1	1.65	12.4	0.4	0.91	31.4	0.4	1.14	0.8	0.0
Knitted Products & Clothing	245.3	4.5	1.80	197.7	2.7	1.66	21.3	0.7	1.49	67.3	0.9	1.48	-1.8	0.2
Furniture & Fixtures	72.3	1.3	1.21	90.0	1.2	1.57	9.3	0.3	0.51	113.7	1.5	1.83	-0.1	1.2
Electrical & Communication Prod.	144.4	2.7	0.75	46.6	0.6	0.31	40.0	1.3	0.42	131.0	1.7	0.35	-2.0	0.4
Grains	147.8	2.7	4.33	126.9	1.7	3.00	499.2	16.2	8.56	401.2	5.2	3.55	-1.0	-11.0
Tobacco & Tobacco Products	0.0	0.0	0.00	0.0	0.0	0.00	0.0	0.0	0.00	0.0	0.0	0.00	0.0	0.0
Mineral Fuels	67.4	1.2	0.2	26.6	0.4	0.1	30.4	1.0	0.2	86.5	1.1	0.2	-0.9	0.1
Autos, Trucks, other Transp. Equip.	159.0	2.9	0.7	407.6	5.6	0.9	233.1	7.6	0.3	992.8	12.8	0.5	2.6	5.3
Petroleum & Coal Products	9.2	0.2	0.0	4.5	0.1	0.0	0.9	0.0	0.1	0.3	0.0	0.0	-0.1	-0.1
Metallic Ores & Concentrates	311.3	5.7	5.5	129.4	1.8	1.8	6.6	0.2	0.1	166.9	2.2	1.1	-4.0	1.9
Agricultural Products excl. Grains	186.8	3.4	2.3	509.1	7.0	3.0	227.3	7.4	7.4	606.6	7.8	5.1	3.5	0.5
Rubber, Leather, Plastic Fab. Prod.	75.9	1.4	0.7	93.9	1.3	0.9	27.3	0.9	0.8	134.3	1.7	1.0	-0.1	0.9
Textile Products	23.9	0.4	0.2	29.2	0.4	0.3	12.9	0.4	0.9	22.1	0.3	0.3	0.0	-0.1
Non-metallic Minerals	8.5	0.2	0.4	38.2	0.5	1.9	15.6	0.5	0.5	17.3	0.2	0.8	0.4	-0.3
Services Incidental to Mining	0.4	0.0	0.0	8.9	0.1	0.3	N/A	—	—	N/A	—	—	0.1	—
Residual	0.1	0.0	—	-0.1	0.0	—	46.9	1.5	—	99.8	1.3	—	0.0	-0.2
Total	5,422.8	100.0	1.00	7,310.9	100.0	1.00	3,079.6	100.0	1.00	7,732.6	100.0	1.00		

Provincial Trade ($ million)

Sector	Canada Interprovincial Exports 1986 value	1986 % of total	1996 value	1996 % of total	Canada International Exports 1986 value	1986 % of total	1996 value	1996 % of total
Fruit, Veg., Feed, Misc. Food Prod.	5,800	5.1	8,144	5.1	1,487	1.1	4,533	1.5
Transportation Services	11,165	9.9	13,699	8.6	8,769	6.5	14,705	5.0
Meat, Fish & Dairy Products	4,525	4.0	6,759	4.2	3,253	2.4	4,965	1.7
Financial Services	7,786	6.9	13,596	8.5	1,151	0.9	2,878	1.0
Wholesale Services	8,604	7.6	16,766	10.5	4,193	3.1	10,798	3.7
Paper & Paper Products	3,967	3.5	3,443	2.1	10,612	7.9	18,589	6.4
Communication Services	3,809	3.4	6,783	4.2	379	0.3	1,139	0.4
Lumber, Sawmill, Other Wood Prod.	1,717	1.5	2,145	1.3	5,777	4.3	14,994	5.1
Personal & Other Misc. Services	5,039	4.5	8,164	5.1	4,253	3.2	10,119	3.5
Business Services	3,478	3.1	7,836	4.9	2,090	1.6	7,509	2.6
Chemicals & Chemical Products	6,512	5.8	8,032	5.0	4,248	3.2	12,858	4.4
Utilities, incl. electricity, water, gas	489	0.4	822	0.5	1,096	0.8	1,024	0.3
Retail Services	1,584	1.4	2,882	1.8	N/A	–	N/A	–
Metal Fabricated Products	3,423	3.0	3,930	2.5	2,008	1.5	5,701	1.9
Primary Metal Products	3,446	3.1	5,358	3.3	7,763	5.8	15,291	5.2
Machinery & Equipment	1,770	1.6	1,600	1.0	5,211	3.9	16,525	5.6
Beverages	670	0.6	919	0.6	741	0.6	1,695	0.6
Non-metallic Mineral Products	1,184	1.1	974	0.6	932	0.7	2,047	0.7
Misc. Manufactured Products	1,334	1.2	1,211	0.8	2,578	1.9	5,752	2.0
Fishing & Trapping Products	129	0.1	229	0.1	495	0.4	398	0.1
Forestry Products	185	0.2	951	0.6	216	0.2	129	0.0
Printing & Publishing	2,217	2.0	3,003	1.9	595	0.4	1,038	0.4
Knitted Products & Clothing	2,831	2.5	2,613	1.6	621	0.5	1,724	0.6
Furniture & Fixtures	1,247	1.1	1,256	0.8	792	0.6	2,357	0.8
Electrical & Communication Prod.	4,022	3.6	3,342	2.1	4,128	3.1	14,068	4.8
Grains	709	0.6	927	0.6	2,539	1.9	4,272	1.5
Tobacco & Tobacco Products	1,015	0.9	1,640	1.0	154	0.1	246	0.1
Mineral Fuels	7,022	6.2	7,873	4.9	7,216	5.4	17,387	5.9
Autos, Trucks, other Transp. Equip.	4,816	4.3	9,756	6.1	36,438	27.2	69,099	23.6
Petroleum & Coal Products	4,033	3.6	4,876	3.0	2,338	1.7	6,119	2.1
Metallic Ores & Concentrates	1,169	1.0	1,543	1.0	5,282	3.9	6,013	2.1
Agricultural Products excl. Grains	1,677	1.5	3,766	2.4	1,340	1.0	4,487	1.5
Rubber, Leather, Plastic Fab. Prod.	2,272	2.0	2,258	1.4	1,558	1.2	5,148	1.8
Textile Products	2,264	2.0	2,043	1.3	605	0.5	2,413	0.8
Non-metallic Minerals	431	0.4	446	0.3	1,313	1.0	815	0.3
Residual	390	0.3	592	0.4	1,909	1.4	5,819	2.0
Total	**112,731**	**99.7**	**160,177**	**99.6**	**134,080**	**98.6**	**292,654**	**98.0**

Note: RCA Index = Industry's share in province's exports to rest of Canada / Industry's share in total Canadian interprovincial trade.

pulling against gravity

Notes

1. Consultations with Frank McKenna, September 1999.

2. "Premier McKenna's Speech at Atlantic Vision Conference," Moncton, 9 October 1997. A copy of the speech is in the provincial archives.

3. Consultation with Frank McKenna, Moncton, New Brunswick, April 2000.

4. Based on data from Statistics Canada.

5. Consultation with a business leader, Moncton, New Brunswick, January 2000.

6. Consultations with a business and community leader, Moncton, New Brunswick, February 2000.

7. Consultations with Professor George Perlin, Queen's University, who carried out public opinion surveys in New Brunswick throughout the McKenna years.

8. Interview with Frank McKenna, Moncton, New Brunswick, 2 March 2000.

9. Quoted in Jennifer J. Salopek, "Rural Electronification," *Training and Development* (October 1999), p. 28.

10. Quoted in "Frank McKenna's Mid-Term Report," *Atlantic Business*, Vol. 5, no. 2 (March 1994), p. 11.

11. "Run, Frank, Run," *Ottawa Citizen*, 27 July 1999, editorial page.

12. David Adams Richards, "The Road Less Taken," in Josh Beutel (ed.), *True (Blue) Grit: A Frank McKenna Review*, pp. 133-34.

13. Quoted in "Frank McKenna's Mid-Term Report," p. 11.

14. "Magazine Campaign 'ads' up for New Brunswick," *Telegraph Journal*, Saint John, 29 May 1995, p. B1.

15. Claude Snow, *La démckennisation* (Caraquet: La Petite Imprimerie, 1999), p. 9 (my translation).

16. See letter from Frank McKenna to the Right Hon. Brian Mulroney, 29 August 1990, provincial archives.

17. See, for example, Donald J. Savoie, *Aboriginal Economic Development in New Brunswick* (Moncton: The Canadian Institute for Research on Regional Development, 2000).

18. Gérald La Forest and Graydon Nicholas, *Report of the Task Force on Aboriginal Issues*, Fredericton, March 1999.

19. La Forest and Nicholas, *Report of the Task Force on Aboriginal Issues*.

20. Televised Leaders Debate, CPAC, 6 September 1995.

21. See, for example, the appointment of David Agnew in 1992 in Ontario, which is highlighted in Graham White's chapter in Evert Lindquist (ed.), *Government Restructuring and Career Public Service* (Toronto: Institute of Public Administration of Canada, 2000).

22. *The New Brunswick Economy: A Report to the Legislative Assembly* (Fredericton: Department of Finance, 1999), p. 53.

23. Based on data received from Statistics Canada.

24. *The New Brunswick Economy*, p. 41.

25. See, among others, "New Brunswick loosens fiscal belt with tax cuts," *The Globe and Mail*, 11 December 1996, p. A1.

26. "New Brunswick loosens fiscal belt with tax cuts," p. A1.

27. Consultations with New Brunswick government officials, Fredericton, March 2000.

28. "New Brunswick: Growth to Improve in 1997," Ottawa, The Conference Board of Canada, Vol. 12, no 1 (Winter 1997), p. 22.

29. "New Brunswick: Growth to Improve in 1997," p. 35.

30. Based on data provided by IRPP, December 2000.

31. *Atlantic Canada: Catching Tomorrow's Wave*, prepared by Senator John S. Bryden, Senator Wilfred Moore, Joe McGuire, MP, Charles Hubbard, MP, on behalf of the Atlantic Caucus, Liberal Party, Ottawa, 31 May 1999, p. 32.

32. Donald J. Savoie, *Rethinking Canada's Regional Development Policy* (Moncton: Canadian Institute for Research on Regional Development, 1997), p. 40.

33. Quoted in Technology Partnerships Canada, *Annual Report 1997-1998: Investing in Innovation*, "Message from the Minister."

34. *Atlantic Canada: Catching Tomorrow's Wave*, p. 130.

35. *Atlantic Canada: Catching Tomorrow's Wave*, p. 131.

36. Technology Partnerships Canada, Current Statistics, *TPC Newsletter*, 31 December 1999.

37. Sébastien Breau, *Profile and Prospects of the Biopharmaceutical Industry in Atlantic Canada* (Moncton: Canadian Institute for Research on Regional Development, 2001).

38. Quoted from a slide presentation on "Industry Portfolio Innovation," Moncton, NB, Atlantic Canada Opportunities Agency, 24 February 2000.

39. Quoted from a slide presentation on "Industry Portfolio Innovation."

40. Eric Reguly, "Leave the funding of tech firms to venture capitalists," *The Globe and Mail*, 25 March 2000, p. B10.

41. See, among others, *The Economic and Fiscal Update: Strong Economy, Strong Society* (Ottawa: Department of Finance, 15 October 1997), p. 44.

42. Consultations with federal government officials, Ottawa and Moncton, February-March 2000.

43. Letter from Premier Frank McKenna to Prime Minister Jean Chrétien, provincial archives, 15 July 1997.

44. Letter from Premier Frank McKenna to Prime Minister Jean Chrétien, provincial archives, 22 January 1997.

45. See, for example, "Rural Electronification," *Training and Development*, October 1999, pp. 30-35.

46. See, among others, "Rural Electronification," p. 30.

47. Quoted in "Rural Electronification," p. 36.

48. Comparative Cost Analysis for Financial Services Call Centre Operations (Princeton, N.J.: The Boyd Company Inc., undated), pp. 9-10.

49. "Keep the buzz alive, expert says," *Telegraph Journal*, Saint John, New Brunswick, 26 April 2000, p. C1.

50. Quoted in "Whatever happened to Tory vision," *Times and Transcript*, Moncton, 2 June 2000, p. A2.

174

7

Lessons Learned

Many have said, "In politics, timing is everything." When McKenna came to power, the province's economic circumstances suited his policy agenda. They actually lent themselves quite nicely to his *projet de société*, as did national economic circumstances and neoconservatism, the latest fashion in public policy. The province's public finances needed close attention, the federal government's cutbacks in transfer payments to the provinces had serious implications for the have-less provinces like New Brunswick, and voices were increasingly being heard to let market forces call the economic adjustment tune. Many economic and political observers claimed the problem in places like New Brunswick was that there was too much government intervention, not too little. What New Brunswick needed above all was a good dose of market discipline.

McKenna subscribed to this view. He insisted that as long as he was premier, New Brunswick would not, as it had in the past, be regarded as the bellyache of Canada. He wanted New Brunswick to pull itself up by its own bootstraps, to be more self-reliant and to have a strong, vibrant private sector. In the introduction, we quoted McKenna on this theme: "Ultimately, a province such as ours can be what it wants to be. With a flourishing work ethic and entrepreneurship, you can stay as wealthy as you want to be."[1]

McKenna's view eventually resonated in Toronto's business community, in the financial press and no doubt in the departments of Finance and Industry in Ottawa. In fact, when the federal government introduced cuts to its employment insurance program, senior ministers made the case that the cuts were not just in the interest of wrestling down the deficit, but that they were also in the long-term economic interest of Atlantic Canada. The cuts would make the region more self-reliant and promote "real" economic development. They approved of the inherent message in McKenna's approach: No point in dredging up old grievances to solve today's problems – just get on with the job. McKenna's claim that "you can stay as wealthy as you want to be" and that New Brunswick would no longer be "the bellyache of Canada" would also absolve them of any responsibility for the province's have-less status.

McKenna's views also squared quite nicely with the neoconservative ideology, which was very much in vogue in the western countries, notably in Anglo-American democracies. Politicians singing the praises of the neoconservative agenda have also applauded McKenna's approach to economic development. Tony Clement, a minister in the Mike Harris government in Ontario and co-chair of the "Unite the Right" movement in Canada declared that the new party should borrow a page from Frank McKenna in defining its economic development policies.[2] McKenna, however, argues he has always felt uncomfortable being identified as a neoconservative. He maintains he did what he had to do to promote economic development and repair the province's balance sheet, which was in bad shape when he came to power. Neoconservatism, he insists, had nothing to do with his agenda. He reports that, if only because of his own roots, he has "never believed in punishing the poor and the little guy," which he sees as "part of the neoconservative agenda."[3]

178   Still, McKenna's agenda was clearly business-friendly. He understood the business community well and no one was surprised when corporate Canada embraced him the moment he left office, appointing him to some of its most sought after boards of directors, including, among others, the Bank of Montreal and Noranda. One can hardly imagine other former premiers from the region, Joey Smallwood, Alex Campbell, Louis J. Robichaud or John Buchanan being so feted. The Globe and Mail described McKenna as "one of the rare bright stars of the Canadian political firmament."[4] There is no question McKenna had that most highly sought after quality in politics – charisma. But he also had energy, enthusiasm, a deeply felt commitment to the development of his province and an ability to connect with New Brunswick or any audience, whether he was speaking to the Bankers Association in Toronto, the Bathurst Chamber of Commerce or a meeting of Liberal partisans in Bouctouche. The situation, as we observed in the introduction, could well be described as *come the moment, come the man.*

William Milne wrote that under McKenna New Brunswick became a "testing ground, a research laboratory in public policy."[5] To be sure, McKenna put a number of economic development ideas to the test. This, in turn, enables us to answer a number of questions: How effective is a business-friendly agenda in promoting economic development in a smaller have-less province? What are the merits of pursuing a neoconservative policy in a province like New Brunswick? More generally, what lessons we can learn from this study? What are the prospects for the future?

Leaving a Trace

McKenna did leave a trace. He left a trace in the national media, which in itself is no small achievement for a New Brunswick premier. He left a trace in the public service, moving it, however slightly, to a business management model. In fact, the McKenna government repaired the province's balance sheet not so much by cutting programs, as in "doing more with less," but by tightening government operations and by having program managers emulate the private sector. He left a trace in job creation and in the province's state of economic development. McKenna also left a trace in that he succeeded in changing the way in which New Brunswickers see themselves, and in which other Canadians see New Brunswick.

Data produced for the previous chapter reveal that McKenna did make a difference on several fronts. New Brunswick made impressive gains during his stay in office and in many instances outperformed provinces of similar size, according to several standard indicators of economic performance. This is true even though New Brunswick suffered from federal spending cuts more than most provinces. As we saw, New Brunswick made the most progress in lessening its dependence on federal transfer payments of one kind or another at a time when Ottawa was making deep cuts to its operations in New Brunswick.

Does a business-friendly agenda hold promise in the economic field in a province like New Brunswick? The short answer is yes. Indeed, few could have pursued the agenda with more energy and enthusiasm than McKenna. But there are limits. Though New Brunswick made significant improvements to its economy, one can hardly claim its economy has been transformed. For one thing, the population remains stagnant, a telling sign. David Foot went to the heart of the matter when he wrote about the "interaction between population and economic development" and "the economic consequences of declining population growth."[6] The state of New Brunswick's population alone makes it clear the province's economy has hardly been transformed. In addition, there are signs the province is not well positioned to catch the next important wave of economic development. A key to the new economy is research and development and, as this study makes clear, New Brunswick still trails most other provinces on this front.

Economics as if History Does Not Matter

Those who sing the virtues of self-help and believe regions like New Brunswick have been treated too softly by misguided government programs are convinced that a sharp dose of market discipline can solve their economic problems. Moreover, proponents of the neoconservative approach suggest government intervention should be kept to a strict minimum. One is thus left to assume that strong economic regions in Canada became strong on their own merit, with little government intervention. To be sure, the economically comfortable regions want to believe this. One can also easily appreciate their pleasure that someone from New Brunswick wanted to meet them as an aspiring equal, not as a supplicant. The message, as we already noted, not only lets them off the hook, but also confirms their belief that market forces and their own abilities explain their economic success.

But history does matter. Economic history matters. Indeed, in economic development it is hardly possible to understand the present without drawing on history. As we saw in Chapter 2, the implementation of Sir John A. Macdonald's National Policy benefited the economic interests of central Canada a great deal and was, as any economic historian will attest, severely detrimental to the interests of the Maritimes. History mattered when C.D. Howe and his officials decided not to locate a single crown corporation in the Maritimes in support of the war effort. These crown corporations later gave rise to an important component of Canada's manufacturing sector. History also mattered when the federal government put in place a post-war industrial development strategy geared toward assisting wartime production facilities make the transition to peacetime production. This strategy greatly assisted central Canadian firms take root and prosper. Those in the Maritimes were left on the outside, looking in.

History certainly mattered in the development of the high-tech sector around Ottawa and in nearby Kanata. Charlotte Gray documents by just how much in a recent *Saturday Night* magazine article. She writes that the federal government "is the reason that technology companies took root here [Ottawa and Kanata]. It all began over half a century ago, during the Second World War, when the federally-funded National Research Council attracted a generation of high-calibre scientists to Ottawa."[7] Gray also explains that Northern Electronic Co. (now Nortel) in 1961 decided to locate its research laboratory just outside Ottawa "because it wanted its engineers to be close to the government-sponsored

180

scientific community."[8] Gray could have added that the federal government helped this Ottawa-based industry with strategic purchases and research and development grants throughout the 1970s and 1980s.[9]

History matters even now as Ottawa's Foundation for Innovation and various R&D initiatives from the federal Industry department are giving shape to the new economy, again leaving Atlantic Canada outside. The fund had, by 31 March 2001, allocated only 3.2 percent of its total resources to the four Atlantic provinces.[10] We saw in the previous chapter that Industry Canada's Technology Partnership Program (TPC) has been largely insignificant to Atlantic Canada, with less than two percent of its funding now allocated to the region. It is important to note that Atlantic Canada's share of the national population in 2000 stood at 7.7 percent (down from 10.4 percent in 1961) and that the region's share of Canada's GDP was about 5.85 percent in 1999.[11] Another important note at this point is that Canada's constitution (section 36, 1b) commits the government of Canada and the provincial governments to "furthering economic development to reduce disparity in opportunities."

History matters because, as we saw, the federal government will always be quick to respond to the first hint of economic trouble in central Canada. In Chapter 3 we saw that the prime minister and the Department of Finance decided to reorient economic policy in the early 1980s because they foresaw economic optimism in the East and energy mega-projects fueling the economy of western Canada, but unprecedented softness in the manufacturing sector in central Canada. The Department of Regional Economic Expansion was scrapped and a new, stronger department was born with programs designed to promote development in every political constituency in Canada. We also saw that economic optimism in the east was short-lived and Ottawa's National Energy Program served to cool down the economic buoyancy in western Canada. Meanwhile, the "unprecedented softness" in the manufacturing sector in central Canada disappeared as quickly as the economic recession of the early 1980s did, but the programs to deal with it remained until the late 1980s.

History matters because Ottawa decided in the early 1970s to reorient its regional development policies, initially designed by the Diefenbaker government for the benefit of Atlantic Canada, to assist its national unity efforts. First Montreal, then virtually every single community in Canada could turn to federal regional development policies for a helping hand. In fact, we reached the point, however ridiculous it may appear to some, where these programs in Atlantic Canada could no longer "compete" with similar federal government programs in other regions, including Ontario.[12] In other words, every region, strong or weak, has had its hand in the federal regional development pot. As

181

a result, regional development programs have gained a "bad reputation." The public perception, fueled by the popular press, however, is still that the federal regional development policy is for the benefit of Atlantic Canada. Thus, Atlantic Canada gets most of the bad press but not most of the benefit.[13] The Atlantic Provinces Economic Council recently produced a revealing study. It pointed out that "Provincial and federal subsidies to business, *measured on a per capita basis*, in 1998, the most recent year for which data is available, are lower in New Brunswick (170.0) than in any other province in Canada (Ontario stands at 202.2 and Quebec at 527.5)"[14] (See Figure 5).

Figure 5
1998 Business Subsidies Per Capita

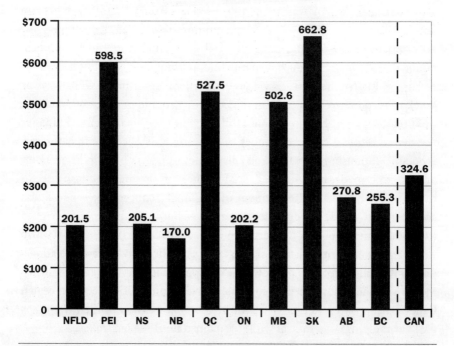

Source: Centre for the Study of Living Standards, *Value Added Per Person-Hour as Percentage of Canadian Average*, 2000.

I stress that we are talking about federal regional policy here, not tax policy, tax expenditures, various R&D measures or federal government operations. As already noted, New Brunswick and the other Atlantic provinces, for the most part, hardly appear on the radar screen of these programs and New Brunswick in particular suffered more than the others from cutbacks in federal government operations.

History also reveals federal measures initially designed for slow-growth regions are invariably pulled and pushed to other areas of the country, particularly to the vote-rich provinces of Ontario and Quebec. The Transitional Jobs Fund (TJF), which hardly enjoyed good press, is a case in point. The fund was established in 1996 to ease the implementation of employment insurance reforms, which hit rural areas of Atlantic Canada hard. New Brunswick, as we already noted, remains one of the most rural provinces in Canada. To ease the transition to a new employment insurance program, the TJF was to make funding available to create jobs.[15]

The fund was initially designed for areas of high unemployment. In announcing the fund, the federal government explained that it would apply to economic regions with 12 percent unemployment or more. The 12 percent rule proved short-lived. Ottawa decided that the 12 percent rule could be adjusted to include small pockets of unemployment in any given area. It is always important to bear in mind that Quebec has more than twice the number of seats in the House of Commons than the four Atlantic provinces combined (75 vs. 31). Government officials readily admit that if the 12 percent criteria had been respected, Atlantic Canada would have received a greater share of TJF funds.[16]

History also mattered when Ottawa, unable to secure the necessary constitutional amendments, decided to carve a larger role for itself through its spending power. With the aid of hindsight, it is now clear that Harold Innis was on to something when he observed that Keynesian economics would serve the economic interests of Ontario and Quebec to the detriment of the smaller provinces. He put forward his view in no uncertain terms when he described Keynesian-inspired full employment policies as a "racket on the part of the central provinces for getting and keeping what they can."[17] Inspired by Keynes or not, we know Ottawa would use its spending power to invest in wealth-generating activities (located mostly in central Canada) and then use it again to share the wealth (through transfer payments). These transfer payments were designed to assist have-less provinces underwrite some of their costs while leaving unchallenged the basic causes that promoted uneven economic development in the first place. Many Canadians and a number of economic observers appear to have forgotten the very *raison d'être* of these transfer payments, viewing them now only from an economic dependency perspective and on their costs to the federal treasury.

In fact, the "have" provinces, especially Ontario, have become openly critical of their treatment by Ottawa on many of these transfer payments. First, Bob Rae and now Mike Harris with Tom Courchene (arguably Canada's leading

183

neoconservative economist at his side), have pushed for "fair share federalism." The agenda has met with some success in Ottawa, as attested to by the 1999 and 2000 federal budget papers and changes to the Canada Health and Social Transfer (CHST). The changes favoured Ontario's interests. Courchene writes about "discriminatory fiscal treatment [against Ontario] at the hands of the federal government." He adds, "If the centre has abandoned the heartland, the heartland under Harris is willing to take matters in its own hands and to pursue the role of an economic region state within North America."[18] In other words, either Ottawa changes its tune on transfer payments or Ontario will take its bat and ball and go play somewhere else. Canadian economic history has contributed immensely to Ontario's economic might and the province now has the capacity to do just that. However, I have never heard premier Rae or Harris (or Courchene) talk about "fair share federalism" when it comes to Canada's economic history, to Ottawa's investing in Canada's manufacturing sector between 1942 and 1960 or now as Ottawa pours substantial sums of money into Ontario's R&D infrastructure.

To be sure, Ottawa has, over the years, appointed royal commissions and task forces to identify solutions for New Brunswick and, more generally, Atlantic Canada's slow growth. But these exercises have been consistently designed to find "practical solutions." They have never been permitted to go to the heart of the matter – and certainly not to define measures which could be perceived as being at the expense of Ontario's economic interests. The Duncan Commission, it will be recalled, was instructed not to deal with tariffs and trade issues or the impact of the region's declining representation in the House of Commons and its implications for the Maritimes.

Facts are one thing, but perceptions are quite another. And perceptions matter a great deal in politics, public policy and economic development. Notwithstanding the fact that New Brunswick trails all provinces in provincial and federal subsidies to business on a per capita basis, the perception remains, as APEC recently argued, that New Brunswick and Atlantic Canada are "a backwater where nothing happens unless it is subsidized to the hilt by federal dollars."[19]

The national media has hardly helped matters. Jeffrey Simpson, a widely respected national columnist, wrote before the last federal election that the federal government went on a "spending spree in Atlantic Canada" when it announced, in June 2000, $700 million of new funding for the Atlantic Canada Opportunity Agency.[20] It is still not clear how much of the $700 million is actually new funding and how much of it is recycled existing program money. We know this much: $290 million was already part of ACOA's five-year fiscal plan and about $140 million was reallocated from Atlantic Canada's share of the

Canada Job Fund. It appears that less than half of the $700 million is new money. Included in the new funding is $110 million allocated to the National Research Council (NRC) to promote research in Atlantic Canada. Though it holds promise, time will tell if the fund will have much of an impact on Atlantic Canada's research and development activities. Simpson, however, chose not to write about a spending spree in Ontario when Prime Minister Chrétien announced, on 20 October 2000, two days before he called a general election, that Ottawa would provide $500 million in new funding "to fund the first phase of the Toronto Waterfront Revitalization."[21] Chrétien also announced, on the very same day, federal funding of $680 million over six years to complement the government of Ontario's investment in community infrastructure.[22]

Jeffrey Simpson is certainly not alone in the national media in practicing the art of *deux poids, deux mesures*. It is ingrained, it appears, in the national media and in Ottawa. One has only to read the reactions of the *National Post* columnists and journalists in the aftermath of Chrétien's June 2000 announcement of special funding for the Atlantic Canada Opportunities Agency to appreciate this.

I was struck, as probably many Maritimers were by the reactions in the media, when John Manley was moved out of the Industry portfolio. Edward Greenspon praised Manley in *The Globe and Mail* for his ability to think "national" and pointedly asked whether his replacement, Brian Tobin, will "be an Atlantic minister or a national minister?"[23] A few days later Campbell Morrison, a columnist, wrote in the Moncton *Times and Transcript* that "If Brian Tobin succeeds at nothing else, at least he has dislodged John Manley from the key Industry portfolio.... [Manley's] primary concern has been the high-tech sector, which by happy coincidence is based largely in Ottawa, and the aerospace sector in Montreal and Toronto."[24] Manley also practiced the art of *deux poids, deux mesures*. Witness, for example, his failed efforts to come to the rescue of the Ottawa Senators with federal funding. Surely, one would be hard pressed to make the case that a hockey team is part of the new economy while the shipbuilding industry is not.

Things "national" in Canada invariably refer to the economic interests of Ontario and Quebec, while things regional refer to the economic interests of Western and Atlantic Canada.

Yes, history matters.

National Political Institutions Also Matter

Several years ago, I invited Professor Niles Hansen from the Department of Economics at the University of Texas and one of the leading students of regional economics and regional development policy to spend some time at the Université

185

de Moncton. After studying Canada's regional development efforts for a few months, he came to a conclusion that went something like this:

> I have finally figured it out...When I first came here, I believed that Canada had a strong regional development policy and we in the U.S. did not, leaving aside some programs under the Tennessee Valley Authority (TVA). Now, I am convinced that we have a strong regional policy and you do not. We have the U.S. Senate and you have a pot-pourri of measures and subsidies that often fall short of the target.[25]

With each state having two elected senators in a Senate that has both policy and program clout, state or regional interests have been and continue to be equally defended at the centre of government. It explains, at least in part, why military establishments and R&D activities related to the military are spread out in all regions of the country.[26] Canada, meanwhile, has mainly looked to regional development programs and to a form of tentative economic *dirigisme* to address the "regional" issue in national policy rather than to its national political institutions. In addition, the regional issue has been overtaken by national unity concerns, with the result that federal regional development programs, at least as they apply in Atlantic Canada, have for the most part lost their way.

There is probably no need to explain how our Senate has failed Canada's regions. Its near total irrelevance is now obvious to the great majority of Canadians. A better informed Canadian public no longer harbours any hope that the Senate, as currently constituted, can ever generate anything worthwhile or even serve to articulate regional interests and then have any kind of impact. Any illusion that the Canadian Senate has any legitimate role in this respect was recently put to rest when the federal government decreed in its "clarity bill" that "the Commons would have the final word on whether any referendum question on Quebec sovereignty passed the clarity test."[27]

Ottawa has been looking at the wrong end of the problem, as its never-ending parade of new regional agencies and program acronyms would suggest. Every time a new ARDA, FRED, DREE, MSERD or ACOA is introduced, the prime minister of the day will invariably explain that it will succeed where all the previous schemes have failed. But these changes are never the solution. Promoting regional interests is not a matter of the machinery of government or of administration: it is a political matter to be resolved at the political level. Yet, "this" and "that" have been tried with the machinery of government and the public service, all while the workings of our political institutions have been ignored. Though there is no denying the public service does exert a great deal of influence on policies and programs, it does not have the power to make policy, to strike new programs or to make important policy or even program decisions. Only elected politicians on the government side hold this power. The fact that the federal public service is still organized along functional or sectoral lines, with line departments pursuing specific sectoral objectives, not regional ones, is a political matter, not an administrative one. The fact that the great majority of senior public service positions and virtually all officials occupying them are located in Ottawa, not the regions, is a political decision, not an administrative one. The fact that no sustained effort has ever been made to document and understand the effect of departmental policies and programs on specific regions is a political failure, not an administrative one. This, despite firm commitments made by prime ministers Trudeau and Mulroney that such investigations would be done. And the fact that Ottawa has abandoned its policy of decentralizing federal government jobs from Ottawa to slow-growth regions was a political decision, not an administrative one.

The economic interests of Ontario and Quebec have been particularly well articulated within the federal government because of the nature of our national political institutions. They hold effective power because they hold the great majority of seats and no political party can aspire to power without support from one or both of these provinces. Canadian prime ministers have, for the most part, come from either Ontario or Quebec ever since Canada was born. In addition, since the 1970s, they have, for a host of reasons, "governed from the centre."[28] That is, political power in Ottawa has been increasingly concentrated in the hands of the prime minister and a few advisors. The federal Cabinet, according to a member of the Chrétien Cabinet, "is no longer a decision-making body: it is a focus group for the prime minister."[29] But in their attempts to "focus on" and "manage" major political developments, they have made matters worse, at least on the regional front. That is, concentrating effective political power in the hands of a few people has greatly inhibited the ability of national political institutions to understand regional forces, let alone accommodate them in policy and decision making.

Any issue affecting Ontario and Quebec is inevitably regarded in Ottawa as a national concern, requiring the close attention of the national government. The same is not true for the Maritimes. An example makes this point clear. The Supreme Court decision in the Marshall case, which gave broad fishing rights to the Micmac nation, had far-reaching political and economic consequences in the Maritimes. For some unexplained reason, Atlantic Canada's representative on the Supreme Court did not participate in the Marshall decision. One can hardly imagine a case before the Supreme Court having a strong impact on one

187

of Ontario's key economic sectors (e.g., the automotive or financial services sector) which would not have all of Ontario's representatives on the court participate in the decision. In addition, by all accounts, the government of Canada had no contingency plan in place to deal with any political fallout resulting from the Marshall decision. Contrast this to the federal government's setting up a special ad hoc unit in the Privy Council Office to deal with any political fallout at the time the Supreme Court tabled its decision on the Quebec reference. Yet, Ottawa has jurisdiction over both the fishery and Aboriginal affairs.

Canadian prime ministers live in Ottawa and their principal policy advisors have, for the most part, been born, educated and spent much of their working lives in either Ontario or Quebec. With very rare exceptions, clerks of the Privy Council Office, secretaries to the Cabinet, the heads of the federal public service and the prime minister's main advisors have been from either Ontario or Quebec ever since Arnold Heeney expanded the scope of the position during the Second World War.[30] This combined with the fact that the Senate is for the most part of no political consequence, other than serving the prime minister as a rich source of partisan political appointments, enables the prime minister to concentrate on the vote-rich provinces of Ontario and Quebec which dominate the House of Commons and from which he draws his power and his chances of re-election.

In some ways, Ottawa's actual regional development policy has been remarkably successful over the years. The federal government's national economic policy has consistently been geared to the economic interests of Ontario and Quebec. In this sense, it has worked well. Southern Ontario and, albeit to a lesser extent, southern Quebec, are two of the world's economic hot spots. Surely, the most ardent neoconservative will recognize that public policy measures, including many defined in Ottawa since the implementation of the National Policy and continuing to this day, have been vitally important to the economic development of southern Ontario and Quebec.

Michael Marzolini, the Chrétien government's pollster, made a presentation to the Liberal biennial convention in Ottawa in March 2000, pointing out, perhaps to the surprise of some delegates, that "the Liberals do well in Ontario because voters there see no difference between the national and provincial interests." He added that New Brunswickers, however, believe the federal government does not act in the interest of their region or province.[31] Chrétien, in his address to the convention, declared that his government "will win more seats in Atlantic Canada in the next general election. Apparently, I will have to fix the problem with U.I. there."[32] This statement again speaks to Ottawa's willingness to share some of the wealth in a period of economic expansion and government surplus. The prime minister said very little about finding ways to assist the region in finding its way in the new economy or, in partnership with the local private sector, in working to increase R&D spending in the region. Chrétien also did not explain what had changed, given that five years earlier some of his senior ministers were claiming cuts to the unemployment insurance program were in the long-term economic interest of Atlantic Canada, lessening the province's dependency on the federal government.

Frank McKenna, in his last speech as premier, took aim at the federal government for its apparent inability to accommodate his province's economic interests. He had pressed Ottawa for months to bring forward a "shipbuilding" policy, to no avail. He claimed that had the shipbuilding industry been located in Ontario, Ottawa would have hurried to define a shipbuilding policy. Said McKenna,

> The auto industry makes sense for Ontario; it certainly makes sense now because they have the industry there. And I think that aerospace probably makes sense for the province of Quebec. But just as sensibly as those industries can go in those provinces, shipbuilding belongs to us on the Atlantic Coast of Canada. But friends, this is not an artificial creation, we've been building ships for hundreds of years, before this country was ever created we were building ships. This is the land of the *Marco Polo* and the *Bluenose*. This is the story of our civilization as we developed here. We build ships and we build good ships. Unfortunately, we live in the only country in the industrialized world that does not have a shipbuilding policy to support those who build ships. And I can tell you, if you could get ships in Oshawa, Ontario, or Ottawa, they would have a shipbuilding policy for this country...what we're looking for is not subsidization and handouts which is the solution that people keep prescribing to Atlantic Canada. What we need is solid, repayable financing for purchasers of our craftsmanship. That is what we need.[33]

The region is still waiting.

It may seem surprising then that, given the circumstances, McKenna, like other Maritime politicians, has consistently supported a strong central government. We noted in an earlier chapter that McKenna, initially at least, opposed the Meech Lake package in part because he felt that "Canada must have a strong national government." Ottawa has always been able to count on the four Atlantic premiers, with the exception of Brian Peckford, former premier of Newfoundland and Labrador, to jump to its defence when discussing the role

189

of the federal government in the economy and in social policy. The region has always been there to show its support whenever Ottawa has sought either to expand its role or to protect the status quo in federal-provincial programs. I put this question to McKenna: "Why did you support a strong central government during the Meech Lake debate in light of your statement on shipbuilding policy?" His reply: "The tradition in the region is to support a strong central government. Hatfield supported a strong central government and so did Robichaud. Given our province's linguistic composition, it was also important to support a strong central government, in the interest of balance."[34]

But a strong central government has *never* been in the economic interest of New Brunswick or Atlantic Canada. To be sure, federal transfer payments of one kind or another have enabled them to provide a high level of public service, but this came with a price – economic dependency. At the same time, it allowed Ottawa to concentrate its real efforts on vote-rich Ontario and southern Quebec. And now that the modern economic infrastructure has been put in place and that globalization, with all its implications, has arrived, Ontario is much less inclined to continue its implicit part of the bargain: support transfer payments to individuals and provincial governments in slow-growth regions.

Things have also changed on the language front. McKenna had to use all his powers of persuasion to convince Mulroney to introduce legislation in Parliament to entrench in the Constitution the principles of New Brunswick's Act recognizing the equality of the province's two official linguistic communities. Thus, in a turnabout, it was one small province, not the federal government, that was now pushing for linguistic equality.[35] Ottawa, of course, was concerned about possible political fallout in Quebec, in light of the failed efforts to amend the Canadian constitution.

Times change. It will be recalled that the Royal Commission on Bilingualism and Biculturalism, combined with the election of the Trudeau government in 1968, constituted a turning point, a defining moment in English-French relations in Canada. Trudeau himself summed up the task at hand and the resulting benefits if fully implemented when he declared that "once francophone-language rights across Canada are constitutionally entrenched, the French Canadian nation will stretch from coast to coast.... Nobody will be able to say [in Quebec], 'I need more power because I speak for the French-Canadian nation.'"[36] For Trudeau and others of like mind, the challenge was, and remains, to secure a strong future for the French-Canadian community, a community that extends beyond Quebec's borders. "*La survivance*" was the cry. But no sooner had Trudeau secured French-language rights than the picture changed. While francophones outside Quebec still see it as one of la *survivance*, for many French-speaking

Quebecers, l'épanouissement national now better reflects their purpose. That is, they wish to develop their society to its full potential and, in doing so, to have a free hand in shaping their political and cultural institutions.

The result is that French Canada itself no longer exists as a community: it has become regionalized. The language issue itself now has new regional borders. The cleavage and the political tensions between Québécois and Acadians are today probably as pronounced as they are between English-speaking Ontarians and Québécois. Indeed, there is a growing and disturbing tension between French-speaking communities across Canada, including Quebec, and it is now increasingly difficult to find a commonality of interests within what was once labeled Canada's French-Canadian community. When, for example, the New Brunswick Acadian community wanted to play host to the VIII International Francophone Summit, it soon discovered it could not count on support from its Quebec cousins. Those who would have been its most natural ally, say, forty years ago, now wished to downplay the French-speaking presence outside Quebec in order to further their own objectives. Thus, French Canada no longer speaks with one voice even on the language issue and it is in this sense that there are now at least two regional French Canadas pursuing vastly different objectives. The implications for New Brunswick are clear: Ottawa is less able to speak to the interests of a French Canada and make them stick. Given all of the above, New Brunswickers, and indeed every Maritimer, need to address the following question with a sense of urgency: Should we continue to support a strong role for the federal government?

What Now?

It is not too much of an exaggeration to write that New Brunswickers and Maritimers have been duped into supporting a strong central government. History reveals, time and again, that at crucial moments in Canada's economic development, Ottawa looked to Ontario's economic interests to shape its policies and efforts. New Brunswick was cut off from its markets to the south and forced to trade east-west where it had to operate at a marked disadvantage. Without Confederation, New Brunswick would have been able to continue to trade north-south. To be sure, it would have had to deal with high tariffs, but not on imported goods the province needed to export competitively. In addition, it would not have been caught up in a large federation where the exchange rate would be set by a more powerful centre.

Also important to recognize is that Ottawa gave Ontario what it denied New Brunswick – access to the United States, and it did not employ subsidies. Rather, it pursued the Auto Pact, which gave Ontario access to the US market.

donald j. savoie

Meanwhile, Ottawa gave New Brunswick and the other Atlantic provinces various transfers that have been wholly inappropriate, notably the unemployment insurance scheme which gave rise to the twelve-week-work syndrome in the region. Furthermore, business subsidies initially designed to promote economic development for Atlantic Canada have been pushed and pulled to other regions of the country, notably Ontario and Quebec, to the point where Atlantic Canada became "uncompetitive" in federal government subsidies for business.

The above is not to suggest that New Brunswickers should spend all their time lamenting the lack of an historical perspective on the part of many economists and political observers or moaning about how Confederation dealt their province a bad hand. This just creates despair. Frank McKenna was right when he told the Canadian Bankers Association that New Brunswickers do not want to wait "passively...for transfer payments from Ottawa. There is a new vision in New Brunswick: self-sufficiency for individuals. Self-sufficiency for the province." McKenna was pursuing the most promising avenue available when he lent his support to the business community, given the hand he had to play at the time. In fact, probably no one else could have promoted it more effectively.

Political leaders in have-less provinces can borrow a page from McKenna in their efforts to promote economic development: Articulate a vision and stick to it; embrace a business-friendly agenda; pursue new investment opportunities with energy and determination; identify the province's comparative advantages (in the case of New Brunswick, bilingualism and an innovative and dynamic telephone company); challenge the public service to identify new ways to deliver services; and introduce measures to improve the image citizens have of their province.

But as this study makes clear, this approach has limits. Economic development in New Brunswick requires a constant pulling against gravity. Gravity does not come solely from market forces or from the province's inherent inability to compete. It also comes from a federal government incapable or unwilling to accommodate regional economic interests in its policies other than those of vote-rich Ontario and southern Quebec. In this sense, gravity is not natural, but rather artificial, the product of national public policies.

Given this reality, New Brunswickers should no longer support a strong role for the federal government in a society dominated by Ontario and Quebec. The only benefits they have drawn from it have been transfer payments of one kind or another. To borrow a saying from the introduction, transfer payments have given New Brunswickers a fish, feeding them for a day; they must be taught how to fish, to feed themselves for life.

Now that these transfer payments are on the wane and some opinion leaders in Ontario are suggesting they want to move the province from being Canada's heartland to being a North American region-state, New Brunswick may as well prepare for the economic future that awaits it. Ontario knows where its economic interests will lie in the new economic order and in a global economy, and it will undoubtedly take the necessary steps to protect its own interests. As one Ontario-based economist observed in a paper commissioned by the federal Industry department, Ontario's support for interregional transfers never stemmed from "an inter-regional altruism intrinsic to Canadian culture."[37] Central Canada exported manufactured goods to Atlantic Canada and transfers enabled the region to purchase the goods, since local natural resources did not yield sufficient rent. In addition, transfer payments were the price to pay for federal government economic policies that favoured the economic interests of central Canada. Ontario is adjusting to the requirements of the global economy and so should New Brunswick.

Rather than nurturing a sense of betrayal from Confederation, New Brunswick should join forces with western Canada and promote new attempts to reform national political institutions. Indeed, the above is not to make the case that New Brunswickers should live off a history of victimization. Rather, it makes the case that New Brunswickers and Atlantic Canadians should no longer support the status quo, a strong role for Ottawa in economic development, unless important changes are introduced. Our continued support for a strong role for Ottawa should now be conditional to the introduction of a federalizing institution to combat the centralizing power of Ontario and to ensure that the national government is responsive to all regions. A "triple E" Senate should become as much a part of Atlantic Canada's political agenda as it is a part of western Canada's. Currently, national political institutions are hopelessly incapable of articulating the regional factor in national policy making. Australia, a federal system with a parliamentary form of government, has made the transition to an elected and effective Senate and there is no reason why Canada cannot do the same.

The results of the last federal election campaign again brought home the point that Canadians are highly divided along regional lines. The comprehensive public opinion survey carried out during the campaign by political scientists André Blais et al. is quite revealing. The survey concluded that "the electoral regional divide is a very serious one in Canada," and that it overshadows other issues, including ideological ones.[38] The survey revealed that regional grievances are deep and that, if anything, they are growing. It is worth stating one of its main conclusions here.

193

There is one issue where regional differences are really substantial: people's perceptions about how their province is treated by the federal government. In the West, 55 percent of respondents told us that their particular province is treated worse than other provinces. In Ontario, *only 12 percent* [emphasis added] felt their province was treated worse.... In Atlantic Canada, 45 percent say their province is treated worse than others. And in Quebec, 37 percent feel this way.... It is this Western regional frustration that fuels support for the Alliance: 63 percent of those who think the West is not fairly treated indicated they would vote Alliance. And that frustration is increasing. The proportion of Westerners who believe their province is not fairly treated has risen 17 points, from 38 percent, in 1997.[39]

What this suggests is that regional grievances in Canada cannot be dismissed as simply Maritimers or Westerners nurturing a sense of betrayal or victimization. The issue is much deeper and one has to ask how long can the political centre in Ottawa continue to believe the status quo in the operations of our national political institutions can be sustained?

There are also new forces at play that New Brunswick should not ignore. We know two things for certain. First, north-south economic ties and trade flows are increasing faster than east-west ones. As Serge Coulombe writes, "In the future, the regional distributions of Canada's economy will be affected by the...continuing development of north-south patterns of trade in place of more traditional east-west patterns."[40] This suggests Atlantic Canada is poised to enter a new phase in its relations not only with central Canada but also with other regions, notably New England and other regions in the United States. Indeed, there is every reason to believe economic ties with New England will be growing stronger, and one has only to look at the energy sector to see concrete evidence of this. In this sense, McKenna's miracle was his rediscovery of north-south trade links, and his willingness to stand up to intense pressure from his own political party, including the premier of Ontario, to support the Canada-US Free Trade Agreement.

As Atlantic Canada redefines its economic relationships with other regions, it will have to do it from a competitive basis. Put differently, the region will have to a) generate new economic activities and become competitive in world markets to maintain current living standards and levels of public services, or b) adjust its economic expectations. There will be no transfer payments from New England, or from elsewhere in the United States or Europe, to compensate for the region's inability to support its public service activities and lifestyle.

194

Simply fixing the employment insurance program will not do. The region needs to rebuild Atlantic Rim trade links, including those with New England. It needs to rebuild its infrastructure, its ports, highways and railways. It needs to recognize the importance of research and development and promote them. The region's economic circumstances clearly do not lend themselves to national R&D programs. We need to understand why and to adjust public policy measures to accommodate them to our region's economic realities.

The most important lessons to be learned for small have-less provinces, at the risk of sounding repetitive, is that national political institutions are in a state of disrepair and have never, nor do they now, work in their economic interests. Residents of have-less provinces are not solely to blame for their region's economic woes. In this sense the pull of economic activities in Canada has been shaped as much, if not more so, by national public policies introduced by a national government dominated by the political presence of Ontario and Quebec more than by economic forces. National economic programs have an inherent bias in favour of Ontario and Quebec. McKenna pushed and pulled all the economic levers he could, as far as he could and probably better than anyone else could, in promoting economic development in the province. His effort did have an impact. But one can only imagine the kind of impact there would have been had the federal government also pushed and pulled in the same direction. McKenna stood alone with the local telephone company in developing a call centre industry for his province, an industry now employing over 12,000 people. Ottawa could have put its shoulder to the wheel by locating some of its call-centre activities (such as those of Revenue Canada, for example) in New Brunswick. Instead, the federal Department of Industry stood on the sidelines, saying its programs were not designed for this industry. The department has never had such problems when it came to helping Ottawa's and Kanata's high-tech industry or Montreal's industrial interests.

I do not mean to suggest here that small have-less provinces should give up on Canada. Rather, the solution is to apply pressure to repair our national political institutions. In the meantime, New Brunswick and the other Atlantic provinces would be well advised to vote strategically in general elections, as they did in the heyday of the Maritime Rights Movement. Partisan party loyalty does not serve the region's economic interests. Best to make full use of the limited political clout the region still has in the House of Commons until such time as national political institutions can actually accommodate regional economic interests.

Notes

1. Quoted in John Lownsbrough, "The Energizer Premier," *Report on Business*, Toronto, March 1993, p. 31.

2. "Conservative coalition sees McKenna initiatives as model," *Telegraph Journal*, Saint John, 1 February 2000, p. A1.

3. Consultations with Frank McKenna, Moncton, New Brunswick, April 2000.

4. "McKenna bets his job on jobs," *The Globe and Mail*, 9 September 1995, p. A1.

5. William J. Milne, *The McKenna Miracle: Myth or Reality?* (Toronto: University of Toronto, monograph series on public policy and public administration, 1996), p. 9.

6. David K. Foot, *Canada's Population Outlook: Demographic Futures and Economic Challenges* (Ottawa: Canadian Institute for Economic Policy, 1982), p. xxiii.

7. Charlotte Gray, "Ottawa dot com," *Saturday Night*, Toronto (March 2000), p. 46.

8. Gray, "Ottawa dot com," p. 46.

9. See, among others, Donald J. Savoie, *Regional Economic Development: Canada's Search for Solutions* (Toronto: University of Toronto Press, 1992), chap. 10.

10. I obtained this information from the fund's Web site (*www.innovation.ca*) on 10 April 2001.

11. Statistics Canada, Cansim.

12. See Savoie, *Regional Economic Development*, p. 245.

13. See, among many others, an editorial in *The Globe and Mail*, "Patron saints of pork," 16 October 1996, p. A20.

14. Atlantic Provinces Economic Council, "Challenging Some Myths About Atlantic Canada," Halifax, Vol. 35, no. 2 (Summer 2000), p. 7.

15. *Backgrounder*: The Transitional Jobs Fund Story (Ottawa: Human Resources Development, 1999), pp. 1-3.

16. Consultations with senior HRD officials, Ottawa, November 1999.

17. Innis, "Decentralization and Democracy," in H. Innis (ed.), *Essays in Canadian Economic History* (Toronto: University of Toronto Press, 1956), p. 371.

18. Thomas J. Courchene (with Colin R. Telmer), *From Heartland to North American Region State: The Social, Fiscal and Federal Evolution of Ontario* (Toronto:

Centre for Public Management, University of Toronto, 1998), p. 152.

19. APEC, "Challenging Some Myths About Atlantic Canada," p. 7.

20. "And let us say, Oh the pain, the bliss of gain," *The Globe and Mail*, 20 October 2000, p. A17.

21. "Prime minister announces $500 million for Toronto 2000 Olympic Bid and Waterfront Revitalization," Office of the Prime Minister, Ottawa, 20 October 2000.

22. "Prime minister announces the signing of the Infrastructure Canada–Ontario Partnership and Investments" of more than $2.5 billion in Ontario Communities, Release, Office of the Prime Minister, Ottawa, 20 October 2000.

23. "Eastern Canada's new boss of bosses," *The Globe and Mail*, 17 October 2000, p. A19.

24. Quoted in Campbell Morrison, *Times and Transcript*, Moncton, 25 October 2000.

25. We co-authored a book on regional development policy. See Niles Hansen, Benjamin Higgins and Donald J. Savoie, *Regional Policy in a Changing World* (New York: Plenum Press, 1990). The book has chapters on U.S. and Canadian regional development policy.

26. Hansen, Higgins and Savoie, *Regional Policy in a Changing World*, chap. 5.

27. "PM Aims to Silence Senate on Clarity," *National Post*, 3 March 2000, p. A1.

28. Donald J. Savoie, *Governing from the Centre: The Concentration of Power in Canadian Politics* (Toronto: University of Toronto Press, 1999).

29. Quoted in Savoie, *Governing from the Centre: The Concentration of Power in Canadian Politics*, p. 240.

30. See, for example, Savoie, *Governing from the Centre*.

31. "Liberals aim to improve Atlantic image," *Times and Transcript*, Moncton, 18 March 2000, p. A9.

32. Quoted from the prime minister's speech, heard on CBC's *Newsworld*, 17 March 2000.

33. Premier Frank McKenna's speech at the Atlantic Vision Conference, Moncton, New Brunswick, 9 October 1997, mimeo, p. 5.

34. Consultations with Frank McKenna, Moncton, New Brunswick, March 2000.

35. The archives contain several letters from Frank McKenna to the prime minister, urging him to proceed with legislation on this matter.

36. "French from Coast to Coast," *The Globe and Mail*, 21 March 1970, p. A7.

37. Serge Coulombe, *Vision Paper: Regional Questions* (Ottawa: Department of Industry, August 1996), p. 43.

38. André Blais et al., "What is it that divides us?", *The Globe and Mail*, Toronto, 18 April 2000, p. A13.

39. Blais et al., "What is it that divides us?", p. A13.

40. Coulombe, *Regional Questions*, preface.

197

Donald J. Savoie

Dr. Savoie currently holds the Clément-Cormier Chair in Economic Development at l'Université de Moncton and he is senior scholar at IRPP. Professor Savoie has degrees in politics and economics from l'Université de Moncton, the University of New Brunswick, and Oxford. He has extensive work experience in both government and academia. He held senior positions with the government of Canada, and in 1983 he founded the Canadian Institute for Research on Regional Development at l'Université de Moncton where he was also appointed Professor of Public Administration. He has received numerous honours, including honorary doctorates from two Canadian universities and a Doctor of Letters from Oxford. He was made an Officer of the Order of Canada (1993) and a Fellow of the Royal Society of Canada (1992). His work has won prizes in Canada, the United States and France. He has served as an advisor to a number of federal, provincial and territorial government departments and agencies, the private sector, independent associations, OECD, the World Bank and the United Nations.

AGMV Marquis

MEMBRE DU GROUPE SCABRINI
Québec, Canada
2001